MY PATH TO ATHEISM

MY PATH TO ATHEISM

BY
ANNIE BESANT

GYAN

ISBN: 978-81-212-1902-0 (HB)
First Published, 1878
Published, 2018
Published by

Gyan Publishing House
5, Ansari Road
Daryaganj, New Delhi-110002
Phone: 011-47034999, 9811692060
www.gyanbooks.com
E-mail: books@gyanbooks.com

Printed at: G. Print Process, Delhi.

PREFACE TO FIRST EDITION.

THE Essays which form the present book have been written at intervals during the last five years, and are now issued in a single volume without alterations of any kind. I have thought it more useful—as marking the gradual growth of thought—to reprint them as they were originally published, so as not to allow the later development to mould the earlier forms. The essay on "Inspiration" is, in part, the oldest of all; it was partially composed some seven years ago, and re-written later as it now stands.

The first essay on the "Deity of Jesus of Nazareth" was written just before I left the Church of England, and marks the point where I broke finally with Christianity. I thought then, and think still, that to cling to the name of Christian after one has ceased to be the thing is neither bold nor straightforward, and surely the name ought, in all fairness, to belong to those historical bodies who have made it their own during many hundred years. A Christianity without a Divine Christ appears to me to resemble a republican army marching under a royal banner—it misleads both friends and foes. Believing that in giving up the deity of Christ I renounced Christianity, I place this essay as the starting-point of my travels outside the Christian pale. The essays that follow it deal with some of the leading Christian dogmas, and are printed in the order in which they were written. But in the gradual thought-development they really precede the essay on the "Deity of Christ". Most inquirers who begin to study by themselves, before they have read any heretical works, or heard any heretical controversies, will have been awakened to thought by the discrepancies and inconsistencies of the Bible itself. A thorough knowledge of the Bible is the groundwork of heresy. Many who think they read their Bibles never read them at all. They go through a chapter every day as a matter of duty, and forget what is said in Matthew before they read what is said in John; hence they never mark the contradictions and never see the discrepancies. But those who *study* the Bible are in a fair way to become heretics. It was the careful compilation of a harmony of the last chapters of the four Gospels—a harmony intended for devotional use—that gave the first blow to my own faith; although I put the doubt away and refused even to look at the question again, yet the effect remained—the tiny seed, which was slowly to germinate and to grow up, later, into the full-blown flower of Atheism.

The trial of Mr. Charles Voysey for heresy made me remember my own puzzle, and I gradually grew very uneasy, though trying not to think, until the almost fatal illness of my little daughter brought a sharper questioning as to the reason of suffering and the reality of the love of God. From that time I began to study the doctrines of Christianity from a critical point of view; hitherto I had confined my theological reading to devotional and historical treatises, and the only controversies with which I was familiar were the controversies which had divided Christians; the writings of the Fathers of the Church and of the modern school which is founded on them had been carefully studied, and I had weighed the points of difference between the Greek, Roman, Anglican, and Lutheran communions, as well as the views of orthodox dissenting schools of thought; only from Pusey's "Daniel", and Liddon's "Bampton Lectures", had I gathered anything of wider controversies and issues of more vital interest. But now all was changed, and it was to the leaders of the Broad Church school that I first turned in the new path. The shock of pain had been so rude when real doubts assailed and shook me, that I had steadily made up my mind to investigate, one by one, every Christian dogma, and never again to say "I believe" until I had tested the object of faith; the dogmas which revolted me most were those of the Atonement and of Eternal Punishment, while the doctrine of Inspiration of Scripture underlay everything, and was the very foundation of Christianity; these, then, were the first that I dropped into the crucible of investigation. Maurice, Robertson, Stopford Brooke, McLeod, Campbell, and others, were studied; and while I recognised the charm of their writings, I failed to find any firm ground whereon they could rest: it was a many-colored beautiful mist—a cloud landscape, very fair, but very unsubstantial. Still they served as stepping-stones away from the old hard dogmas, and month by month I grew more sceptical as to the possibility of finding certainty in religion. Mansel's Bampton lectures on "The Limits of Religious Thought" did much to increase the feeling; the works of F. Newman, Arnold, and Greg carried on the same work; some efforts to understand the creeds of other nations, to investigate Mahommedanism, Buddhism, and Hinduism, all led in the same direction, until I concluded that inspiration belonged to all people alike, and there could be no necessity of atonement, and no eternal hell prepared for the unbeliever in Christianity. Thus, step by step, I renounced the dogmas of Christianity until there remained only, as distinctively Christian, the Deity of Jesus which had not yet been analysed. The whole tendency of the Broad Church stream of thought was to increase the manhood at the expense of the deity of Christ; and with hell and atonement gone, and inspiration everywhere, there appeared no *raison d'être* for the Incarnation. Besides, there were so many incarnations, and the Buddhist absorption seemed a grander idea. I now first met with Charles Voysey's works, and those of Theodore Parker and Channing, and the belief in the Deity of Jesus followed the other dead creeds. Renan I had read much earlier, but did not care for him; Strauss I did not meet with until afterwards; Scott's "English Life of Jesus", which I read at this period, is as useful a book on this subject as could be put into the hands of an inquirer. From Christianity into simple Theism I had found my way; step by step the Theism melted into Atheism; prayer was gradually discontinued, as utterly at variance with any dignified idea of God, and as in contradiction to all the results of scientific investigation. I had taken a keen interest in the later scientific discoveries, and Darwin had done much towards freeing me from my old bonds. Of John Stuart Mill I had read much, and I now took him up again; I studied Spinoza, and re-read Mansel, together with many other writers on the Deity, until the result came which is found in the essay entitled "The Nature and Existence of God". It was just before this was written that I read Charles Bradlaugh's "Plea for Atheism" and his "Is there a God?". The essay on "Constructive Rationalism" shows how we replace the old faith and build our house anew with stronger materials.

The path from Christianity to Atheism is a long one, and its first steps are very rough and very painful; the feet tread on the ruins of the broken faith, and the sharp edges cut into the bleeding flesh; but further on the path grows smoother, and presently at its side begins to peep forth the humble daisy of hope that heralds the spring-tide, and further on the roadside is fragrant with all the flowers of summer, sweet and brilliant and gorgeous, and in the distance we see the promise of the autumn, the harvest that shall be reaped for the feeding of man.

Annie Besant.

1878.

ON THE

DEITY OF JESUS OF NAZARETH

"WHAT think ye of Christ, whose son is he?" Human child of human parents, or divine Son of the Almighty God? When we consider his purity, his faith in the Father, his forgiving patience, his devoted work among the offscourings of society, his brotherly love to sinners and outcasts—when our minds dwell on these alone,—we all feel the marvellous fascination which has drawn millions to the feet of this "son of man," and the needle of our faith begins to tremble towards the Christian pole. If we would keep unsullied the purity of our faith in God alone, we are obliged to turn our eyes some times—however unwillingly—towards the other side of the picture and to mark the human weaknesses which remind us that he is but one of our race. His harshness to his mother, his bitterness towards some of his opponents, the marked failure of one or two of his rare prophecies, the palpable limitation of his knowledge—little enough, indeed, when all are told,—are more than enough to show us that, however great as man, he is not the All-righteous, the All-seeing, the All-knowing, God.

No one, however, whom Christian exaggeration has not goaded into unfair detraction, or who is not blinded by theological hostility, can fail to revere portions of the character sketched out in the three synoptic gospels. I shall not dwell here on the Christ of the fourth Evangelist; we can scarcely trace in that figure the lineaments of the Jesus of Nazareth whom we have learnt to love.

I propose, in this essay, to examine the claims of Jesus to be more than the man he appeared to be during his life-time: claims—be it noted—which are put forward on his behalf by others rather than by himself. His own assertions of his divinity are to be found only in the unreliable fourth gospel, and in it they are destroyed by the sentence there put into his mouth with strange inconsistency: "If I bear witness of myself, my witness is not true."

It is evident that by his contemporaries Jesus was not regarded as God incarnate. The people in general appear to have looked upon him as a great prophet, and to have often debated among themselves whether he were their expected Messiah or not. The band of men who accepted him as their teacher were as far from worshipping him as God as were their fellow-countrymen: their prompt desertion of him when attacked by his enemies, their complete hopelessness when they saw him overcome and put to death, are sufficient proofs that though they regarded him—to quote their own words—as a "prophet mighty in word and deed," they never guessed that the teacher they followed, and the friend they lived with in the intimacy of social life was Almighty God Himself. As has been well pointed out, if they believed their Master to be God, surely when they were attacked they would have fled to him for protection, instead of endeavouring to save themselves by deserting him: we may add that this would have been their natural instinct, since they could never have imagined beforehand that the Creator Himself could really be taken captive by His creatures and suffer death at their hands. The third class of his contemporaries, the learned Pharisees and Scribes, were as far from regarding him as divine as were the people or his disciples. They seem to have viewed the new teacher somewhat contemptuously at first, as one who unwisely persisted in expounding the highest doctrines to the many, instead of—a second Hillel—adding to the stores of their own learned circle. As his influence spread and appeared to be undermining their own,—still more, when he placed himself in direct opposition, warning the people against them,—they were roused to a course of active hostility, and at length determined to save themselves by destroying him. But all through their passive contempt and direct antagonism, there is never a trace of their deeming him to be anything more than a religious enthusiast who finally became dangerous: we never for a moment see them assuming the manifestly absurd position of men knowingly measuring their strength against God, and endeavouring to silence and destroy their Maker. So much for the opinions of those who had the best opportunities of observing his ordinary life. A "good man," a "deceiver," a "mighty prophet," such are the recorded opinions of his contemporaries: not one is found to step forward and proclaim him to be Jehovah, the God of Israel.

One of the most trusted strongholds of Christians, in defending their Lord's Divinity, is the evidence of prophecy. They gather from the sacred books of the Jewish nation the predictions of the longed-for Messiah, and claim them as prophecies fulfilled in Jesus of Nazareth. But there is one stubborn fact which destroys the force of this argument: the Jews, to whom these writings belong, and who from tradition and national peculiarities may reasonably be supposed to be the best exponents of their own prophets, emphatically deny that these prophecies are fulfilled in Jesus at all. Indeed, one main reason for their rejection of Jesus is precisely this, that he does not resemble in any way the predicted Messiah. There is no doubt that the Jewish nation were eagerly looking for their Deliverer when Jesus was born: these very longings produced several pseudo-Messiahs, who each gained in turn a considerable following, because each bore some resemblance to the expected Prince. Much of the popular rage which swept Jesus to his death was the re-action of disappointment after the hopes raised by the position of authority he assumed. The sudden burst of anger against one so benevolent and inoffensive can only be explained by the intense hopes excited by his regal entry into Jerusalem, and the utter destruction of those hopes by his failing to ascend the throne of David. Proclaimed as David's son, he came riding on an ass as king of Zion, and allowed himself to be welcomed as the king of Israel: there his short fulfilling of the prophecies ended, and the people, furious at his failing them, rose and clamoured for his death. Because he did *not* fulfil the ancient Jewish oracles, he died: he was too noble for the *rôle* laid down in them for the Messiah, his ideal was far other than that of a conqueror, with "garments rolled in blood." But even if, against all evidence, Jesus was one with the Messiah of the prophets, this would destroy, instead of implying, his Divine claims. For the Jews were pure monotheists; their Messiah was a prince of David's line, the favoured servant, the anointed Jehovah, the king who should rule in His name: a Jew would shrink with horror from the blasphemy of seating Messiah on Jehovah's throne remembering how their prophets had taught them that their God "would not give His honour to another." So that, as to prophecy, the case stands thus: If Jesus be the Messiah prophesied of in the old Jewish books, then he is not God: if he be not the Messiah, Jewish prophecy is silent as regards him altogether, and an appeal to prophecy is absolutely useless.

After the evidence of prophecy Christians generally rely on that furnished by miracles. It is remarkable that Jesus himself laid but little stress on his miracles; in fact, he refused to appeal to them as credentials of his authority, and either could not or would not work them when met with determined unbelief. We must notice also that the people, while "glorifying God, who had given such power unto *men*," were not inclined to admit his miracles as proofs of his right to claim absolute obedience: his miracles did not even invest him with such sacredness as to protect him from arrest and death. Herod, on his trial, was simply anxious to see him work a miracle, as a matter of curiosity. This stolid indifference to marvels as attestations of authority is natural enough, when we remember that Jewish history was crowded with miracles, wrought for and against the favoured people, and also that they had been specially warned against being misled by signs and wonders. Without entering into the question whether miracles are possible, let us, for argument's sake, take them for granted, and see what they are worth as proofs of Divinity. If Jesus fed a multitude with a few loaves, so did Elisha: if he raised the dead, so did Elijah and Elisha; if he healed lepers, so did Moses and Elisha; if he opened the eyes of the blind, Elisha smote a whole army with blindness and afterwards restored their sight: if he cast out devils, his contemporaries, by his own testimony, did the same. If miracles prove Deity, what miracle of Jesus can stand comparison with the divided Red Sea of Moses, the stoppage of the earth's motion by Joshua, the check of the rushing waters of the Jordan by Elijah's cloak? If we are told that these men worked by *conferred* power and Jesus by *inherent*, we can only answer that this is a gratuitous assumption, and begs the whole question. The Bible records the miracles in equivalent terms: no difference is drawn between the manner of working of Elisha or Jesus; of each it is sometimes said they prayed; of each it is sometimes said they spake. Miracles indeed must not be relied on as proofs of divinity, unless believers in them are prepared to pay divine honours not to Jesus only, but also to a crowd of others, and to build a Christian Pantheon to the new found gods.

So far we have only seen the insufficiency of the usual Christian arguments to establish a doctrine so stupendous and so *primâ facie* improbable as the incarnation of the Divine Being: this kind of negative testimony, this insufficient evidence, is not however the principle reason which compels Theists to protest against the central dogma of Christianity. The stronger proofs of the simple manhood of Jesus remain, and we now proceed to positive evidence of his not being God. I propose to draw attention to the traces of human infirmity in his noble character, to his absolute mistakes in prophecy, and to his evidently limited knowledge. In accepting as substantially true the account of Jesus given by the evangelists, we are taking his character as it appeared to his devoted followers. We have not to do with slight blemishes, inserted by envious detractors of his greatness; the history of Jesus was written when his disciples worshipped him as God, and his manhood, in their eyes, reached ideal perfection. We are not forced to believe that, in the gospels, the life of Jesus is given at its highest, and that he was, at least, not more spotless than he appears in these records of his friends. But here again, in order not to do a gross injustice, we must put aside the fourth gospel: to study his character "according to S. John" would need a separate essay, so different is it from that drawn by the three; and by all rules of history we should judge him by the earlier records, more especially as they corroborate each other in the main.

The first thing which jars upon an attentive reader of the gospels is the want of affection and respect shown by Jesus to his mother. When only a child of twelve he lets his parents leave Jerusalem to return home, while he repairs alone to the temple. The fascination of the ancient city and the gorgeous temple services was doubtless almost overpowering to a thoughtful Jewish boy, more especially on his first visit: but the careless forgetfulness of his parents' anxiety must be considered as a grave childish fault, the more so as its character is darkened by the indifference shown by his answer to his mother's grieved reproof. That no high, though mistaken, sense of duty kept him in Jerusalem is evident from his return home with his parents; for had he felt that "his

Father's business" detained him in Jerusalem at all, it is evident that this sense of duty would not have been satisfied by a three days' delay. But the Christian advocate would bar criticism by an appeal to the Deity of Jesus: he asks us therefore to believe that Jesus, being God, saw with indifference his parents' anguish at discovering his absence; knew all about that three days' agonised search (for they, ignorant of his divinity, felt the terrible anxiety as to his safety, natural to country people losing a child in a crowded city); did not, in spite of the tremendous powers at his command, take any steps to re-assure them; and finally, met them again with no words of sympathy, only with a mysterious allusion, incomprehensible to them, to some higher claim than theirs, which, however, he promptly set aside to obey them. If God was incarnate in a boy, we may trust that example as a model of childhood: yet, are Christians prepared to set this "early piety and desire for religious instruction" before their young children as an example they are to follow? Are boys and girls of twelve to be free to absent themselves for days from their parents' guardianship under the plea that a higher business claims their attention? This episode of the childhood of Jesus should be relegated to those "gospels of the infancy" full of most unchildlike acts, which the wise discretion of Christendom has stamped with disapproval. The same want of filial reverence appears later in his life: on one occasion he was teaching, and his mother sent in, desiring to speak to him: the sole reply recorded to the message is the harsh remark: "Who is my mother?" The most practical proof that Christian morality has, on this head, outstripped the example of Jesus, is the prompt disapproval which similar conduct would meet with in the present day. By the strange warping of morality often caused by controversial exigencies, this want of filial reverence has been triumphantly pointed out by Christian divines; the indifference shown by Jesus to family ties is accepted as a proof that he was more than man!. Thus, conduct which they implicitly acknowledge to be unseemly in a son to his mother, they claim as natural and right in the Son of God, to His! In the present day, if a person is driven by conscience to a course painful to those who have claims on his respect, his recognised duty, as well as his natural instinct, is to try and make up by added affection and more courteous deference for the pain he is forced to inflict: above all, he would not wantonly add to that pain by public and uncalled-for disrespect.

The attitude of Jesus towards his opponents in high places was marked with unwarrantable bitterness. Here also the lofty and gentle spirit of his whole life has moulded Christian opinion in favour of a course different on this head to his own, so that abuse of an opponent is now commonly called *un*-Christian. Wearied with three years' calumny and contempt, sore at the little apparent success which rewarded his labour, full of a sad foreboding that his enemies would shortly crush him, Jesus was goaded into passionate denunciations: "Woe unto you, Scribes and Pharisees, hypocrites . . . ye fools and blind . . . ye make a proselyte twofold more the child of hell than yourselves . . . ye serpents, ye generation of vipers, how can ye escape the damnation of hell!" Surely this is not the spirit which breathed in, "If ye love them which love you, what thanks have ye? . . . Love your enemies, bless them that curse you, pray for them that persecute you." Had he not even specially forbidden the very expression, "Thou fool!" Was not this rendering "evil for evil, railing for railing?"

It is painful to point out these blemishes: reverence for the great leaders of humanity is a duty dear to all human hearts; but when homage turns into idolatry, then men must rise up to point out faults which otherwise they would pass over in respectful silence, mindful only of the work so nobly done.

I turn then, with a sense of glad relief, to the evidence of the limited knowledge of Jesus, for here no blame attaches to him, although *one* proved mistake is fatal to belief in his Godhead. First as to prophecy: "The Son of man shall come in the glory of his Father with his angels: and then shall he reward every man according to his works. Verily I say unto you, There be some standing here which shall not taste of death till they see the Son of man coming in his kingdom." Later, he amplifies the same idea: he speaks of a coming tribulation, succeeded by his own return, and then adds the emphatic declaration: "Verily I say unto you, This generation shall not pass till all these things be done." The non-fulfilment of these prophecies is simply a question of fact: let men explain away the words now as they may, yet, if the record is true, Jesus did believe in his own speedy return, and impressd the same belief on his followers. It is plain, indeed, that he succeeded in impressing it on them, from the references to his return scattered through the epistles. The latest writings show an anxiety to remove the doubts which were disturbing the converts consequent on the non-appearance of Jesus, and the fourth gospel omits any reference to his coming. It is worth remarking, in the latter, the spiritual sense which is hinted at—either purposely or unintentionally—in the words, "The hour . . . *now* is when the dead shall hear the voice of the Son of God, and they that hear shall live." These words may be the popular feeling on the advent of the resurrection, forced on the Christians by the failure of their Lord's prophecies in any literal sense. He could not be mistaken, *ergo* they must spiritualise his words. The limited knowledge of Jesus is further evident from his confusing Zacharias the son of Jehoiada with Zacharias the son of Barachias: the former, a priest, was slain in the temple court, as Jesus states; but the son of Barachias was Zacharias, or Zachariah, the prophet.* He himself owned a limitation of his knowledge, when he confessed his ignorance of the day of his own return, and said it was known to the "Father only." Of the same class of sayings is his answer to the mother of James and John, that the high seats of the coming kingdom "are not mine to give." That Jesus believed in the fearful doctrine of eternal punishment is evident, in spite of the ingenious attempts to prove that the doctrine is not scriptural: that he, in common with his countrymen, ascribed many diseases to the immediate power of Satan, which we should now probably refer to natural causes, as epilepsy, mania, and the like, is also self-evident. But on such points as these it is useless to dwell, for the Christian believes them on the authority of Jesus, and the subjects, from their nature, cannot be brought to the test of ascertained facts. Of the same character are some of his sayings: his discouraging "Strive to enter in at the strait gate, *for* many," etc.; his using in defence of partiality Isaiah's awful prophecy, "that seeing they may see and not perceive," etc.; his using Scripture at one time as binding, while he, at another, depreciates it; his fondness for silencing an opponent by an ingenious retort: all these things are blameworthy to those who regard him as man, while they are shielded from criticism by his divinity to those who worship him as God. There morality is a question of opinion, and it is wasted time to dwell on them when

* See Appendix, page 12.

arguing with Christians, whose moral sense is for the time held in check by their mental prostration at his feet. But the truth of the quoted prophecies, and the historical fact of the parentage of Zachariah, can be tested, and on these Jesus made palpable mistakes. The obvious corollary is, that being mistaken—as he was—his knowledge was limited, and was therefore human, not divine.

In turning to the teaching of Jesus (I still confine myself to the three gospels), we find no support of the Christian theory. If we take his didactic teaching, we can discover no trace of his offering himself as an object of either faith or worship. His life's work, as teacher, was to speak of the Father. In the sermon on the Mount he is always striking the keynote, "your heavenly Father;" in teaching his disciples to pray, it is to "Our Father," and the Christian idea of ending a prayer "through Jesus Christ" is quite foreign to the simple filial spirit of their master. Indeed, when we think of the position Jesus holds in Christian theology, it seems strange to notice the utter absence of any suggestion of duty to himself throughout this whole code of so-called Christian morality. In strict accordance with his more formal teaching is his treatment of inquirers: when a young man comes kneeling, and, addressing him as "Good Master," asks what he shall do to inherit eternal life, the loyal heart of Jesus first rejects the homage, before he proceeds to answer the all-important question: "Why callest thou *me* good: there is none good but one, that is, God." He then directs the youth on the way to eternal life, and *he sends that young man home without one word of the doctrine on which, according to Christians, his salvation rested.* If the "Gospel" came to that man later, he would reject it on the authority of Jesus, who had told him a different "way of salvation;" and if Christianity is true, the perdition of that young man's soul is owing to the defective teaching of Jesus himself. Another time, he tells a Scribe that the first commandment is that God is one, and that all a man's love is due to Him; then adding the duty of neighbourly love, he says: "There is *none other* commandment greater than these:" so that belief in Jesus, if incumbent at all, must come after love to God and man, and is not necessary, by his own testimony, to "entering into life." On Jesus himself then rests the primary responsibility of affirming that belief in him is a matter of secondary importance, at most, letting alone the fact that he never inculcated belief in his Deity as an article of faith at all. In the same spirit of frank loyalty to God are his words on the unpardonable sin : in answer to a gross personal affront, he tells his insulters that they shall be forgiven for speaking against him, a simple son of man, but warns them of the danger of confounding the work of God's Spirit with that of Satan, "because they said" that works done by God, using Jesus as His instrument, were done by Beelzebub.

There remains yet one argument of tremendous force, which can only be appreciated by personal meditation. We find Jesus praying to God, relying on God, in his greatest need crying in agony to God for deliverance, in his last struggle, deserted by his friends, asking why God, his God, had also forsaken him. We feel how natural, how true to life, this whole account is: in our heart's reverence for that noble life, that "faithfulness unto death," we can scarcely bear to think of the insult offered to it by Christian lips: they take every beauty out of it by telling us that through all that struggle Jesus was the Eternal, the Almighty, God: it is all apparent, not real : in his temptation he could not fall: in his prayers he needed no support: in his cry that the cup might pass away he foresaw it was inevitable: in his agony of desertion and loneliness he was present everywhere with God. In all that life, then, there is no hope for man, no pledge of man's victory, no promise for humanity. This is no *man's* life at all, it is only a wonderful drama enacted on earth. What God could do is no measure of man's powers: what have we in common with this "God-man?" This Jesus, whom we had thought our brother, is, after all, removed from us by the immeasurable distance which separates the feebleness of man from the omnipotence of God. Nothing can compensate us for such a loss as this. We had rejoiced in that many-sided nobleness, and its very blemishes were dear, because they assured us of his brotherhood to ourselves : we are given an ideal picture where we had studied a history, another Deity where we had hoped to emulate a life. Instead of the encouragement we had found, what does Christianity offer us?—a perfect life? But we knew before that God was perfect: an example? it starts from a different level: a Saviour? we cannot be safer than we are with God: an Advocate? we need none with our Father: a Substitute to endure God's wrath for us? we had rather trust God's justice to punish us as we deserve, and his wisdom to do what is best for us. As

God, Jesus can give us nothing that we have not already in his Father and ours: as man, he gives us all the encouragement and support which we derive from every noble soul which God sends into this world, "a burning and a shining light":

> "Through such souls alone
> God stooping shows sufficient of His light
> For us in the dark to rise by."

As God, he confuses our perceptions of God's unity, bewilders our reason with endless contradictions, and turns away from the Supreme all those emotions of love and adoration which can only flow towards a single object, and which are the due of our Creator alone: as man, he gives us an example to strive after, a beacon to steer by; he is one more leader for humanity, one more star in our darkness. As God, all his words would be truth, and but few would enter into heaven, while hell would overflow with victims: as man, we may refuse to believe such a slander on our Father, and take all the comfort pledged to us by that name. Thank God, then, that Jesus is only man, human child of human parents; that we need not dwarf our conceptions of God to fit human faculties, or envelope the illimitable spirit in a baby's feeble frame. But though only man, he has reached a standard of human greatness which no other man, so far as we know, has touched: the very height of his character is almost a pledge of the truthfulness of the records in the main: his life had to be lived before its conception became possible, at that period and among such a people. They could recognise his greatness when it was before their eyes: they would scarcely have imagined it for themselves, more especially that, as we have seen, he was so different from the Jewish ideal. His code of morality stands unrivalled, and he was the first who taught the universal Fatherhood of God publicly and to the common people. Many of his loftiest precepts may be found in the books of the Rabbis, but it is the glorious prerogative of Jesus that he spread abroad among the many the wise and holy maxims that had hitherto been the sacred treasures of the few. With him none were too degraded to be called the children of the Father: none too simple to be worthy of the highest teaching. By example, as well as by precept, he taught that all men were brothers, and all the good he had he showered at their feet. "Pure in heart," he saw God, and what he saw he called all to see:

he longed that all might share in his own joyous trust in the Father, and seemed to be always seeking for fresh images to describe the freedom and fulness of the universal love of God. In his unwavering love of truth, but his patience with doubters—in his personal purity, but his tenderness to the fallen—in his hatred of evil, but his friendliness to the sinner—we see splendid virtues rarely met in combination. His brotherliness, his yearning to raise the degraded, his lofty piety, his unswerving morality, his perfect self-sacrifice, are his indefeasible titles to human love and reverence. Of the world's benefactors he is the chief, not only by his own life, but by the enthusiasm he has known to inspire in others: "Our plummet has not sounded his depth:" words fail to tell what humanity owes to the Prophet of Nazareth. On his example the great Christian heroes have based their lives: from the foundation laid by his teaching the world is slowly rising to a purer faith in God. We need now such a leader as he was—one who would dare to follow the Father's will as he did, casting a long-prized revelation aside when it conflicts with the higher voice of conscience. It is the teaching of Jesus that Theism gladly makes its own, purifying it from the inconsistencies which mar its perfection. It is the example of Jesus which Theists are following, though they correct that example in some points by his loftiest sayings. It is the work of Jesus which Theists are carrying on, by worshipping, as he did, the Father, and the Father alone, and by endeavouring to turn all men's love, all men's hopes, and all men's adoration, to that "God and Father of all, who is above all, and through all, and," not in Jesus only, but "*in us all.*"

APPENDIX.

"Josephus mentions a Zacharias, a son of Baruch ('Wars of the Jews,' Book iv., sec. 4), who was slain under the circumstances described by Jesus. His name would be more suitable at the close of the long list of Jewish crimes, as it occurred just before the destruction of Jerusalem. But, as it took place about thirty-four years after the death of Jesus, it is clear that he could not have referred to it; therefore, if we admit that he made no mistake, we strike a serious blow at the credibility of his historian, who then puts into his mouth a remark never uttered."

A COMPARISON

BETWEEN THE

FOURTH GOSPEL AND THE THREE SYNOPTICS.

EVERY one, at least in the educated classes, knows that the authenticity of the fourth gospel has been long and widely disputed. The most careless reader is struck by the difference of tone between the simple histories ascribed to Matthew, Mark, and Luke, and the theological and philosophical treatise which bears the name of John. After following the three narratives, so simple in their structure, so natural in their style, so unadorned by rhetoric, so free from philosophic terms,—after reading these, it is with a feeling of surprise that we find ourselves plunged into the bewildering mazes of the Alexandrine philosophy, and open our fourth gospel to be told that, "In the beginning was the word, and the word was with God, and the word was God." We ask instinctively, "How did John, the fisherman of Galilee, learn these phrases of the Greek schools, and why does he mix up the simple story of his master with the philosophy of that 'world which by wisdom knew not God?'"

The general Christian tradition is as follows: The spread of "heretical" views about the person of Jesus alarmed the "orthodox" Christians, and they appealed to John, the last aged relic of the apostolic band, to write a history of Jesus which should confute their opponents, and establish the essential deity of the founder of their religion. At their repeated solicitations, John wrote the gospel which bears his name, and the doctrinal tone of it is due to its original intention,—a treatise written against Cerinthus, and designed to crush, with the authority of an apostle, the rising doubts as to the pre-existence and absolute deity of Jesus of Nazareth. So far non-Christians and Christians—including the writer of the gospel—are agreed. This fourth gospel is not—say Theists—a simple biography of Jesus written by a loving disciple as a memorial of a departed and cherished friend, but a history written with a special object and to prove a certain doctrine. "St. John's gospel is a polemical treatise," echoes Dr. Liddon. "These are written that ye may believe that Jesus is the Christ, the Son of God," confesses the writer himself. Now, in examining the credibility of any history, one of the first points to determine is whether the historian is perfectly unbiassed in his judgment and is therefore likely give facts exactly as they occurred, uncoloured by views of his own. Thus we do not turn to the pages of a Roman Catholic historian to gain a fair idea of Luther, or of William the Silent, or expect to find in the volumes of Clarendon a thoroughly faithful portraiture of the vices of the Stuart kings; rather, in reading the history of a partisan, do we instinctively make allowances for the recognised bias of his mind and heart. That the fourth gospel comes to us prefaced by the announcement that it is written, not to give us a history, but to prove a certain predetermined opinion, is, then, so much doubt cast at starting on its probable accuracy; and, by the constitution of our minds, we at once guard ourselves against a too ready acquiescence in its assertions, and become anxious to test its statements by comparing them with some independent and more impartial authority. The history may be most accurate, but we require proof that the writer is never seduced into slightly—perhaps unconsciously—colouring an incident so as to favour the object he has at heart. For instance, Matthew, an honest writer enough, is often betrayed into most non-natural quotation of prophecy by his anxiety to connect Jesus with the Messiah expected by his countrymen. This latent wish of his leads him to insert various quotations from the Jewish Scriptures which, severed from their context, have a verbal similarity with the events he narrates. Thus, he refers to Hosea's mention of the Exodus: "When Israel was a child then I loved him and called my son out of Egypt," and by quoting only the last six words gives this as a "prophecy" of an alleged journey of Jesus into Egypt. Such an instance as this shows us how a man may allow himself to be blinded by a pre-conceived determination to prove a certain fact, and warns us to sift carefully any history that comes to us with the announcement that it is written to prove such and such a truth.

Unfortunately we have no independent contemporary history—except a sentence of Josephus—whereby to test the accuracy of the Christian records; we are therefore forced into the somewhat unsatisfactory task of comparing them one with another, and in cases of diverging testimony we must strike the balance of probability between them.

On examining, then, these four biographies of Jesus, we find a remarkable similarity between three of them, amid many divergencies of detail; some regard them, therefore, as the condensation into writing of the oral teaching of the apostles, preserved in the various Churches they severally founded, and so, naturally, the same radically, although diverse in detail. "The synoptic Gospels contain the substance of the Apostles' testimony, collected principally from their oral teaching current in the Church, partly also from written documents embodying portions of that teaching."* Others think that the gospels which we possess, and which are ascribed severally to Matthew, Mark, and Luke, are all three derived from an original gospel now lost, which was probably written in Hebrew or Aramaic, and variously translated into Greek. However this may be, the fact that such a statement as this has been put forward proves the striking similarity, the root identity, of the three "synoptical gospels," as they are called. We gather from them an idea of Jesus which is substantially the same: a figure, calm, noble, simple, generous; pure in life, eager to draw men to that love of the Father and devotion to the Father which were his own distinguishing characteristics; finally, a teacher of a simple and high-toned morality, perfectly unfettered by dogmatism. The effect produced by the sketch of the Fourth Evangelist is totally different. The friend of sinners has disappeared (except in the narrative of the woman taken in adultery, which is generally admitted to be an interpolation), for his whole time is occupied in arguing about his own position; "the common people" who followed and "heard him gladly" and his enemies, the Scribes and Pharisees, are all massed together as "the Jews," with whom he is in constant collision; his simple style of teaching—parabolic indeed, as was the custom of the East, but consisting of parables intelligible to a child—is exchanged for mystical discourses, causing perpetual misunderstandings, the true meaning of which is still wrangled about by Christian theo-

* Alford.

logians; his earnest testimony to "your heavenly Father" is replaced by a constant self-assertion; while his command "do this and ye shall live," is exchanged for "believe on me or perish." "How great is the contrast between that discourse and the Sermon on the Mount. . . . In the last discourse it is His Person rather than his teaching which is especially prominent. His subject in that discourse is Himself. Certainly he preaches himself in His relationship to His redeemed; but still he preaches above all, and in all, Himself. All radiates from Himself, all converges towards Himself. . . . in those matchless words all centres so consistently in Jesus, that it might seem that Jesus Alone is before us."* These and similar differences, both of direct teaching and of the more subtle animating spirit, I propose to examine in detail; but before entering on these it seems necessary to glance at the disputed question of the authorship of our history, and determine whether, if it prove apostolic, it *must* therefore be binding on us.

I leave to more learned pens than mine the task of criticising and drawing conclusions from the Greek or the precise dogma of the evangelist, and of weighing the conflicting testimony of mighty names. From the account contained in the English Bible of John the Apostle, I gather the following points of his character: He was warm-hearted to his friends, bitter against his enemies, filled with a fiery and unbridled zeal against theological opponents; he was ambitious, egotistical, pharisaical. I confess that I trace these characteristics through all the writings ascribed to him, and that they seem to be only softened by age in the fourth gospel. That John was a warm friend is proved by his first epistle; that he was bitter against his enemies appears in his mention of Diotrephes, "I will remember his deeds which he doeth, prating against us with malicious words;" his unbridled zeal was rebuked by his master; the same cruel spirit is intensified in his "Revelation;" his ambition is apparent in his anxiety for a chief seat in Messiah's kingdom; his egotism appears in the fearful curse he imprecates on those who alter *his* revelation; his pharisaism is marked in such a feeling as, "we know *we* are of God, and the whole world lieth in wickedness." Many of these qualities appear to me to mark the gospel which bears his name; the same restricted tenderness, the same bitterness

* Liddon.

against opponents, the same fiery zeal for "the truth," *i.e.*, a special theological dogma, are everywhere apparent. The same egotism is most noticeable, for in the other gospels John shares his master's chief regard with two others, while here he is "*the* disciple whom Jesus loved," and he is specially prominent in the closing scenes of Jesus' life as the *only* faithful follower. We should also notice the remarkable similarity of expression and tone between the fourth gospel and the first epistle of John, a similarity the more striking as the language is peculiar to the writings attributed to John. It is, however, with the utmost diffidence that I offer these suggestions, well knowing that the greatest authorities are divided on this point of authorship, and that the balance is rather against the apostolic origin of the gospel than for it. I am, however, anxious to show that, *even taking it as apostolic*, it is untrustworthy and utterly unworthy of credit. If John be the writer, we must suppose that his long residence in Ephesus had gradually obliterated his Jewish memories, so that he speaks of "the Jews" as a foreigner would. The stern Jewish monotheism would have grown feebler by contact with the subtle influence of the Alexandrine tone of thought; and he would have caught the expressions of that school from living in a city which was its second home. To use the Greek philosophy as a vehicle for Christian teaching would recommend itself to him as the easiest way of approaching minds imbued with these mystic ideas. Regarding the master of his youth through the glorifying medium of years, he gradually began to imagine him to be one of the emanations from the Supreme, of which he heard so much. Accustomed to the deification of Roman emperors, men of infamous lives, he must have been almost driven to claim divine honours for *his* leader. If his hearers regarded *them* as divine, what could he say to exalt *him* except that he was ever with God, nay, was himself God? If John be the writer of this gospel, some such change as this must have passed over him, and in his old age the gradual accretions of years must have crystallised themselves into a formal Christian theology. But if we find, during our examination, that the history and the teaching of this gospel is utterly irreconcilable with the undoubtedly earlier synoptic gospels, we must then conclude that, apostolic or not, it must give place to them, and be itself rejected as a trustworthy account of the life and teaching of Jesus of Nazareth.

The first striking peculiarity of this gospel is that all the people in it talk in exactly the same style and use the same markedly peculiar phraseology. (*a*) "The Father loveth the Son and hath given all things into his hand." (*b*) "For the Father loveth the Son and showeth him all things that Himself doeth." (*c*) "Jesus, knowing that the Father had given all things into his hand." These sentences are evidently the outcome of the same mind, and no one, unacquainted with our gospel, would guess that (*a*) was spoken by John the Baptist, (*b*) by Jesus, (*c*) by the writer of the gospel. When the Jews speak, the words still run in the same groove: "If any man be a worshipper of God, and doeth His will, him He heareth," is not said, as might be supposed, by Jesus, but by the man who was born blind. Indeed, commentators are sometimes puzzled, as in John iii. 10-21, to know where, if at all, the words of Jesus stop and are succeeded by the commentary of the narrator. In an accurate history different characters stand out in striking individuality, so that we come to recognise them as distinct personalities, and can even guess beforehand how they will probably speak and act under certain conditions. But here we have one figure in various disguises, one voice from different speakers, one mind in opposing characters. We have here no beings of flesh and blood, but airy phantoms, behind whomwe see clearly the solitary preacher. For Jesus and John the Baptist are two characters as distinctas can well be imagined, yet their speeches are absolutely indistinguishable, and their thoughts run in the same groove. Jesus tells Nicodemus: "We speak that we do know and testify that we have seen, and ye receive not our witness; and no man hath ascended up to heaven, but he that came down from heaven." John says to his disciples: "He that cometh from heaven is above all, and what he hath seen and heard that he testifieth, and no man receiveth his testimony." But it is wasting time to prove so self-evident a fact: let us rather see how a Christian advocate meets an argument whose force he cannot deny. "The character and diction of our Lord's discourses entirely penetrated and assimilated the habits of thought of His beloved Apostle; so that in his first epistle he writes in the very tone and spirit of those discourses; and when reporting the sayings of his former teacher, the Baptist, he gives them, consistently with the deepest inner truth (!) of narration, the forms and cadences so familiar and habitual to himself."* It must be left to each individual to judge if a careful and accurate historian thus tampers with the words he pretends to narrate, and thus makes them accord with some mysterious inner truth; each too must decide as to the amount of reliance it is wise to place on a historian who is guided by so remarkable a rule of truth. But further, that the "character and diction" of this gospel are moulded on that of Jesus, seems a most unwarrantable assertion. Through all the recorded sayings of Jesus in the three gospels, there is no trace of this very peculiar style, except in one case (Matt. xi. 27), a passage which comes in abruptly and unconnectedly, and stands absolutely alone in style in the three synoptics, a position which throws much doubt on its authenticity. It has been suggested that this marked difference of style arises from the different auditories addressed in the three gospels and in the fourth; on this we remark that (*a*), we intuitively recognise such discourses as that in Matt. x. as perfectly consistent with the usual style of Jesus, although this is addressed to "his own;" (*b*), in this fourth gospel the discourses addressed to "his own" and to the Jews are in exactly the same style; so that, neither in this gospel, nor in the synoptics do we find any difference—more than might be reasonably expected—between the style of the discourses addressed to the disciples and those addressed to the multitudes. But we *do* find a very marked difference between the style attributed to Jesus by the three synoptics and that put into his mouth by the fourth evangelist; this last being a style so remarkable that, if usual to Jesus, it is impossible that its traces should not appear through all his recorded speeches. From which fact we may, I think, boldly deduce the conclusion that the style in question is not that of Jesus, the simple carpenter's son, but is one caught from the dignified and stately march of the oratory of Ephesian philosophers, and is put into his mouth by the writer of his life. And this conclusion is rendered indubitable by the fact above-mentioned, that all the characters adopt this poetically and musically-rounded phraseology.

Thus our first objection against the trustworthiness of our historian is that all the persons he introduces, however different in character, speak exactly alike, and that this style, when put into the mouth of Jesus, is totally different from

* Alford.

that attributed to him by the three synoptics. We conclude, therefore, that the style belongs wholly to the writer, and that he cannot, consequently, be trusted in his reports of speeches. The major part, by far the most important part, of this gospel is thus at once stamped as untrustworthy.

Let us next remark the partiality attributed by this gospel to Him Who has said—according to the Bible—"*all* souls are Mine." We find the doctrine of predestination, *i.e.*, of favouritism, constantly put forward. "*All that the Father giveth me* shall come to me." "No man can come to me except the Father draw him." "That of all *which He hath given me* I should lose nothing." "Ye believe not, *because* ye are not of my sheep." "Though he had done so many miracles before them, yet they believed not on him: *that the saying* of Esaias the prophet *might be fulfilled.*" "*Therefore, they could not believe because* that Esaias said," &c. "I have chosen you out of the world." "Thou hast given him power over all flesh, that he should give eternal life to *as many as Thou hast given him.*" "Those that thou gavest me I have kept and none of them is lost, but the son of perdition, *that the Scriptures might be fulfilled.*" These are the most striking of the passages which teach that doctrine which has been the most prolific parent of immorality and the bringer of despair to the sinner. Frightfully immoral as it is, this doctrine is taught in all its awful hopelessness and plainness by this gospel: some "*could not* believe" because an old prophet prophesied that they should not. So, "according to St. John," these unbelieving Jews were pre-ordained to eternal damnation and the abiding wrath of God. They were cast into an endless hell, which "they *could not*" avoid. We reject this gospel, secondly, for the partiality it dares to attribute to Almighty God.

We will now pass to the historical discrepancies between this gospel and the three synoptics, following the order of the former.

It tells us (ch. 1) that at the beginning of his ministry Jesus was at Bethabara, a town near the junction of the Jordan with the Dead Sea; here he gains three disciples, Andrew and another, and then Simon Peter: the next day he goes into Galilee and finds Philip and Nathanael, and on the following day—somewhat rapid travelling—he is present, with these disciples, at Cana, where he performs his first miracle, going afterwards with them to Capernaum and

Jerusalem. At Jerusalem, whither he goes for "the Jews' passover," he drives out the traders from the temple, and remarks, "Destroy this temple, and in three days I will raise it up:" which remark causes the first of the strange misunderstandings between Jesus and the Jews, peculiar to this Gospel, simple misconceptions which Jesus never troubles himself to set right. Jesus and his disciples then go to the Jordan, baptising, whence Jesus departs into Galilee with them, because he hears that the Pharisees know he is becoming more popular than the Baptist (ch. iv. 1-3). All this happens before John is cast into prison, an occurrence which is a convenient note of time. We turn to the beginning of the ministry of Jesus as related by the three. Jesus is in the south of Palestine, but, hearing that John is cast into prison, he departs into Galilee, and resides at Capernaum. There is no mention of any ministry in Galilee and Judæa before this; on the contrary, it is only "from that time" that "Jesus *began* to preach." He is alone, without disciples, but, walking by the sea, he comes upon Peter, Andrew, James, and John, and calls them. Now if the fourth gospel is true, these men had joined him in Judæa, followed him to Galilee, south again to Jerusalem, and back to Galilee, had seen his miracles and acknowledged him as Christ, so it seems strange that they had deserted him and needed a second call, and yet more strange is it that Peter (Luke v. 1-11) was so astonished and amazed at the miracle of the fishes. The driving out of the traders from the temple is placed by the synoptics at the very end of his ministry, and the remark following it is used against him at his trial: so was probably made just before it. The next point of contact is the history of the 5000 fed by five loaves (ch. vi.), the preceding chapter relates to a visit to Jerusalem unnoticed by the three: indeed, the histories seem written of two men, one the "prophet of Galilee" teaching in its cities, the other concentrating his energies on Jerusalem. The account of the miraculous feeding is alike in all: not so the succeeding account of the conduct of the multitude. In the fourth gospel, Jesus and the crowd fall to disputing, as usual, and he loses many disciples: among the three, Luke says nothing of the immediately following events, while Matthew and Mark tell us that the multitudes—as would be natural—crowded round him to touch even the hem of his garment. This is the same as always: in the three the crowd loves him; in the fourth it carps at and argues with him. We must again miss the sojourn of Jesus in Galilee, according to the three, and his visit to Jerusalem, according to the one, and pass to his entry into Jerusalem in triumph. Here we notice a most remarkable divergence: the synoptics tell us that he was going up to Jerusalem from Galilee, and, arriving on his way at Bethphage, he sent for an ass and rode thereon into Jerusalem: the fourth gospel relates that he was dwelling at Jerusalem, and leaving it, for fear of the Jews, he retired, not into Galilee, but "beyond Jordan, into the place where John at first baptised," *i.e.*, Bethabara, "and *there he abode*." From there he went to Bethany and raised to life a putrefying corpse: this stupendous miracle is never appealed to by the earlier historians in proof of their master's greatness, though "much people of the Jews" are said to have seen Lazarus after his resurrection: this miracle is also given as the reason for the active hostility of the priests, "from that day forward." Jesus then retires to Ephraim near the wilderness, from which town he goes to Bethany, and thence in triumph to Jerusalem, being met by the people "for that they heard that he had done this miracle." The two accounts have absolutely nothing in common except the entry into Jerusalem, and the preceding events of the synoptics exclude those of the fourth gospel, as does the latter theirs. If Jesus abode in Bethabara and Ephraim, he could not have come from Galilee; if he started from Galilee, he was not abiding in the south. John xiii.-xvii. stand alone, with the exception of the mention of the traitor. On the arrest of Jesus, he is led (ch. xviii. 13) to Annas, who sends him to Caiaphas, while the others send him direct to Caiaphas, but this is immaterial. He is then taken to Pilate: the Jews do not enter the judgment-hall, lest, being defiled, they could not eat the passover, a feast which, according to the synoptics, was over, Jesus and his disciples having eaten it the night before. Jesus is exposed to the people at the sixth hour (ch. xix. 14), while Mark tells us he was crucified three hours before—at the third hour—a note of time which agrees with the others, since they all relate that there was darkness from the sixth to the ninth hour, *i.e.*, there was thick darkness at the time when, "according to St. John," Jesus was exposed. Here our evangelist is in hopeless conflict with the three. The accounts about the resurrection are irreconcilable in all the gospels, and mutually destructive. It remains to notice, among these discrepancies, one or two points which did not come in conveniently in the course of the narrative. During the whole of the fourth gospel, we find Jesus constantly arguing for his right to the title of Messiah. Andrew speaks of him as such (i. 41); the Samaritans acknowledge him (iv. 42); Peter owns him (vi. 69); the people call him so (vii. 26, 31, 41); Jesus claims it (viii. 24); it is the subject of a law (ix. 22); Jesus speaks of it as already claimed by him (x. 24, 25); Martha recognises it (xi. 27). We thus find that, from the very first, this title is openly claimed by Jesus, and his right to it openly canvassed by the Jews. But —in the three—the disciples acknowledge him as Christ, and he charges them to "tell *no man* that he was Jesus the Christ" (Matt. xvi. 20; Mark viii. 29, 30; Luke ix. 20, 21); and this in the same year that he blames the Jews for not owning this Messiahship, since he had told them who he was "from the beginning" (ch. viii. 24, 25); so that, if "John" was right, we fail to see the object of all the mystery about it, related by the synoptics. We mark, too, how Peter is, in their account, praised for confessing him, for flesh and blood had not revealed it to him, while in the fourth gospel, "flesh and blood," in the person of Andrew, reveal to Peter that the Christ is found; and there seems little praise due to Peter for a confession which had been made two or three years earlier by Andrew, Nathanael, John Baptist, and the Samaritans. Contradiction can scarcely be more direct. In John vii. Jesus owns that the Jews know his birthplace (28), and they state (41, 42) that he comes from Galilee, while Christ should be born at Bethlehem. Matthew and Luke distinctly say Jesus was born at Bethlehem; but here Jesus confesses the right knowledge of those who attribute his birthplace to Galilee, instead of setting their difficulty at rest by explaining that though brought up at Nazareth, he was born in Bethlehem. But our writer was apparently ignorant of their accounts. We reject this gospel, thirdly, because its historical statements are in direct contradiction to the history of the synoptics.

The next point to which I wish to direct attention is the relative position of faith and morals in the three synoptics and the fourth gospel. It is not too much to say that on this point their teaching is absolutely irreconcilable, and one or the other must be fatally in the wrong. Here the fourth gospel clasps hands with Paul, while the others take the side of James. The opposition may be most plainly shown by parallel columns of quotations:

"Except your righteousness exceed that of the scribes and Pharisees, ye shall *in no case* enter. . Heaven."—Matt. v. 20.	"He that *believeth on the* Son hath everlasting life."—iii. 36.
"Have we not prophesied in thy name and in thy name done many wonderful works?" "Then will I profess unto them . . . Depart . . . ye that work iniquity."—Matt. vii. 22, 23.	"He that believeth on Him *is not condemned*."—iii. 18.
"If thou wilt enter into life, keep the commandments."—Mark x. 17-28.	"He that believeth not the Son shall not see life."—iii. 36.
"Her sins, which are many, are forgiven, *for she loved* much."—Luke vii. 47.	"If ye *believe not that I am he*, ye shall die in your sins."—viii. 24.

These few quotations, which might be indefinitely multiplied, are enough to show that, while in the three gospels *doing* is the test of religion, and no profession of discipleship is worth anything unless shown by "its fruits," in the fourth *believing* is the cardinal matter: in the three we hear absolutely nothing of faith in Jesus as requisite, but in the fourth we hear of little else: works are thrown completely into the background and salvation rests on believing—not even in God—but in Jesus. We reject this gospel, fourthly, for setting faith above works, and so contradicting the general teaching of Jesus himself.

The relative positions of the Father and Jesus are reversed by the fourth evangelist, and the teaching of Jesus on this head in the three gospels is directly contradicted. Throughout them Jesus preaches the Father only: he is always reiterating "your heavenly Father;" "that ye may be the children of your Father," is his argument for forgiving others; "your Father is perfect," is his spur to a higher life; "your Father knoweth," is his anodyne in anxiety; "it is the Father's good pleasure," is his certainty of coming happiness; "*one* is your Father, which is in heaven," is, by an even extravagant loyalty, made a reason for denying the very name to any other. But in the fourth gospel all is changed: if the Father is mentioned at all, it is only as the sender of Jesus, as *his* Witness and *his* Glorifier. All love, all devotion, all homage, is directed to Jesus and to Jesus only: even "on the Christian hypothesis the Father is eclipsed by His only begotten Son."* "All judgment" is in the hands of the Son: he has "life in himself;" "the

* Voysey.

work of God" is to believe on him; he gives "life unto the world;" he will "raise" us "up at the last day;" except by eating him there is "no life;" he is "the light of the world;" he gives true freedom; he is the "one shepherd: none can pluck" us out of his hand; he will "draw all men unto" himself: he is the "Lord and Master," "the truth and the life;" what is even asked of the Father, *he* will do; he will come to his disciples and abide in them; his peace and joy are their reward. Verily, we need no more: he who gives us eternal life, who raises us from the dead, who is our judge, who hears our prayers, and gives us light, freedom, and truth, He, He only, is our God; none can do more for us than he: in Him only will we trust in life and death. So, consistently, the Son is no longer the drawer of believers to the Father, but the Father is degraded into becoming the way to the Son, and none can come to Jesus unless Almighty God draws them to him. Jesus is no longer the way into the Holiest, but the Eternal Father is made the means to an end beyond himself.

For this fifth reason, more than for anything else, we reject this gospel with the most passionate earnestness, with the most burning indignation, as an insult to the One Father of spirits, the ultimate Object of all faith and hope and love.

And who is this who thus dethrones our heavenly Father? It is not even the Jesus whose fair moral beauty has exacted our hearty admiration. To worship *him* would be an idolatry, but to worship him—were he such as "John" describes him—would be an idolatry as degrading as it would be baseless. For let us mark the character pourtrayed in this fourth gospel. His public career begins with an undignified miracle: at a marriage, where the wine runs short, he turns water into wine, in order to supply men who have already "well drunk" (ch. ii. 10). [We may ask, in passing, what led Mary to expect a miracle, when we are told that this was the first, and she could not, therefore, know of her son's gifts.] The next important point is the conversation with Nicodemus, where we scarcely knew which to marvel at most, the stolid stupidity of a "Master in Israel" misunderstanding a metaphor that must have been familiar to him, or the aggressive way in which Jesus speaks as to the non-reception of his message before he had been in public many months, and as to non-belief in his person before belief had become possible. We then come to the series of discourses related in ch. v. 10. Perfect egotism pervades them all; in all appear the same strange misunderstandings on the part of the people, the same strange persistence in puzzling them on the part of the speaker. In one of them the people honestly wonder at his mysterious words: "How is it that he saith, I come down from heaven," and, instead of any explanation, Jesus retorts that they should not murmur, since no man *can* come to him unless the Father draw him; so that, when he puts forward a statement apparently contrary to fact—"his father and mother we know," say the puzzled Jews—he refuses to explain it, and falls back on his favourite doctrine: "Unless you are of those favoured ones whom God enlightens, you cannot expect to understand me." Little wonder indeed that "many of his disciples walked no more with" a teacher so perplexing and so discouraging; with one who presented for their belief a mysterious doctrine, contrary to their experience, and then, in answer to their prayer for enlightenment, taunts them with an ignorance he admits was unavoidable. The next important conversation occurs in the temple, and here Jesus, the friend of sinners, the bringer of hope to the despairing—this Jesus has no tenderness for some who "believed on him;" he ruthlessly tramples on the bruised reed and quenches the smoking flax. First he irritates their Jewish pride with accusations of slavery and low descent; then, groping after his meaning, they exclaim, "We have one Father, even God," and he—whom we know as the tenderest preacher of that Father's universal love—surely he gladly catches at their struggling appreciation of his favourite topic, and fans the hopeful spark into a flame? Yes! Jesus of Nazareth would have done so. But Jesus, "according to St. John," turns fiercely on them, denying the sonship he elsewhere proclaims, and retorts, "Ye are of your father, the devil." And this to men who "believed on him;" this from lips which said, "*One* is your Father," and He, in heaven. He argues next with the Pharisees, and we find him arrogantly exclaiming: "*all* that ever came before me were thieves and robbers." What, all? Moses and Elijah, Isaiah and all the prophets? At length, after he has once more repulsed some inquirers, the Jews take up stones to stone him, as Moses commanded, because "thou makest thyself God." He escapes by a clever evasion, which neutralises all his apparent assertions of Divinity. "Other men have been called gods, so surely I do not blaspheme by calling myself God's son." Never let us forget that in this gospel, the stronghold of the Divinity of Jesus, Jesus himself explains his strongest assertion "I and my Father are one" in a manner which can only be honest in the mouth of a man.* We pass to the celebrated "last discourse." In this we find the same peculiar style, the same self-assertion, but we must note, in addition, the distinct tri-theism which pervades it. There are three distinct Beings, each necessarily deprived of some attribute of Divinity: thus, the Deity is Infinite, but if He is divided He becomes finite, since two Infinites are an impossible absurdity, and unless they are identical they must bound each other, so becoming finite. Accordingly "the Comforter" cannot be present till Jesus departs, therefore neither Jesus nor the Comforter can be God, since God is omnipresent. Since, then, prayer is to be addressed to Jesus as God, the low theory of tri-theism, of a plurality of Gods, none of whom is a perfect God, is here taught. In this discourse, also, the Christian horizon is bounded by the figure of Jesus, the office of the Comforter is subservient to this one worship, "he shall glorify me." Jesus, at last, prays for his disciples, markedly excluding from his intercession "the world" he was said to have come to save, and, as throughout this gospel, restricting all his love, all his care, all his tenderness to "these, whom Thou hast given me." Here we come to the essence of the spirit which pervades this whole gospel. "I pray for them; I pray not for the world: not for them who are of their father the devil, nor for my betrayer, the son of perdition." This is the spirit which Christians dare to ascribe to Jesus of Nazareth, the tenderest, gentlest, widest-hearted man who has yet graced humanity. This is the spirit, they tell us, which dwelt in *his* bosom, who gave us the parables of the lost sheep and the prodigal son. "No," we answer, "this is not the spirit of the Prophet of Nazareth, but" (Dr. Liddon will pardon the appropriation) "this is the temper of a man who will not enter the public baths along with the heretic who has dishonoured his Lord." This is the spirit of the writer of

* For a good work we stone thee not, but for blasphemy; and because that thou being a man makest thyself God." Jesus answered them, "Is it not written in your law, I said, ye are gods? If he called them gods unto whom the word of God came (and the scripture cannot be broken), say ye of him whom the Father hath sanctified and sent into the world, Thou blasphemest, because I said I am the son of God?"

the gospel, not of Jesus: the egotism of the writer is reflected in the words put into the mouth of his master; and thus the preacher of the Father's love is degraded into the seeker of his own glory, and bearing witness of himself, his witness becomes untrue. I must also draw attention to one or two cases of unreality attributed to Jesus by this gospel. He prays, on one occasion, "because of the people who stand by:" he cries on his cross, "I thirst," not because of the burning agony of crucifixion, but in order "that the Scriptures might be fulfilled:" a voice answers his prayer, "not because of me, but for your sakes." This calculation of effect is very foreign to the sincere and open spirit of Jesus. Akin to this is the prevarication attributed to him, when he declines to accompany his brethren to Judæa, but "when his brethren were gone up then went he also up to the feast, not openly but as it were in secret." All this strikes us strangely as part of that simple, fearless life.

We reject this gospel, sixthly, for the cruel spirit, the arrogance, the self-assertion, the bigotry, the unreality, attributed by it to Jesus, and we denounce it as a slander on his memory and an insult to his noble life.

We may, perhaps, note, as another peculiarity of this gospel—although I do not enter here into the argument of the divinity of Jesus,—that when Dr. Liddon, in his celebrated Bampton Lectures, is anxious to prove the Deity of Jesus *from his own mouth*, he is compelled to quote exclusively from this gospel. Such a fact as this cannot be overlooked, when we remember that "St. John's gospel is a polemical treatise" written to prove this special point. We cannot avoid noting the coincidence.

We have now gone through this remarkable record and examined it in various lights. At the outset we conceded to our opponents all the advantage which comes from admitting that the gospel *may* be written by the Apostle John; we have left the authorship a moot point, and based our argument on a different ground. Apostolic or non-apostolic, Johannine or Corinthian, we accept it or reject it for itself, and not for its writer. We have found that all its characters speak alike in a marked and peculiar style—a style savouring of the study rather than the street, of Alexandria rather than Jerusalem or Galilee. We have glanced at its immoral partiality. We have noted the numerous discrepancies between the history of this gospel and that of the three synoptics. We have discovered it to be equally opposed to them in morals as in history: in doctrine as in morals. We have seen that, while it degrades God to enthrone Jesus in His stead, it also degrades Jesus, and so lowers his character that it defies recognition. Finally, we have found it stands alone in supporting the Deity of Jesus from his own mouth.

I know not how all this may strike others; to me these arguments are simply overwhelming in their force. I tear out the "Gospel according to St. John" from the writings which "are profitable" "for instruction in righteousness." I reject it from beginning to end, as fatally destructive of all true faith towards God, as perilously subversive of all true morality in man, as an outrage on the sacred memory of Jesus of Nazareth, and as an insult to the Justice, the Supremacy, and the Unity of Almighty God.

ON THE ATONEMENT.

THE Atonement may be regarded as the central doctrine of Christianity, the very *raison d'être* of the Christian faith. Take this away, and there would remain indeed a faith and a morality, but both would have lost their distinctive features: it would be a faith without its centre, and a morality without its foundation. Christianity would be unrecognisable without its angry God, its dying Saviour, its covenant signed with "the blood of the Lamb:" the blotting out of the Atonement would deprive millions of all hope towards God, and would cast them from satisfaction into anxiety, from comfort into despair. The warmest feelings of Christendom cluster round the Crucifix, and he, the crucified one, is adored with passionate devotion, not as martyr for truth, not as witness for God, not as faithful to death, but as the substitute for his worshippers, as he who bears in their stead the wrath of God, and the punishment due to sin. The Christian is taught to see in the bleeding Christ the victim slain in his own place; he himself should be hanging on that cross, agonised and dying; those nail-pierced hands ought to be his; the anguish on that face should be furrowed on his own; the weight of suffering resting on that bowed head should be crushing himself into the dust. In the simplest meaning of the words, Christ is the sinner's substitute, and on him the sin of the world is laid: as Luther expressed it, he "is the greatest and only sinner;" literally "made sin" for mankind, and expiating the guilt which, in very deed, was transferred from man to him.

I wish at the outset, for the sake of justice and candour, to acknowledge frankly the good which has been drawn forth by the preaching of the Cross. This good has been, however, the indirect rather than the direct result of a belief in the Atonement. The doctrine, in itself, has nothing elevating about it, but the teaching closely connected with the doctrine has its ennobling and purifying side. All the enthusiasm aroused in the human breast by the thought of one who sacrificed himself to save his brethren, all the consequent longing to emulate that love by sacrificing all for Jesus and for those for whom he died, all the moral gain caused by the contemplation of a sublime self-devotion, all these are the fruits of the nobler side of the Atonement. That the sinless should stoop to the sinful, that holiness should embrace the guilty in order to raise them to its own level, has struck a chord in men's bosoms which has responded to the touch by a harmonious melody of gratitude to the divine and sinless sufferer, and loving labour for suffering and sinful man. The Cross has been at once the apotheosis and the source of self-sacrificing love. "Love ye one another *as* I have loved you: not in word but in deed, with a deep self-sacrificing love:" such is the lesson which, according to one of the most orthodox Anglican divines, "Christ preaches to us from His Cross." In believing in the Atonement, man's heart has, as usual, been better than his head; he has passed over the dark side of the idea, and has seized on the divine truth that the strong should gladly devote themselves to shield the weak, that labour, even unto death, is the right of humanity from every son of man. It is often said that no doctrine long retains its hold on men's hearts which is not founded on some great truth; this divine idea of self-sacrifice has been the truth contained in the doctrine of the Atonement, which has made it so dear to many loving and noble souls, and which has hidden its "multitude of sins"—sins against love and against justice, against God and against man. Love and self-sacrifice have floated the great error over the storms of centuries, and these cords still bind to it many hearts of which love and self-sacrifice are the glory and the crown.

This said, in candi dhomage to the good which has drawn its inspiration from Jesus crucified, we turn to the examination of the doctrine itself: if we find that it is as dishonouring to God as it is injurious to man, a crime against justice, a blasphemy against love, we must forget all the sentiments which cluster round it, and reject it utterly. It is well to speak respectfully of that which is dear to any religious soul, and to avoid jarring harshly on the strings of religious feeling, even though the soul be misled and the feeling be misdirected; but a time comes when false charity is cruelty, and tenderness to error is treason to truth. For long, men who know its emptiness pass by in silence the shrine consecrated by human hopes and fears, by love and worship, and the "times of this ignorance God (in the bold figure of Paul) also winks at;" but when "the fulness of the time is come," God sends forth some true son of his to dash the idol to the ground, and to trample it into dust. We need not be afraid that the good wrought by the lessons derived from the Atonement in time past will disappear with the doctrine itself; the mark of the Cross is too deeply ploughed into humanity ever to be erased, and those who no longer call themselves by the name of Christ are not the most backward scholars in the school of love and sacrifice.

The history of this doctrine has been a curious one. In the New Testament the Atonement is, as its name implies, a simply making at one God and man: *how* this is done is but vaguely hinted at, and in order to deduce the modern doctrine from the Bible, we must import into the books of the New Testament all the ideas derived from theological disputations. Words used in all simplicity by the ancient writers must have attached to them the definite polemical meaning they hold in the quarrels of theologians, before they can be strained into supporting a substitutionary atonement. The idea, however, of "ransom" is connected with the work of Jesus, and the question arose, "to whom is this ransom paid?" They who lived in those first centuries of Christianity were still too much within the illumination of the tender halo thrown by Jesus round the Father's name, to dream for a moment that their redeemer had ransomed them from the beloved hands of God. No, the ransom was paid to the devil, whose thrall they believed mankind to be, and Jesus, by sacrificing himself, had purchased them from the devil and made them sons of God. It is not worth while to enter on the quaint details of this scheme, how the devil thought he had conquered and could hold Jesus captive, and was tricked by finding that his imagined gain could not be retained by him, and so on. Those who wish to become acquainted with this ingenious device can study it in the pages of the Christian fathers: it has at least one advantage over the modern plan, namely, that we are not so shocked at hearing of pain and suffering as acceptable to the supposed incarnate evil, as at hearing of them being offered as a sacrifice to the supreme good. As the teaching of Jesus lost its power, and became more and more polluted by the cruel thoughts of savage and bigoted men, the doctrine of the atonement gradually changed its character. Men thought the Almighty to be such a one as themselves, and being fierce and unforgiving and revengeful, they projected their own shadows on to the clouds which surrounded the Deity, and then, like the shepherd who meets his own form reflected and magnified on the mountain mist, they recoiled before the image they themselves had made. The loving Father who sent his son to rescue his perishing children by sacrificing himself, fades away from the hearts of the Christian world, and there looms darkly in his place an awful form, the inexorable judge who exacts a debt man is too poor to pay, and who, in default of payment, casts the debtor into a hopeless prison, hopeless unless another pays to the uttermost farthing the fine demanded by the law. So, in this strange transformation-scene God actually takes the place of the devil, and the ransom once paid to redeem men from Satan becomes the ransom paid to redeem men from God. It reminds one of the quarrels over the text which bids us "fear him who is able to destroy both body and soul in hell," when we remain in doubt whom he is we are to fear, since half the Christian commentators assure us that it refers to our Father in heaven, while the other half asseverate that the devil is the individual we are to dread. The seal was set on the "redemption scheme" by Anselm in his great work, "*Cur Deus Homo*," and the doctrine which had been slowly growing into the theology of Christendom was thenceforward stamped with the signet of the Church. Roman Catholics and Protestants, at the time of the Reformation, alike believed in the vicarious and substitutionary character of the atonement wrought by Christ. There is no dispute between them on this point. I prefer to allow the Christian divines to speak for themselves as to the character of the atonement: no one can accuse me of exaggerating their views, if their views are given in their own words. Luther teaches that "Christ did truly and effectually feel for all mankind, the wrath of God, malediction and death." Flavel says that "to wrath, to the wrath of an infinite God without mixture, to the very torments of hell, was Christ delivered, and that by the hand of his own father." The Anglican homily preaches that "sin did pluck God out of heaven to make him feel the horrors and pains of death," and that man, being a firebrand of hell and a bondsman of the devil, "was ransomed by the death of his own only and well-beloved son;" the "heat of his wrath," "his burning wrath," could only be "pacified" by Jesus, "so pleasant was this sacrifice and oblation of his son's death." Edwards, being logical, saw that there was a gross injustice in sin being twice punished, and in the pains of hell, the penalty of sin, being twice inflicted, first on Christ, the substitute of mankind, and then on the lost, a portion of mankind. So he, in common with most Calvinists, finds himself compelled to restrict the atonement to the elect, and declared that Christ bore the sins, not of the world, but of the chosen out of the world; he suffers "not for the world, but for them whom Thou hast given me." But Edwards adheres firmly to the belief in substitution, and rejects the universal atonement for the very reason that "to believe Christ died for all is the surest way of proving that he died for none in the sense Christians have hitherto believed." He declares that "Christ suffered the wrath of God for men's sins;" that "God imposed his wrath due unto, and Christ underwent the pains of hell for," sin. Owen regards Christ's sufferings as "a full valuable compensation to the justice of God for all the sins" of the elect, and says that he underwent "that same punishment which . . . . . they themselves were bound to undergo."

The doctrine of the Christian Church—in the widest sense of that much-fought-over term—was then as follows, and I will state it in language which is studiously moderate, *as compared with the orthodox teaching* of the great Christian divines. If any one doubts this assertion, let him study their writings for himself. I really dare not transfer some of their expressions to my own pages. God the Father having cursed mankind and condemned them to eternal damnation, because of Adam's disobedience in eating an apple—or some other fruit, for the species is only preserved by tradition, and is not definitely settled by the inspired writings—and having further cursed each man for his own individual transgressions, man lay under the fierce wrath of God, unable to escape, and unable to pacify it, for he could not even atone for his own private sins, much less for his share of the guilt incurred by his forefather in Paradise. Man's debt was hopelessly large, and he had "nothing to pay;" so all that remained to him was to suffer an eternity of torture, which sad fate he had merited by the crime of being born into an accursed world. The second person of the Trinity moved to pity by the helpless and miserable state of mankind, interposed between the first person of the Trinity and the wretched sinners; he received into his own breast the fire-tipped arrows of divine wrath, and by suffering inconceivable tortures, equal in amount to an eternity of the torments of hell, he wrung from God's hands the pardon of mankind, or of a portion thereof. God, pacified by witnessing this awful agony of one who had from all eternity been "lying in his bosom" co-equal sharer of his Majesty and glory, and the object of his tenderest love, relents from his fierce wrath, and consents to accept the pain of Jesus as a substitute for the pain of mankind. In plain terms, then, God is represented as a Being so awfully cruel, so implacably revengeful, that pain *as* pain, and death *as* death, are what he demands as a propitiatory sacrifice, and with nothing less than extremest agony can his fierce claims on mankind be bought off. The due weight of suffering he must have, but it is a matter of indifference whether it is undergone by Jesus or by mankind. Did not the old Fathers do well in making the awful ransom a matter between Jesus and the devil?

When this point is pressed on Christians, and one urges the dishonour done to God by painting him in colours from which heart and soul recoil in shuddering horror, by ascribing to him a revengefulness and pitiless cruelty in comparison with which the worst efforts of human malignity appear but childish mischief, they are quick to retort that we are caricaturing Christian doctrine; they will allow, when overwhelmed with evidence, that "strong language" has been used in past centuries, but will say that such views are not now held, and that they do not ascribe such harsh dealing to God the Father. Theists are therefore compelled to prove each step of their accusation, and to quote from Christian writers the words which embody the views they assail. Were I simply to state that Christians in these days ascribe to Almighty God a fierce wrath against the whole human race, that this wrath can only be soothed by suffering and death, that he vents this wrath on an innocent head, and that he is well pleased by the sight of the agony of his beloved Son, a shout of indignation would rise from a thousand lips, and I should be accused of exaggeration, of false witness, of blasphemy. So once more I write down the doctrine from Christian dictation, and, be it remembered, the sentences I quote are from published works, and are therefore, the outcome of serious deliberation; they are not overdrawn pictures taken from the fervid eloquence of excited oratory, when the speaker may perhaps be carried further than he would, in cold blood, consent to.

Stroud makes Christ drink "the cup of the wrath of God." Jenkyn says, "he suffered as one disowned and reprobated and forsaken of God." Dwight considers that he endured God's "hatred and contempt." Bishop Jeune tells us that "after man had done his worst, worse remained for Christ to bear. He had fallen into his father's hands." Archbishop Thomson preaches that "the clouds of God's wrath gathered thick over the whole human race: they discharged themselves on Jesus only;" he "becomes a curse for us, and a vessel of wrath." Liddon echoes the same sentiment: "the apostles teach that mankind are slaves, and that Christ on the Cross is paying their ransom. Christ crucified is voluntarily devoted and accursed:" he even speaks of "the precise amount of ignominy and pain needed for the redemption," and says that the "divine victim" paid more than was absolutely necessary.

These quotations seem sufficient to prove that the Christians of the present day are worthy followers of the elder believers. The theologians first quoted are indeed coarser in their expressions, and are less afraid of speaking out exactly what they believe, but there is no real difference of creed between the awful doctrine of Flavel and the polished dogma of Canon Liddon. The older and the modern Christians alike believe in the bitter wrath of God against "the whole human race." Both alike regard the Atonement as so much pain tendered by Jesus to the Almighty Father in payment of a debt of pain owed to God by humanity. They alike represent God as only to be pacified by the sight of suffering. Man has insulted and injured God, and God must be revenged by inflicting suffering on the sinner in return. The "hatred and contempt" God launched at Jesus were due to the fact that Jesus was the sinner's substitute, and are therefore the feelings which animate the Divine heart towards the sinner himself. God hates and despises the world. He would have "consumed it in a moment" in the fire of his burning wrath, had not Jesus, "his chosen, stood before him in the gap to turn away his wrathful indignation."

Now, how far is all this consistent with justice? Is the

wrath of God against humanity justified by the circumstances of the case, so that we may be obliged to own that some sacrifice was due from sinful man to his Creator, to propitiate a justly incensed and holy God? I trow not. On this first count, the Atonement is a fearful injustice. For God has allowed men to be brought into the world with sinful inclinations, and to be surrounded with many temptations and much evil. He has made man imperfect, and the child is born into the world with an imperfect nature. It is radically unjust, then, that God should curse the work of His hands for being what He made them, and condemn them to endless misery for failing to do the impossible. Allowing that Christians are right in believing that Adam was sinless when he came from his Maker's hands, these remarks apply to every other living soul since born into the world; the Genesis myth will not extricate Christians from the difficulty. Christians are quite right and are justified by facts when they say that man is born into the world frail, imperfect, prone to sin and error; but who, we ask them, made men so? Does not their own Bible tell them that the "potter hath power over the clay," and, further, that "we are the clay and thou art the potter?" To curse men for being men, *i.e.*, imperfect moral beings, is the height of cruelty and injustice; to condemn the morally weak to hell for sin, *i.e.*, for failing in moral strength, is about as fair as sentencing a sick man to death because he cannot stand upright. Christians try and avoid the force of this by saying that men should rely on God's grace to uphold them, but they fail to see that this *very want of reliance* is part of man's natural weakness. The sick man might be blamed for falling because he did not lean on a stronger arm, but suppose he was too weak to grasp it? Further, few Christians believe that it is impossible in practice, however possible in theory, to lead a perfect life; and as to "offend in one point is to be guilty of all," one failure is sufficient to send the generally righteous man to hell. Besides, they forget that infants are included under the curse, although *necessarily* incapable of grasping the idea either of sin or of God; all babies born into the world and dying before becoming capable of acting for themselves would, we are taught, have been inevitably consigned to hell, had it not been for the Atonement of Jesus. Some Christians actually believe that unbaptized babies are not admitted into heaven, and in a Roman Catholic book descriptive of hell, a poor little baby writhes and screams in a red-hot oven.

This side of the Atonement, this unjust demand on men for a righteousness they could not render, necessitating a sacrifice to propitiate God for non-compliance with his exaction, has had its due effect on men's minds, and has alienated their hearts from God. No wonder that men turned away from a God who, like a passionate but unskilful workman, dashes to pieces the instrument he has made because it fails in its purpose, and, instead of blaming his own want of skill, vents his anger on the helpless thing that is only what he made it. Most naturally, also, have men shrunk from the God who "avengeth and is furious" to the tender, pitiful, human Jesus, who loved sinners so deeply as to choose to suffer for their sakes. They could owe no gratitude to an Almighty Being who created them and cursed them, and only consented to allow them to be happy on condition that another paid for them the misery he demanded as his due; but what gratitude could be enough for him who rescued them from the fearful hands of the living God, at the cost of almost intolerable suffering to himself? Let us remember that Christ is said to suffer the very torments of hell, and that his worst sufferings were when "fallen into his father's hands," out of which he has rescued us, and then can we wonder that the crucified is adored with a very ecstasy of gratitude? Imagine what it is to be saved from the hands of him who inflicted an agony admitted to be unlimited, and who took advantage of an infinite capacity in order to inflict an infinite pain. It is well for the men before whose eyes this awful spectre has flitted that the fair humanity of Jesus gives them a refuge to fly to, else what but despair and madness could have been the doom of those who, without Jesus, would have seen enthroned above the wailing universe naught but an infinite cruelty and an Almighty foe.

We see, then, that the necessity for an atonement makes the Eternal Father both unjust in his demands on men and cruel in his punishment of inevitable failure; but there is another injustice which is of the very essence of the Atonement itself. This consists in the vicarious character of the sacrifice: a new element of injustice is introduced when we consider that the person sacrificed is not even the guilty party. If a man offends against law, justice requires that he should be punished: the punishment becomes unjust if it is excessive, as in the case we have been considering above; but it is equally unjust to allow him to go free without punishment. Christians are right in affirming that moral government would be at an end were men allowed to sin with impunity, and did an easy forgiveness succeed to each offence. They appeal to our instinctive sense of justice to approve the sentiment that punishment should follow sin: we acquiesce, and hope that we have now reached a firm standing-ground from which to proceed further in our investigation. But, no; they promptly outrage that same sense of justice which they have called as a witness on their side, by asking us to believe that its ends are attained provided that somebody or other is punished. When we reply that *this* is not justice, we are promptly bidden not to be presumptuous and argue from our human ideas of justice as to the course that ought to be pursued by the absolute justice of God. "Then why appeal to it at all?" we urge; "why talk of justice in the matter if we are totally unable to judge as to the rights and wrongs of the case?" At this point we are commonly overwhelmed with Paul's notable argument—"Nay, but, O man, who art thou that repliest against God?" But if Christians value the simplicity and straightforwardness of their own minds, they should not use words which convey a certain accepted meaning in this shuffling, double sense. When we speak of "justice," we speak of a certain well-understood quality, and we do not speak of a mysterious divine attribute, which has not only nothing in common with human justice, but which is in direct opposition to that which we understand by that name. Suppose a man condemned to death for murder: the judge is about to sentence him, when a bystander—as it chances, the judge's own son—interposes: "My Lord, the prisoner is guilty and deserves to be hanged; but if you will let him go, I will die in his place." The offer is accepted, the prisoner is set free, the judge's son is hanged in his stead. What is all this? Self-sacrifice (however misdirected), love, enthusiasm—what you will; but certainly not *justice*—nay, the grossest injustice, a second murder, an ineffaceable stain on the ermine of the outraged law. I imagine that, in this supposed case, no Christian will be found to assert that justice was done; yet call the judge God, the prisoner mankind, the substitute Jesus, and the trial scene is exactly reproduced. Then, in the name of candour and common sense, why call that just in God which we see would be so unjust and immoral in man? This vicarious nature of the Atonement also degrades the divine name, by making him utterly careless in the matter of punishment: all he is anxious for, according to this detestable theory, is that he should strike a blow *somewhere.* Like a child in a passion, he only feels the desire to hurt somebody, and strikes out vaguely and at random. There is no discrimination used; the thunderbolt is launched into a crowd: it falls on the head of the "sinless son," and crushes the innocent, while the sinner goes free. What matter? It has fallen somewhere, and the "burning fire of his wrath" is cooled. This is what men call the vindication of the justice of the Moral Governor of the universe: this is "the act of God's awful holiness," which marks his hatred of sin, and his immovable determination to punish it. But when we reflect that this justice is consistent with letting off the guilty and punishing the innocent person, we feel dread misgivings steal into our minds. The justice of our Moral Governor has nothing in common with our justice—indeed, it violates all our notions of right and wrong. What if, as Mr. Vance Smith suggests, this strange justice be consistent also with a double punishment of sin; and what if the Moral Governor should bethink himself that, having confused morality by an unjust—humanly speaking, of course—punishment, it would be well to set things straight again by punishing the guilty after all? We can never dare to feel safe in the hands of this unjust—humanly speaking—Moral Governor, or predicate from our instinctive notions of right and wrong what his requirements may be. One is lost in astonishment that men should believe such things of God, and not have manhood enough to rise up rebellious against such injustice—should, instead, crouch at his feet, and while trying to hide themselves from his wrath should force their trembling lips to murmer some incoherent acknowledgment of his mercy. Ah! they do not believe it; they assert it in words, but, thank God, it makes no impression on their hearts; and they would die a thousand deaths rather than imitate, in their dealings with their fellow-men, the fearful cruelty which the Church has taught them to call the justice of the Judge of all the earth.

The Atonement is not only doubly unjust, but it is perfectly futile. We are told that Christ took away the sins of the world; we have a right to ask, "how?" So far as we can judge, we bear our sins in our own bodies still, and the Atonement helps us not at all. Has he borne the physical consequences of sin, such as the loss of health caused by intemperance of all kinds? Not at all, this penalty remains, and, from the nature of things, cannot be transferred. Has he borne the social consequences, shame, loss of credit, and so on? They remain still to hinder us as we strive to rise after our fall. Has he at least borne the pangs of remorse for us, the stings of conscience? By no means; the tears of sorrow are no less bitter, the prickings of repentance no less keen. Perhaps he has struck at the root of evil, and has put away sin itself out of a redeemed world? Alas! the wailing that goes up to heaven from a world oppressed with sin weeps out a sorrowfully emphatic, "no, this he has *not* done." What has he then borne for us? Nothing, save the phantom wrath of a phantom tyrant; all that is real exists the same as before. We turn away, then, from the offered atonement with a feeling that would be impatience at such trifling, were it not all too sorrowful, and leave the Christians to impose on their imagined sacrifice, the imagined burden of the guilt of the accursed race.

Further, the Atonement is, from the nature of things, entirely impossible: we have seen how Christ fails to bear our sins in any intelligible sense, but can he, in any way, bear the "punishment" of sin? The idea that the punishment of sin can be transferred from one person to another is radically false, and arises from a wrong conception of the punishment consequent on sin, and from the ecclesiastical guilt, so to speak, thought to be incurred thereby. *The only true punishment of sin is the injury caused by it to our moral nature:* all the indirect punishments, we have seen, Christ has not taken away, and the true punishment can fall only on ourselves. For sin is nothing more than the transgression of law. All law, when broken, entails *of necessity* an appropriate penalty, and recoils, as it were, on the transgressor. A natural law, when broken, avenges itself by consequent suffering, and so does a spiritual law: the injury wrought by the latter is not less real, although less obvious. Physical sin brings physical suffering; spiritual, moral, mental sin brings each its own appropriate punishment. "Sin" has become such a cant term that we lose sight, in using it, of its real simple meaning, a breaking of law. Imagine any sane man coming and saying, "My dear friend, if you like to put your hand into the fire I will bear the punishment of being burnt, and you shall not suffer." It is quite as absurd to imagine that if I sin Jesus can bear my consequent suffering. If a man lies habitually, for instance, he grows thoroughly untrue: let him repent ever so vigorously, he must bear the consequences of his past deeds, and fight his way back slowly to truthfulness of word and thought: no atonement, nothing in heaven or earth save his own labour, will restore to him the forfeited jewel of instinctive candour. Thus the "punishment" of untruthfulness is the loss of the power of being true, just as the punishment of putting the hand into the fire is the loss of the power of grasping. But in addition to this simple and most just and natural "retribution," theologians have invented certain arbitrary penalties as a punishment of sin, the wrath of God and hell fire. These imaginary penalties are discharged by an equally imaginary atonement, the natural punishment remaining as before; so after all we only reject the two sets of inventions which balance each other, and find ourselves just in the same position as they are, having gained infinitely in simplicity and naturalness. The punishment of sin is not an arbitrary penalty, but an inevitable sequence: Jesus may bear, if his worshippers will have it so, the theological fiction of the "*guilt* of sin," an idea derived from the ceremonial uncleanness of the Levitical law, but let him leave alone the solemn realities connected with the sacred and immutable laws of God.

Doubly unjust, useless, and impossible, it might be deemed a work of supererogation to argue yet further against the Atonement; but its hold on men's minds is too firm to allow us to lay down a single weapon which can be turned against it. So, in addition to these defects, I remark that, viewed as a propitiatory sacrifice to Almighty God, it is thoroughly inadequate. If God, being righteous, as we believe Him to be, regarded man with anger because of man's sinfulness, what is obviously the required propitiation? Surely the removal of the cause of anger, *i.e.*, of sin itself, and the seeking by man of righteousness. The old Hebrew prophet saw this plainly, and his idea of atonement is the true one: "*wherewith* shall I come before the Lord," he is asked, with burnt-offerings or—choicer still—parental anguish over a first-born's corpse? "What doth the Lord require of thee," is the reproving answer, "but to do justly and to love mercy, and to walk humbly with thy God?" But what is the propitiatory element in the Christian Atonement? let Canon Liddon answer: "the ignominy and pain *needed* for the redemption." Ignominy, agony, blood, death, these are what Christians offer up as an acceptable sacrifice to the Spirit of Love. But what have all these in common with the demands of the Eternal Righteousness, and how can pain atone for sin? they have no relation to each other; there is no appropriateness in the offered exchange. These terrible offerings are in keeping with the barbarous ideas of uncivilized nations, and we understand the feelings which prompt the savage to immolate tortured victims on the altars of his gloomy gods; they are appropriate sacrifices to the foes of mankind, who are to be bought off from injuring us by our offering them an equivalent pain to that they desire to inflict, but they are offensive when given to Him who is the Friend and Lover of Humanity. An Atonement which offers suffering as a propitiation can have nothing in common with God's will for man, and must be utterly beside the mark, perfectly inadequate. If we must have Atonement, let it at least consist of something which will suit the Righteousness and Love of God, and be in keeping with his perfection; let it not borrow the language of ancient savagery, and breathe of blood and dying victims, and tortured human frames, racked with pain.

Lastly, I impeach the Atonement as injurious in several ways to human morality. It has been extolled as "meeting the needs of the awakened sinner" by soothing his fears of punishment with the gift of a substitute who has already suffered his sentence for him; but nothing can be more pernicious than to console a sinner with the promise that he shall escape the punishment he has justly deserved. The Atonement may meet the first superficial feelings of a man startled into the consciousness of his sinfulness, it may soothe the first vague fears and act as an opiate to the awakened conscience; but it does *not* fulfil the cravings of a heart deeply yearning after righteousness; it offers a legal justification to a soul which is longing for purity, it offers freedom from *punishment* to a soul longing for freedom from *sin*. The true penitent does not seek to be shielded from the consequences of his past errors: he accepts them meekly, bravely, humbly, learning through pain the lesson of future purity. An atonement which steps in between us and this fatherly discipline ordained by God, would be a curse and not a blessing; it would rob us of our education and deprive us of a priceless instruction. The force of temptation is fearfully added to by the idea that repentance lays the righteous penalty of transgression on another head; this doctrine gives a direct encouragement to sin, as even Paul perceived when he said, "shall we continue in sin that grace may abound?" Some one has remarked, I think, that though Paul ejaculates, "God forbid," his fears were well founded and have been widely realised. To the Atonement we owe the morbid sentiment which believes in the holy death of a ruffianly murderer, because, goaded by ungovernable terror, he has snatched at the offered safety and been "washed in the blood of the lamb." To it we owe the unwholesome glorying in the pious sentiments of such an one, who ought to go out of this life sadly and silently, without a sickening parade of feelings of love towards the God whose laws, as long as he could, he has broken and despised. But the Christian teachers will extol the "saving grace" which has made the felon die with words of joyful assurance, meet only for the lips of one who crowns a saintly life with a peaceful death. The Atonement has weakened that stern condemnation of sin which is the safeguard of purity; it has softened down moral differences, and placed the penitent above the saint; it has dulled the feeling of responsibility in the soul; it has taken away the help, such as it is, of fear of punishment for sin; it has confused man's sense of justice, outraged his feeling of right, blunted his conscience, and misdirected his repentance. It has chilled his love to God by representing the universal father as a cruel tyrant and a remorseless and unjust judge. It has been the fruitful parent of all asceticism, for, since God was pacified by suffering once, he would, of course, be pleased with suffering at all times, and so men have logically ruined their bodies to save their souls, and crushed their feelings and lacerated their hearts to propitiate the awful form frowning behind the cross of Christ. To the Atonement we owe it that God is served by fear instead of by love, that monasticism holds its head above the sweet sanctities of love and home, that religion is crowned with thorns and not with roses, that the *miserere* and not the *gloria* is the strain from earth to heaven. The Atonement teaches men to crouch at the feet of God, instead of raising loving, joyful faces to meet his radiant smile; it shuts out his sunshine from us, and veils us in the night of an impenetrable dread. What is the sentiment with which Canon Liddon closes a sermon on the death of Christ? I quote it to show the slavish feeling engendered by this doctrine in a very noble human soul: "In ourselves, indeed, there is nothing that should stay His (God's) arm or invite his mercy. But may he have respect to the acts and the sufferings of his sinless son? Only while contemplating the inestimable merits of the Redeemer can we dare to hope that our heavenly Father will overlook the countless provocations which he receives at the hands of the redeemed." Is this a wholesome sentiment, either as regards our feelings towards God or our efforts towards holiness? Is it well to look to the purity of another as a makewight for our personal shortcomings? All these injuries to morality done by the atonement are completed by the crowning one, that it offers to the sinner a veil of "imputed righteousness." Not only does it take from him his saving punishment, but it nullifies his strivings after holiness by offering him a righteousness which is not his own. It introduces into the solemn region of duty to God the legal fiction of a gift of holiness, which is imputed, not won. We are taught to believe that we can blind the eyes of God and satisfy him with a pretended purity. But that every one whose purity we seek to claim as ours, that fair blossom of humanity, Jesus of Nazareth, whose mission we so misconstrue, launched his anathema at whited sepulchres, pure without and foul within. What would he have said of the whitewash of "imputed righteousness?" Stern and sharp would have been his rebuke, methinks, to a device so untrue, and well-deserved would have been his thundered "woe" on a hypocrisy that would fain deceive God as well as man.

These considerations have carried so great a weight with the most enlightened and progressive minds among Christians themselves, that there has grown up a party in the Church whose repudiation of an atonement of agony and death is as complete as even we could wish. They denounce with the utmost fervour the hideous notion of a "bloody sacrifice," and are urgent in their representations of the dishonour done to God by ascribing to him "pleasure in the death of him that dieth," or satisfaction in the sight of pain. They point out that there is no virtue in blood to wash away sin, not even "in the blood of a God." Maurice eloquently pleads against the idea that the suffering of the "well-beloved Son" was in itself an acceptable sacrifice to the Almighty Father, and he sees the atoning element in the "holiness and graciousness of the Son." Writers of this school perceive that a moral and not a physical sacrifice can be the only acceptable offering to the Father of spirits, but the great objection lies against their theory also, that the Atonement is still vicarious. Christ still suffers *for* man, in order to make men acceptable to God. It is, perhaps, scarcely fair to say this of the school as a whole, since the opinions of Broad Church divines differ widely from each other, ranging from the orthodox to the Socinian standing-point. Yet, roughly speaking, we may say that while they have given up the error of thinking that the death of Christ reconciles God to us, they yet believe that his death, in some mysterious manner, reconciles us to God. It is a matter of deep thankfulness that they give up the old cruel idea of propitiating God, and so prepare the way for a higher creed. Their more humane teaching reaches hearts which are as yet sealed against us, and they are the John Baptist of the Theistic Christ. We must still urge on them that an atonement at all is superfluous, that all the parade of reconciliation by means of *a* mediator is perfectly unnecessary as between God and his child, man; that the notion put forward that Christ realised the ideal of humanity and propitiated God by showing what a man *could* be, is objectionable in that it represents God as needing to be taught what were the capacities of his creatures, and is further untrue, because the powers of God in man are not really the equivalent of the capabilities of a simple man. Broad Churchmen are still hampered by the difficulties surrounding a divine Christ, and are puzzled to find for him a place in their theology which is at once suitable for his dignity, and consistent with a reasonable belief. They feel obliged to acknowledge that some unusual benefit to the race must result from the incarnation and death of a God, and are swayed alternately by their reason, which places the crucifixion of Jesus in the roll of martyrs' deaths, and by their prejudices, which assign to it a position unique and unrivalled in the history of the race. There are, however, many signs that the deity of Jesus is, as an article of faith, tottering from its pedestal in the Broad Church school. The hold on it by such men as the Rev. J. S. Brooke is very slight, and his interpretation of the incarnation is regarded by orthodox divines with unmingled horror. Their *moral* atonement, in turn, is as the dawn before the sunrise, and we may hope that it will soon develop into the real truth: namely, that the dealings of Jesus with the Father were a purely private matter between his own soul and God, and that his value to mankind consists in his being one of the teachers of the race, one "with a genius for religion," one of the schoolmasters appointed to lead humanity to God.

The theory of M'Leod Campbell stands alone, and is highly interesting and ingenious—it is the more valuable and hopeful as coming from Scotland, the home of the dreariest belief as to the relations existing between man and God. He rejects the penal character of the Atonement, and makes it consist, so to speak, in leading God and man to understand one another. He considers that Christ witnessed to men on behalf of God, and vindicated the father's heart by showing what he could be to the son who trusted in him. He witnessed to God on behalf of men—and this is the weakest point in the book, verging, as it does, on substitution—showing in humanity a perfect sympathy with God's feelings towards sin, and offering to God for man a perfect repentance for human transgression. I purposely say "verging," because Campbell does not *intend* substitution; he represents this sorrow of Jesus as what he must inevitably feel at seeing his brother-men unconscious of their sin and danger, so no fiction is supposed as between God and Christ. But he considers that God, having seen the perfection of repentance in Jesus, accepts the repentance of man, imperfect as it is, because it is *in kind* the same as that of Jesus, and is the germ of that feeling of which his is the perfect flower; in this sense, and only in this sense, is the repentance of man accepted "for Christ's sake." He considers that men must share in the mind of Christ as towards God and towards sin, in order to be benefited by the work of Christ, and that each man must thus actually take part in the work of atonement. The sufferings of Jesus he regards as necessary in order to test the reality of the life of sonship towards God, and brotherhood towards men, which he came to earth to exemplify. I trust I have done no injustice in this short summary to a very able and thoughtful book, which presents, perhaps, the only view of the Atonement compatible with the love and the justice of God; and this only, of course, if the idea of *any* atonement can fairly be said to be consistent with justice. The merits of this view are practically that this work of Jesus is not an "atonement" in the theological sense at all. The defects of Campbell's book are inseparable from his creed, as he argues from a belief in the deity of Jesus, from an unconscious limitation of God's knowledge (as though God did not understand man till he was revealed to him by Jesus) and from a wrong conception of the punishment due to sin.

I said, at starting, that the Atonement was the *raison d'être* of Christianity, and, in conclusion, I would challenge all thoughtful men and women to say whether good cause has or has not been shown for rejecting this pillar "of the faith." The Atonement has but to be studied in order to be rejected. The difficulty is to persuade people to *think* about their creed, Yet the question of this doctrine must be faced and answered. "I have too much faith in the common sense and justice of Englishmen when once awakened to face any question fairly, to doubt what that answer will be."

ON THE

MEDIATION AND SALVATION OF ECCLESIASTICAL CHRISTIANITY.

THE whole Christian scheme turns on the assumption of the inherent necessity of some one standing between the Creator and the creature, and shielding the all-weak from the power of the All-mighty. "It is a fearful thing to fall into the hands of the living God;" such is the key-note of the strain which is chanted alike by Roman Catholicism, with its thousand intercessors, and by Protestantism, with its "one Mediator, the man Christ Jesus." "Speak *thou* for me," cries man to his favourite mouthpiece, whoever it may be; "go *thou* near, but let me not see the face of God, lest I die." The heroes, the saints, the idols of humanity, have been the men who have dared to search into the Unseen, and to gaze straight up into the awful Face of God. They have dashed aside all that intervened between their souls and the Eternal Soul, and have found it, as one of them quaintly phrases it, "a profitable sweet necessity to fall on the naked arm of Jehovah." Then, because they dared to trust Him who had called them into existence, and to stretch out beseeching hands to the Everlasting Father, they have been forced into a position they would have been the very first to protest against, and have been made into mediators for men less bold, for children less confiding. Those who dared not seek God for themselves have clung to the garments of the braver souls, who have thus become, involuntarily, veils between their brother-men and the Supreme. There is, perhaps, no better way of demonstrating the radical errors from which spring all the so-called "schemes of redemption" and "economies of Divine grace" than by starting from the Christian hypothesis.

We will admit, for argument's sake, the Deity of Jesus, in order that we may thus see the more distinctly that a mediator of any kind between God and man is utterly uncalled for. It is mediation, in itself, that is wrong in principle; we object to it as a whole, not to any special manifestation of it. Divine or human mediators, Jesus or his mother, saint, angel, or priest, we reject them each and all; our birthright as human beings is to be the offspring ot the Universal Father, and we refuse to have any interloper pressing in between our hearts and His.

We will take mediation first in its highest form, and speak of it as if Jesus were really God as well as man. All Christians agree in asserting that the coming of the Son into the world to save sinners was the result of the love of the Father for these sinners; *i.e.*, "*God* so loved the world that *He* sent His Son." The motive-power of the redemption of the world is, then, according to Christians, the deep love of the Creator for the work of His hands. This it was that exiled the Son from the bosom of the Father, and caused the Eternal to be born into time. But now a startling change occurs in the aspect of affairs. Jesus has "atoned for the sins of the world;" he "has made peace through the blood of his cross; and having done so, he suddenly appears as the mediator for men. What does this pleading of the Son on behalf of sinners imply? Only this—*a complete change in the Father's mind towards the world.* After the yearning love of which we have heard, after this absolute sacrifice to win His children's hearts, He at last succeeds. He sees His children at His feet, repentant for the past, eager to make amends in the future; human hands appealing to Him, human eyes streaming with tears. He turns His back on the souls He has been labouring to win; He refuses to clasp around His penitents the arms outstretched to them so long, unless they are presented to Him by an accredited intercessor, and come armed with a formal recommendation. The inconsistency of such a procedure must be palpable to all minds; and in order to account for one absurdity, theologians have invented another; having created one difficulty, they are forced to make a second, in order to escape from the first. So they represent God as loving sinners, and desiring to forgive and welcome them. This feeling is the Mercy of God; but, in opposition to the dictates of Mercy, Justice starts up, and forbids any favour to the sinner unless its own claims are first satisfied to the utmost. A Christian writer has represented Mercy and Justice as standing before the Eternal: Mercy pleads for forgiveness and pity, Justice clamours for punishment. Two attributes of the Godhead are personified and placed in opposition to each other, and require to be reconciled. But when we remember that each personified quality is really but a portion, so to speak, of the Divine character, we find that God is divided against Himself. Thus, this theory introduces discord into the harmonious mind which inspires the perfect melodies of the universe. It sees warring elements in the Serenity of the Infinite One; it pictures successive waves of love and anger ruffling that ineffable Calm; it imagines clouds of changing motives sweeping across the sun of that unchanging Will. Such a theory as this must be rejected as soon as realised by the thoughtful mind. God is not a man, to be swayed first by one motive and then by another. His mercy and justice ever point unwaveringly in the same direction: perfect justice requires the same as perfect mercy. If God's justice could fail, the whole moral universe would be in confusion, and that would be the greatest cruelty that could be inflicted on intelligent beings. The weak pliability, miscalled mercy, which is supposed to be worked upon by a mediator, is a human infirmity which men have transferred to their idea of God.

A man who has announced his intention to punish may be persuaded out of his resolution. New arguments may be adduced for the condemned one's innocence, new reasons for clemency may be suggested; or the judge may have been over-strict, or have been swayed by prejudice. Here a mediator may indeed step in, and find good work to do; but, in the name of the Eternal Perfection, what has all this to do with the judgment of God? Can His knowledge be imperfect, His mercy increased? Can His sentence be swayed by prejudice, or made harsh by over-severity? But if His judgment is already perfect, any change implies imperfection, and all left for the mediator to do is to persuade God to make a change, *i.e.*, to become imperfect; or, God having decided that sin shall be punished, the mediator steps in, and actually so works upon God's feelings that He revokes His decision, and—most cruel of mercies—lets it go unnoticed. Like an unwise parent, God is persuaded not to punish the erring child. But such is not the case. God is just, and because He is just He is most truly merciful: in that justice rests the certainty of the due punishment of sin, and, therefore of the purification of the sinner! and no mediator—thanks be to God for it!—shall ever cause to waver for one instant that Rock of Justice on which reposes the hope of Humanity.

But the theory we are considering has another fatal error in it: it ascribes imperfection to Almighty God. For God is represented as desiring to forgive sinners, and this desire must be either right or wrong. If it be right, it can at once be gratified; but if Justice opposes this forgiveness, then the desire to forgive is not wholly right. Theologians are thus placed in this dilemma: if God is perfect—as He is—any desire of His must likewise be flawlessly perfect, and its fulfilment must be the very best thing that could happen to His whole creation; on the other hand, if there is any barrier of right—and Justice *is* right—interposed between God and His desire, then His Will is not the most perfect Good. Theologians must then choose between admitting that the desire of God to welcome sinners is just, or detracting from the Eternal Perfection.

It is obvious that we do not weaken our case by admitting, for the moment, the Deity of Jesus; for we are striking at the root-idea of mediation. That the mediator should be God is totally beside the question, and in no way strengthens our adversaries' hands. His Deity does nothing more than introduce a new element of confusion into the affair; for we become entangled in a maze of contradictions. God, who is One, even according to Christians, is at one and the same time estranged from sinners, pleading for sinners, and admitting the pleading. God pleads to Himself—but we are confounding the persons: one God pleads to another—but we are dividing the substance. Alas and alas for the creed which compels its votaries to deny their reason, and degrade their Maker! which babbles of a Nature it cannot comprehend, and forces its foolish contradictions on indignant souls! If Jesus be God, his mediation is at once impossible and unnecessary; if he be God, his will is the will of God; and if he wills to welcome sinners, it is God who wills to welcome them. If he, who is God, is content to pardon and embrace, what further do sinners require? Christians tell us that Jesus is one with God: it is well, we reply; for you say he is the Friend of sinners, and the Redeemer of the lost. If he be God, we both agree as to the friendliness of God to sinners. You need no mediator between you and Jesus; and, since he is God, you need no mediator with God. This reasoning is irrefragable, unless Christians are content to assign to their mediator some place which is less than divine; for they certainly derogate from his dignity when they imagine him as content to receive those whom Almighty God chases from before His face. And in making this difference between Jesus and the Father they make a fatal admission that he is distinct in feeling from God, and therefore cannot be the One God. It is the proper perception of this fact which has introduced into the Roman Church the human mediators whose intercession is constantly implored. Jesus, being God, is too awful to be approached: his mother, his apostles, some saint or martyr, must come between. I have read a Roman Catholic paper about the mediation of Mary which would be accepted by the most orthodox Protestant were Mary replaced by Jesus, and Jesus by the Father. For Jesus is there painted, as the Father is painted by the orthodox, in stern majesty, hard, implacable, exacting the uttermost farthing; and Mary is represented as standing between him and the sinners for whom she pleads. It is only a further development of the idea which makes the man Jesus the Mediator between God and man. As the deification of Mary progresses, following in slow but certain steps the deification of Jesus, a mediator will be required through whom to approach *her;* and then Jesus, too, will fade out of the hearts of men, as the Father has faded out of the hearts of Christians, and this superstition of mediation will sink lower and lower, till it is rejected by all earnest hearts, and is loathed by human souls which are aching for the living God.

We see, then, that mediation implies an absurd and inexplicable change in the supposed attitude of God towards man, and destroys all confidence in the justice of the Supreme Ruler. We should further take into consideration the strange feeling towards the Universal *Heart* implied in man's endeavour to push some one in between himself and the Eternal Father. As we study Nature and try to discover from its workings something of the characteristics of the Worker therein, we find not only a ruling Intelligence —*a Supreme Reason*, before which we bow our heads in an adoration too deep for words—but we catch also beautiful glimpses of a ruling Love—*a Supreme Heart*, to which our hearts turn with a glad relief from the dark mysteries of pain and evil which press us in on every side. Simple belief in God at all, that is to say, in a Power which works in the Universe, is quite sufficient to disperse any of that feeling of fear which finds its fit expression in the longing for a mediator. For being placed here without our request, and even without our consent, we have surely, as a simple matter of justice, a right to demand that the Power which placed us here shall provide us with means by which we can secure our happiness. I speak, of course, as of a *conscious* Power, because a blind Force is necessarily irresponsible; but those who believe in a God are bound to acknowledge that He is responsible for their well-being. If any one should suggest that to say thus is to criticise God's dealings and to speak with presumptuous irreverence, I retort that the irreverence lies with those who ascribe to the Supreme a course of action towards His creatures that they themselves would be ashamed to pursue towards their own children, and that they who fling at us the reproach of blasphemy because we will not bow the knee before their idol, would themselves lie open to the charge, were it not that their ignorance shields them from the sterner censure. All good in man—poor shallow streamlet though it be—flows down from the pure depths of the Fountain of Good, and any throb of Love on earth is a pulsation caused by the ceaseless beating of the Universal Father-Heart. Yet men fear to trust that Heart, lest it should cease beating; they fear to rest on God, lest He should play them false. When will they catch even a glimpse of that great ocean of love which encircles the universe as the atmosphere the earth, which is infinite because God is infinite? If there is no spot in the universe of which it can be said, "God is not here," then is there also no spot where love does not rule; if there is no life existing without the support of the Life-Giver and the Life-Sustainer, then is there also no life which is not cradled in the arms of Love. Who then will dare to push himself in between man and a God like this? In the light of the Universal Reason and the Universal Heart mediation stands confessed as an impertinent absurdity. Away with any and all of those who interfere in the most sacred concerns of the soul, who press in between the Creator and His offspring; between the heart of man and the parent Heart of God. Whoever it may be, saint or martyr, or the king of saints and martyrs, Jesus of Nazareth, let him come down from a position which none can rightly hold. To elevate the noblest son of man into this place of mediator is to make him into an offence to his brethren, and to cause their love to turn into anger, and their reverence into indignation. If men persist in talking about the need of a mediator before they dare to approach God, we must remind them that, if there be a God at all, He *must* be just, and that, therefore, they are perfectly safe in His hands; if they begin to babble about forgiveness "*for the sake of Jesus Christ*," we must ask them what in the world they mean by the "forgiveness of sin?" Surely they do not think that God is like man, quick to revenge affront and jealous of His dignity; even were it possible for man to injure, in any sense, the Majesty of God, do they conceive that God is an irascible and revengeful Potentate? Those who think thus of God can never—I assert boldly—have caught the smallest glimpse of *God*. They may have seen a "magnified man," but they have seen nothing more; they have never prostrated themselves before that Universal Spirit who dwells in this vast universe; they have never felt their own littleness in a place so great. How *can* sin be forgiven? can a past act be undone, or the hands go back on the sun-dial of Time? All God's so-called chastisements are but the natural and inevitable results of broken laws—laws invariable in their action, neither to be escaped or defied. Obedience to law results in happiness, and the suffering consequent on the transgression of law is not inflicted by an angry God, but is the simple natural outcome of the broken law itself. Put your hand in the fire, and no mediator can save you from burning; cry earnestly to God to save you, and then cast yourself from a precipice, and will a mediator come between you and the doom you have provoked? We should do more wisely if we studied laws and tried to conform ourselves to them, instead of going blundering about with our eyes shut, trusting that some one will interpose to shield us from the effects of our own folly and stupidity. Happily for mankind, mediation is impossible in that beautiful realm of law in which we are placed; when men have quite made up their minds that their happiness depends entirely on their own exertions, there will at last be some chance for the advancement of Humanity, for then they will work for things instead of praying for them. It is of real practical importance that this Christian notion of mediation should be destroyed, because on it hang all the ideas about trusting to some one else to do our own work. *This plan has not answered:* we judge it by results, and it has failed. Surely we may hope that as men get to see that prayer has not succeeded in its efforts to "move the arm which moves the world, to bring salvation down," they may turn to the more difficult, but also the more hopeful task, of moving their own arms to work out their own salvation. For the past, it *is* past, and none can reverse it; none can stay the action of the eternal law which links sorrow with transgression, and joy and peace with obedience. When we slip back on our path upward, we may repent and call on God or man for forgiveness as we list, but only through toil and suffering can the lost way be recovered, and the rugged path must be trodden with bleeding feet; for there is none who can lift the sinner over the hindrances he has built up for himself, or carry him over the rocks with which he has strewed his road.

Does the sentimental weakness of our age shrink from this doctrine, and whimper out that it is cold and stern? Ay, it is cold with the cold of the bracing sea-breeze, stringing to action the nerves enfeebled by hot-houses and soft-living; ay, it is stern with the blessed sternness of changeless law, of law which never fails us, never varies a hair's breadth. But in that law is strength; man's arm is feeble, but let him submit to the laws of steam, and his arm becomes dowered with a giant's force; conform to a law, and the mighty power of that law is on your side; "humble yourself under the mighty hand of God," who is the Universal Law, "*and He shall lift you up.*"

So much for mediation. We turn with a still deeper repugnance to study the Christian idea of "Salvation." Mediation at least leaves us God, however it degrades and blasphemes Him, but salvation takes us altogether out of His Hands. Not content with placing a mediator between themselves and God, Christians cry out that He is still too near them; they must push Him yet further back, they must have a Saviour too, through whom all His benefits shall filter.

"Saviour," is an expression often found in the Old Testament, where it bears a very definite and noble meaning. God is the Saviour of men from the power of sin, and although we may consider that God does *not* save from sin in this direct manner, we are yet bound to acknowledge that there is nothing in this idea which is either dishonouring or repulsive. But the word "Saviour" has been degraded by Christianity, and the salvation He brings is not a salvation from sin. "The Lord and Saviour, Jesus Christ" is the Saviour of men, not because he delivers them from sin, but because he saves them from hell, and from the fiery wrath of God. Salvation is no longer the equivalent of righteousness, the antithesis of sin; in Christian life it means nothing more than the antithesis of damnation. It is true that Christians may retort that Jesus "saves his people from their sins;" we gladly acknowledge the nobleness and the beauty of many a Christian life, but nevertheless this is *not* the primary idea attached by popular Christianity to the word "salvation." "Being saved" is to be delivered out of "those hands of the living God," into which, as they are taught by their Bible, it is so fearful a thing to fall. "Being saved is the *immediate* result of conversion, and is the opposite of "being lost." "Being saved" is being hidden "in the riven side of Jesus," and so preserved from the awful flames of the destroying wrath of God. Against all this we, believers in an Almighty Love, in a Universal Father, enter our solemn and deliberate protest, with a depth of abhorrence, with a passion of indignation which is far too intense to find any adequate expression in words. There is no language strong enough to show our deeply-rooted repugnance to the idea that we can be safer anywhere or at any time than we are already here; we cannot repell with sufficient warmth the officious interference which offers to take us out of the hands of God. To push some one in between our souls and Him was bad enough; but to go further and to offer us salvation from our Maker, to try and threaten us away from the arms of His Love, to suggest that another's hands are more tender, another's heart more loving than the Supreme Heart,—these are blasphemies to which we will not listen in silence. It is true that to *us* these suggestions are only matters of laughter; dimly as we guess at the Deity, we know enough not to be afraid of Him, and these crude and childish conceptions about Him are among ourselves too contemptible to refute.

"Non ragione di lor, mai guardo e passo."

But we see how these ideas colour men's thoughts and lives, how they cripple their intellect and outrage their hearts, and we rise to trample down these superstitions, not because they are in themselves worth refuting, but simply because they degrade our brother-men. We believe in no wisdom that improves on Nature's laws, and one of those laws, written on our hearts, is that sorrow shall tread on the heels of sin. We are conscious that men should learn to welcome this law, and not to shrink from it. To fly from the suffering following on broken law is the last thing we should do; we ought to have no gratitude for a "Saviour" who should bear our punishment, and so cheat us out of our necessary lesson, turn us into spoiled children, and check our moral growth; such an offer as this, could it really be made, ought to be met with stern refusal. We should trust the Supreme so utterly, and adore His wisdom with a humility so profound, that if we could change His laws we should not dare to interfere; nor ought we, even when our lot is saddest, to complain of it, or do anything more than labour to improve it in steadfast obedience to law. We should ask for no salvation; we should desire to fall—were it possible that we *could* be out of them—into the hands of God.

Further, is it impossible to make Christians understand that were Jesus all they say he is, we should still reject him; that were God all they say He is, we would, in that case, throw back His salvation. For were this awful picture of a soul-destroying Jehovah, of a blood-craving Moloch, endowed with a cruelty beyond human imagination, a true description of the Supreme Being, then would we take the advice of Job's wife, we would "curse God and die;" we would hide in the burning depths of His hell rather than dwell within sight of Him whose brightness would mock at the gloom of His creatures, and whose bliss would be a sneer at their despair. Were it thus indeed—

> "O King of our salvation,
> Many would curse to thee, and I for one!
> Fling Thee Thy bliss, and snatch at Thy damnation,
> Scorn and abhor the rising of Thy sun."

"Is it not worth while to believe," blandly urges a Christian writer, "if it is true, as it is true, that they who deny will suffer everlasting torments?" No! we thunder back at him, *it is not worth while;* it is not worth while to believe a lie, or to acknowledge as true that which our hearts and intellects alike reject as false; it is not worth while to sell our souls for a heaven, or to defile our honesty to escape a hell; it is not worth while to bow our knee to a Satan or bend our heads before a spectre. Better, far better, to "dwell with everlasting burnings" than to degrade our humanity by calling a lie, truth, and cruelty, love, and unreasonableness, justice; better to suffer in hell, than to have our hearts so hard that we could enjoy while others suffer; could rejoice while others are tormented, could sing alleluias to the music of golden harps, while our lyrics are echoed by the anguished wailing of the lost. God Himself—were He such as Christians paint Him—could not blot out of our souls our love of truth, of righteousness, of justice. While we have these we are *ourselves*, and we can suffer and be happy; but we cannot afford to pay down these as the price of our admission to heaven. We should be miserable even as we paced the golden streets, and should sit in tears beside the river of the water of life. Yet *this* is salvation; *this* is what Christians offer us in the name of Jesus; *this* is the glad tidings brought to us as the gospel of the Saviour, as the "good news of God;" and this we reject, wholly and utterly, laughing it to scorn from the depths of our glad hearts which the Truth has made free; this we denounce, with a stern and bitter determination, in the name of the Universal Father, in the name of the self-reliance of humanity, in the name of all that is holy, and just, and loving.

But happily many, even among Christians, are beginning to shrink from this idea of salvation from the God in whom they say they place all their hopes. They put aside the doctrine, they gloss it over, they prefer not to speak of it. Free thought is leavening Christianity, and is moulding the old faith against its will. Christianity now hides its own cruel side, and only where the bold opponents of its creeds have not yet spread, does it dare to show itself in its real colours; in Spain, in Mexico, we see Christianity unveiled; here, in England, liberty is too strong for it, and it is forced into a semblance of liberality. The old wine is being poured into new bottles; what will be the result? We may, however, rejoice that nobler thoughts about God are beginning to prevail, and are driving out the old wicked notions about Him and His revenge. The Face of the Father is beginning, however dimly, to shine out from His world, and before the Beauty of that Face all hard thoughts about Him are fading away. Nature is too fair to be slandered for ever, and when men perceive that God and Nature are One, all that is ghastly and horrible must die and drop into forgetfulness. The popular Christian ideas of mediation and salvation must soon pass away into the limbo of rejected creeds which is being filled so fast; they are already dead, and their pale ghosts shall soon flit no longer to vex and harass the souls of living men.

ON ETERNAL TORTURE.

SOME time ago a Clergyman was proving to me, by arguments many and strong that hell was right, necessary and just; that it brought glory to God and good to man; that the holiness of God required it as a preventive, and the justice of God exacted it as a penalty, of sin. I listened quietly till all was over and silence fell on the reverend denunciator; he ceased, satisfied with his arguments, triumphant in the consciousness that they were crushing and unassailable. But my eyes were fixed on the fair scene without the library window, on the sacrament oi earth, the visible sign of the invisible beauty, and the contrast between God's works and the Church's speech came strongly upon me. And all I found to say in answer came in a few words: "If I had not heard you mention the name of God, I should have thought you were speaking of the Devil." The words, dropped softly and meditatively, had a startling effect. Horror at the blasphemy, indignation at the unexpected result of laboured argument, struggled against a dawning feeling that there must be something wrong in a conception which laid itself open to such a blow; the short answer told more powerfully than half an hour's reasoning.

The various classes of orthodox Christian doctrines should be attacked in very different styles by the champions of the great army of free-thinkers, who are at the present day besieging the venerable superstitions of the past. Around the Deity of Jesus cluster many hallowed memories and fond associations; the worship of centuries has shed around his figure a halo of light, and he has been made into the ideal of Humanity; the noblest conceptions of morality, the highest flights of enlightened minds, have been enshrined in a human personality and called by the name of Christ; the Christ-idea has risen and expanded with every development of human progress, and the Christ of the highest Christianity of the day is far other than the Christ of Augustine, of Thomas à Kempis, of Luther, or Knox; the strivings after light, after knowledge, after holiness, of the noblest sons of men have been called by them a following of Jesus; Jesus is baptized in human tears, crucified in human pains, glorified in human hopes. Because of all this, because he is dear to human hearts and identified with human struggles, therefore he should be gently spoken of by all who feel the bonds of the brotherhood of man; the dogma of his Deity must be assailed, must be overthrown, because it is false, because it destroys the unity of God, because it veils from us the Eternal Spirit, the source of all things, but he himself should be reverently spoken of, so far as truthfulness permits, and this dogma, although persistently battled against, should be attacked without anger and without scorn.

There are other doctrines which, while degrading in regard to man's conception of God, and therefore deserving of reprobation, yet enshrine great moral truths and have become bound up with ennobling lessons; such is the doctrine of the Atonement, which enshrines the idea of selfless love and of self-sacrifice for the good of humanity. There are others again against which ridicule and indignation may rightly be brought to bear, which are concessions to human infirmity, and which belong to the childhood of the race; man may be laughed out of his sacraments and out of his devils, and indignantly reminded that he insults God and degrades himself by placing a priesthood or mediator between God and his own soul. But there is one dogma of Orthodox Christianity which stands alone in its atrocity, which is thoroughly and essentially bad, which is without one redeeming feature, which is as blasphemous towards God as it is injurious to man; on it therefore should be poured out unsparingly the bitterest scorn and the sharpest indignation. There is no good human emotion enlisted on the side of an Eternal Hell; it is not hallowed by human love or human longings, it does not enshrine human aspirations, nor is it the outcome of human hopes. In support of this no appeal can be made to any feeling of the nobler side of our nature, nor does eternal fire stimulate our higher faculties: it acts only on the lower, baser, part of man; it excites fear, distrust of God, terror of his presence; it may scare from evil occasionally, but can never teach good; it sees God in the lightning-flash that slays, but not in the sunshine which invigorates; in the avalanche which buries a village in its fall, but not in the rich promise of the vineyard and the joyous beauty of the summer day. Hell has driven thousands half-mad with terror, it has driven monks to the solitary deserts, nuns to the sepulchre of the nunnery, but has it ever caused one soul of man to rejoice in the Father of all, and pant, "as the hart panteth after the water-springs, for the presence of God"?

It is only just to state, in attacking this as a Christian doctrine, that, though believed in by the vast majority of Christians, the most enlightened of that very indefinite body repudiate it with one voice. It is well known how the great Broad-Church leader, Frederick Denison Maurice, endeavoured to harmonize, on this point, his Bible and his strong moral sense, and failed in so doing, as all must fail who would reconcile two contradictories. How he fought with that word "eternal," struggled to prove that whatever else it might mean it did *not* mean everlasting in our modern sense of the word: that "eternal death" being the antithesis to "eternal life" must mean a state of ignorance of the Eternal One, even as its opposite was the knowledge of God: that therefore men could rise from eternal death, aye, did so rise every day in this life, and might so rise in the life to come. Noble was his protest against this awful doctrine, fettered as he was by undue reverence for, and clinging to, the Bible. His appeal to the moral sense in man as the arbiter of all doctrine has borne good fruit, and his labours have opened a road to free thought greater than he expected or even hoped. Many other clergymen have followed in his steps. The word "eternal" has been wrangled over continually, but, however they arrive there, all Broad Churchmen unite in the conclusion that it does not, cannot, shall not, mean literally lasting for ever. This school of thought has laid much stress on the fondness of Orientals for imagery; they have pointed out that the Jewish word Gehenna is the same as Ge Hinnom, or valley of Hinnom, and have seen in the state of that valley the materials for "the worm that dieth not and the fire that is not quenched:" they show how by a natural transition the place into which were thrown the bodies of the worst criminals became the type of punishment in the next world, and the valley where children were sacrificed to Moloch gave its name to the infernal abode of devils. From that valley Jesus drew his awful picture, suggested by the pale lurid fires ever creeping there, mingling their ghastly flames with the decaying bodies of the dishonoured dead. In all this there is probably much truth, and many Broad Churchmen are content to accept this explanation, and so retain their belief in the supernatural character of the Bible, while satisfying their moral sense by rejecting its most immoral dogma.

Among the evangelicals, only one voice, so far as I know, is heard to protest against eternal torture; and all honour is due to the Rev. Samuel Minton, for his rare courage in defying on this point the opinion of his "world," and braving the censure which has been duly inflicted on him. He seems to make "eternal" the equivalent of "irremediable" in some cases and of "everlasting" in others. He believes that the wicked will be literally destroyed, burnt up, consumed; the fact that the fire is eternal by no means implies, he remarks, that that which is cast into the fire should be likewise eternal, and that the fire is unquenchable does not prove that the chaff is unconsumable. "Eternal destruction" he explains as irreparable destruction, final and irreversible extinction. This theory should have more to recommend it to all who believe in the supernatural inspiration of the Bible, than the Broad Church explanation; it uses far less violence towards the words of Scripture, and, indeed, a very fair case may be made out for it from the Bible itself.

It is scarcely necessary to add to this small list of dissentients from orthodox Christianity, the Unitarian body; I do not suppose that there is such a phenomenon in existence as a Unitarian Christian who believes in an eternal hell.

With these small exceptions the mass of Christians hold this dogma, but for the most part carelessly and uncomprehendingly. Many are ashamed of it even while duteously confessing it, and gabble over the sentences in their creed which acknowledge it in a very perfunctory manner. People of this kind "do not like to talk about hell, it is better to think of heaven." Some Christians, however, hold it strongly, and proclaim their belief boldly; the members of the Evangelical Alliance actually make the profession of it a condition of admittance into their body, while many High Church divines think that a sharp declaration of their belief in it is needed by loyalty towards God and "charity to the souls of men." I wish I could believe that all who profess this dogma did not realize it, and only accepted it because their fathers and mothers taught it to them. But what can one say to such statements as the following, quoted from Father Furniss by W. R. Greg in his splendid "Enigmas of Life:" I take it as a specimen of Roman Catholic *authorized* teaching. Children are asked: "How will your body be when the devil has been striking it every moment for a hundred million years without stopping?'" A girl of eighteen is described as dressed in fire; "she wears a bonnet of fire. It is pressed down all over her head; it burns her head; it burns into the skull; it scorches the bone of the skull and makes it smoke." A boy is boiled: "Listen! there is a sound just like titat of a kettle boiling. . . . The blood is boiling in the scalded veins of that boy. The brain is boiling and bubbling in his head. The marrow is boiling in his bones." Nay, even the poor little babies are not exempt from torture: one is in a red hot oven, "hear how it screams to come out; see how it turns and twists about in the fire. . . . You can see on the face of this little child"—the fair pure innocent baby-face—"what you see on the faces of all in hell—despair, desperate and horrible." Surely this man realized what he taught, but then he was that half-human being—a priest.

Dr. Pusey, too, has a word to say about hell: "Gather in mind all that is most loathsome, most revolting—the most treacherous, malicious, coarse, brutal, inventive, fiendish cruelty, unsoftened by any remains of human feeling, such as thou couldst not endure for a single hour. . . . hear those yells of blaspheming, concentrated hate as they echo along the lurid vault of hell."

Protestantism chimes in, and Spurgeon speaks of hell: "Wilt thou think it is easy to lie down in hell, with the bieath of the Eternal fanning the flames? Wilt thou delight thyself to think that God will invent torments for thee, sinner?" "When the damned jingle the burning irons of their torment, they shall say, 'for ever;' when they howl, echo cries, 'for ever.'"

I may allude, to conclude my quotations, to a description of hell which I myself heard from an eminent prelate of the English Church, one who is a scholar and a gentleman, a man of moderate views in Church matters, by no means a zealot in an ordinary way. In preaching to a country congregation composed mainly of young men and girls, he warned them specially against sins of the flesh, and threatened them with the consequent punishment in hell. Then, in language which I cannot reproduce, for I should not dare to sully my pages by repeating what I then listened to in horrified amazement, there ensued a description drawn out in careful particulars of the state of the suffering body in hell, so sickening in its details that it must suffice to say of it that it was a description founded on the condition of a corpse flung out on a dungheap and left there to putrefy, with the additional horror of creeping, slowly-burning flames; and this state of things was to go on, as he impressed on them with terrible energy, for ever and ever, "decaying but ever renewing."

I should almost ask pardon of tender-hearted men and women for laying before them language so abominable; but I urge on all who are offended by it that this is the teaching given to our sons and daughters in the present day. Father Furniss, Dr. Pusey, Mr. Spurgeon, an English Bishop, surely these are honoured names, and in quoting them I quote from the teaching of Christendom. Not mine the fault if the language be unfit for printing. I *quote*, because if we only assert, Christians are quick to say, "you are misrepresenting our beliefs," and I quote from writers of the present day only, that none may accuse me of hurling at Christians reproaches for a doctrine they have outgrown or softened down. Still, I own that it seems scarcely credible that a man should believe this and remain sane; nay, should preach this, and walk calmly home from his Church with God's sunshine smiling on the beautiful world, and after preaching it should sit down to a comfortable dinner and very likely a quiet pipe, as though hell did not exist, and its awful misery and fierce despair.

It is said that there is no reason that we should not be contented in heaven while others suffer in hell, since we know how much misery there is in this world and yet enjoy ourselves in spite of the knowledge. I say, deliberately, of every one who does realise the misery of this world and remains indifferent to it, who enjoys his own share of the good things of this life, without helping his brother, who does not stretch out his hand to lift the fallen, or raise his voice on behalf of the down-trodden and oppressed, that that man is living a life which is the very antithesis of a Divine life—a life which has in it no beauty and no nobility, but is selfish, despicable, and mean. And is this the life which we are to regard as the model of heavenly beauty? Is the power to lead this life for ever to be our reward for self-devotion and self-sacrifice here on earth? Is a supreme selfishness to crown unselfishness at last? But this *is* the life which is to be the lot of the righteous in heaven. Snatched from a world in flames, caught up in the air to meet their descending Lord, his saints are to return with him to the heaven whence he came; there, crowned with golden crowns, they are to spend eternity, hymning the Lamb who saved them to the music of golden harps, harps whose melody is echoed by the curses and the wailings of the lost; for below is a far different scene, for there the sinners are "tormented with fire and brimstone in the presence of the holy angels and the presence of the Lamb; and the smoke of their torment ascendeth up for ever and ever, and they have no rest day nor night."

It is worth while to gaze for a moment at the scene of future felicity; there is the throne of God and rejoicing crowds: "Rejoice over her, thou heaven, and ye holy apostles and prophets," so goes out the command, and they rejoice because "God has avenged them on her," and again they said Alleluia, and her smoke rose up for ever and ever." Truly God must harden the hearts of his saints in heaven as of old he hardened Pharaoh's heart, if they are to rejoice over the anguished multitude below, and to bear to live amid the lurid smoke ascending from the burning bodies of the lost. To me the idea is so unutterably loathsome that I marvel how Christians endure to retain such language in their sacred books, for I would note that the awful picture drawn above is not of my doing; it is not the scoffing caricature of an unbeliever, *it is heaven as described by St. John the divine.* If this heaven is true I do not hesitate to say that it is the duty of every human being to reject it utterly and to refuse to enter it. We might even appeal to Christians by the example of their own Jesus, who could not be content to remain in heaven himself while men went to hell, but came down to redeem them from endless suffering. Yet they, who ought to imitate him, who do, many of them, lead beautiful lives of self-devotion and compassion, are suddenly, on death, to lose all this which makes them "partakers of the Divine Nature," and are to be content to win happiness for themselves, careless that millions of their brethren are in woe unspeakable. They are to reverse the aim of their past lives, they are to become selfish instead of loving, hard instead of selfless, indifferent instead of loving, hard instead of tender. Which is the better reproduction of the "mind of Christ," the good Samaritan tending the wounded man, or the stern Inquisitor gloating over the fire which consumes heretics to the greater glory of God? Yet the latter is the ideal of heavenly virtue. Never will they who truly love man be content to snatch at bliss for themselves while others suffer, or endure to be crowned with glory while they are crowned with thorns. Better, far better, to suffer in hell and share the pains of the lost, than to have a heart so hard, a nature so degraded, as to enjoy the bliss of heaven, rejoicing over, or even disregarding, the woes of hell.

But there is worse than physical torture in the picture of hell; pain is not its darkest aspect. Of all the thoughts with which the heart of man has outraged the Eternal Righteousness, there is none so appalling, none so blasphemous, as that which declares that even one soul, made by the Supreme Good, shall remain during all eternity, under the power of sin. Divines have wearied themselves in describing the horrors of the Christian hell; but it is *not* the furnace of flames, *not* the undying worm, *not* the fire which never may be quenched, that revolt us most; hideous as are these images, they are not the worst terror of hell. Who does not know how St. Francis, believing himself ordained to be lost everlastingly, fell on his knees and cried, "O my God, if I am indeed doomed to hate thee during eternity, at least suffer me to love thee while I live here." To the righteous heart the agony of hell is a far worse one than physical torture could inflict: it is the existence of men and women who might have been saints, shut out from hope of holiness for evermore; God's children, the work of his hands, gnashing their teeth at a Father who has cast them down for ever from the life he might have given; it is Love everlastingly hated; good everlastingly trampled under foot; God everlastingly baffled and defied; worst of all, it is a room in the Father's house where his children may hunger and thirst after righteousness, but never, never, can be filled.

> "Depart, O sinner, to the chain!
> Enter the eternal cell;
> *To all that's good and true and right,*
> To all that's fair and fond and bright,
> *To all of holiness and right,*
> Bid thou thy last farewell."

Would to God that Christian men and women would ponder

it well and think it out for themselves, and when they go into the worst parts of our great cities and their hearts almost break with the misery there, then let them remember how that misery is but a faint picture of the endless, hopeless, misery, to which the vast majority of their fellow-men are doomed.

Christian reader, do not be afraid to realise the future in which you say you believe, and which the God of Love has prepared for the home of some of his children. Imagine yourself, or any dear to you, plunged into guilt from which there is no redeemer, and where the voice cannot penetrate of him that speaks in righteousness, mighty to save. In the well-weighed words of a champion of Christian orthodoxy, think there is no reason to believe that hell is only a punishment for past offences; in that dark world sin and misery reproduce each other in infinite succession. "What if the sin perpetuates itself, if the prolonged misery may be the offspring of the prolonged guilt?" Ponder it well, and, if you find it true, then cast out from your creed the belief in a Jesus who loved the lost; blot out from your Bible every verse that speaks of a Father's heart; tear from your Prayer-books every page that prays to a Father in heaven. If the lowest of God's creatures is to be left in the foul embraces of sin for ever, God cannot be the Eternal Righteousness, the unconquerable Love. For what sort of Righteousness is that which rests idly contented in a heaven of bliss, while millions of souls capable of righteousness are bound by it in helpless sin; what sort of love is that which is satisfied to be repulsed, and is willing to be hated? As long as God is righteous, as long as God is love, so long is it impossible that men and women shall be left by him for ever in a state to which our worst dens of earth are a very paradise of beauty and purity. Bible writers may have erred, but "Thou continuest holy, O Thou worship of Israel!" There is one revelation that cannot err, and that is written by God's finger on every human heart. What man recoils from doing, even at his lowest, can never be done by his Creator, from whose inspiration he draws every righteous thought. Is there one father, however brutalized, who would deliberately keep his child in sin because of a childish fault? one mother who would aimlessly torture her son, keeping him alive but to torment? Yet this, nothing less,—nay, a thousand times more, for it is this multiplied infinitely by infinite power of torture,—this is what Christians ask us to believe about our Father and our God, a glimmer from the radiance of whose throne falls on to our earth, when men love their enemies and forgive freely those who wrong them If this so-called orthodox belief is right, then is their gospel of the Love of God to the world a delusion and a lie; if this is true, the teaching of Jesus to publicans and harlots of the Fatherhood of God is a cruel mockery of our divinest instincts; the tale of the good Shepherd who could not rest while one sheep was lost is the bitterest irony. But this awful dogma is not true, and the Love of God cradles his creation; not one son of the Father's family shall be left under the power of sin, to be an eternal blot on God's creation, an endless reproach to his Maker's wisdom, an everlasting and irreparable mistake.

No amount of argument, however powerful, should make us believe a doctrine from which our hearts recoil with such shuddering horror as they do from this doctrine of eternal torture and eternal sin. There is a divine instinct in the human heart which may be trusted as an arbiter between right and wrong; no supernatural revelation, no miracle, no angel from heaven, should have power to make us accept as divine that which our hearts proclaim as vile and devilish. It is not true faith to crush down our moral sense beneath the hoof of credulity; true faith believes in God only as a "Power which makes for *Righteousness*," and recks little of threats or curses which would force her to accept that which conscience disapproves. And what is more, if it were possible that God were not what we dream, if he were not "righteous in all his ways and holy in all his works," then were it craven cowardice to worship him at all. It has been well said, "that to worship simple power, without virtue, is nothing but devil-worship;" in that case it were nobler to refuse to praise him and to take what he might send. Then indeed we must say, with John Stuart Mill, in that burst of passion which reads so strangely in the midst of his passionless logic, that if I am told that this is justice and love, and that if I do not call it so, God will send me to hell, then "to hell I'll go."

I have purposely put first my strong reprobation of eternal hell, because of its own essential hideousness, and because, were it ever so true, I should deem myself disgraced by acknowledging it as either loving or good. But it is, however, a satisfaction to note the feebleness of the arguments advanced in support of this dogma, and to find that justice and holiness, as well as love, frown on the idea of an eternal hell.

The first argument put forth is this: "God has made a law which man breaks; man must therefore in justice suffer the penalty of his transgression." This, like so many of the orthodox arguments, sounds just and right, and at first we perfectly agree with it. The instinct of justice in our own breasts confirms the statement, and looking abroad into the world we see its truth proved by facts. Law is around us on every side; man is placed in a realm of law; he may strive against the laws which encircle him, but he will only dash himself to pieces against a rock; he is under a code which he breaks at his peril. Here is perfect justice, a justice absolutely unwavering, deaf to cries, unseducible by flatteries, unalloyed by favouritism: a law exists, break it, and you suffer the inevitable consequences. So far, then, the orthodox argument is sound and strong, but now it takes a sudden leap. "The penalty of the broken law is hell." Why? What common factor is there between a lie, and the "lake of fire in which all liars shall have their part?" Nature is absolutely against the orthodox corollary, because hell as a punishment of sin is purely arbitrary, the punishment might quite as well have been something else; but in nature the penalty of a broken law is always strictly in character with the law itself, and is derived from it. Men imagine the most extraordinary "judgment." A nation is given to excessive drinking, and is punished with cattle-plague; or shows leanings towards popery, and is chastised with cholera. It is as reasonable to believe this as it would be to expect that if a child fell down stairs he would be picked up covered with blisters from burning, instead of his receiving his natural punishment of being bruised. Why, because I lie and forget God, should I be punished with fire and brimstone? Fire is not derivable from truth, nor is brimstone a stimulus to memory. There is also a strange confusion in many minds about the punishment of sin. A child is told not to put his hand into the fire, he does so, and is burnt; the burning is a punishment, he is told; for what? Not for disobedience to the parent, as is generally said, but for disregarding the law of nature which says that fire burns. One often hears it said: "God's punishments for sin are not equal: one man sins once and suffers for it all his life, while another sins twenty times and is not punished at all." By no means: the two men both break a moral law, and suffer a moral degradation; one of them breaks in addition some physical law, and suffers a physical injury. People see injustice where none exists, because they will not take the trouble to distinguish what laws are broken when material punishments follow. There is nothing arbitrary in nature: cause and effect rule in her realm. Hell is then unjust, in the first place, because physical torture has nothing in common with moral guilt.

It is unjust, secondly, because it is excessive. Sin, say theologians, is to be punished infinitely, because sin is an offence committed against an infinite being. Of course, then, good must logically be rewarded infinitely, because it is duty offered to an infinite being. There is no man who has never done a single good act, so every man deserves an infinite reward. There is no man who has never done a single bad act, so every man deserves an infinite punishment. Therefore every man deserves both an infinite reward and an infinite punishment, "which," as Euclid says, "is absurd." And this is quite enough answer to the proposition. But I must protest, in passing, against this notion of "sin against God" as properly understood. If by this expression is only meant that every sin committed is a sin against God, because every sin is done against man's higher nature, which is God in man, then indeed there is no objection to be made to it. But this is not what is generally meant by the phrase. It usually means that we are able, as it were, to injure God in some way, to dishonour him, to affront him, to trouble him. By sin we make him "angry," we "provoke him to wrath;" because of this feeling on his own part he punishes us, and demands "satisfaction." Surely a moment's reflection must prove to any reasonable being that sin against God in this sense is perfectly impossible. What can the littleness of man do against the greatness of the Eternal! Imagine a speck of dust troubling the depths of the ocean, an aphis burdening an oak-tree with its weight: each is far more probable than that a man could ruffle the perfect serenity of God. Suppose I stand on a lawn watching an ant-heap, an ant twinkles his feelers at me scornfully; do I fly into a passion and rush on the insect to destroy it, or seize it and slowly torture it? Yet I am far less above the level of the ant than God is above mine.

But I must add a word here to guard against the misapprehension that in saying this I am depriving man of the strength he finds in believing that he is personally known to

God and an object of his care. Were I the ant's creator, familiar with all the workings of its mind, I might regret, for its sake, the pride and scorn of its maker shown by its action, because it was not rising to the perfection of nature of which it was capable. So, in that nature in which we live and move, which is too great to regard anything as little, which is around all and in all, and which we believe to be conscious of all, there is—I cannot but think—some feeling which, for want of a better term, we must call a desire for the growth of his creatures (because in this growth lies their own happiness), and a corresponding feeling of regret when they injure themselves. But I say this in fear and reverence, knowing that human language has no terms in which to describe the nature we adore, and conscious that in the very act of putting ideas about him into words, I degrade the ideas and they no longer fully answer to the thought in my own mind. Silent adoration befits man best in the presence of his maker, only it is right to protest against the more degrading conceptions of him, although the higher conceptions are themselves far below what he really is. Sin then, being done against oneself only, cannot deserve an eternity of torture. Sin injures man already, why should he be further injured by endless agony? The infliction of pain is only justifiable when it is the means of conveying to the sufferer himself a gain greater than the suffering inflicted; therefore punishment is only righteous when reformatory. But *endless* torture cannot aim at reformation; it has no aim beyond itself, and can only arise, therefore, from vengeance and vindictiveness, which we have shown to be impossible with God. Hell is unjust, secondly, ecause its punishment is excessive and aimless.

It is also unjust, because to avoid it needs an impossible perfection. It is no answer to this to say that there is an escape offered to us through the Atonement made by Jesus Christ. Why should I be called on to escape like a criminal from that which I do not deserve? God makes man imperfect, frail, sinful, utterly unable to keep perfectly a perfect law: he therefore fails, and is—what? To be strengthened? by no means; he is to go to hell. The statement of this suffices to show its injustice. We cavil not at the wisdom which made us what we are, but we protest against the idea which makes God so cruelly unjust as to torture babies because they are unable to walk as steadily as full-grown men. Hell is unjust, in the third place, because man does not deserve it.

To all this it will probably be retorted, "you are arguing as though God's justice were the same as man's, and you were therefore capable of judging it, an assumption which is unwarrantable, and is grossly presumptuous." To which I reply: "If by God's justice you do not mean justice at all, but refer to some Divine attribute of which we know nothing, all my strictures on it fall to the ground; only, do not commit the inconsistency of arguing that hell is *just*, when by 'just' you mean some unknown quality, and then propping up your theories with proofs drawn from human justice. It would perhaps tend to clearness in argument if you gave this Divine attribute some other name, instead of using for it an expression which has already a definite meaning."

The justice of hell disposed of, we turn to the love of God. I have never heard it stated that hell is a proof of his great love to the world, but I take the liberty myself of drawing attention to it in this light. God, we are told, existed alone before ought was created; there perfect in himself, in happiness, in glory, he might have remained, say orthodox theologians. Then, we have a right to ask in the name of charity, why did he, happy himself, create a race of beings of whom the vast majority were to be endlessly and hopelessly miserable? Was this love? "He created man to glorify him." But was it loving to create those who would only suffer for his glory? Was it not rather a gigantic, an inconceivable selfishness?

"Man may be saved if he will." That is not to the point; God foreknew that some would be lost, and yet he made them. With all reverence I say it, God had no right to create sentient beings, if of one of them it can ever be truly said, "good were it for that man that he had never been born." He who creates, imposes on himself, by the very act of creation, duties towards his creatures. If God be self-conscious and moral, it is an absolute certainty that the whole creation is moving towards the final good of every creature in it. We did not ask to be made; we suffered not when we existed not; God, who has laid existence on us without our consent, is responsible for our final good, and is bound by every tie of righteousness and justice, not to speak of love, to make the existence he gave us, unasked, a blessing and not a curse to us. Parents feel this responsibility towards the children they bring into the world, and feel themselves bound to protect and to make happy those who, without them, had not been born. But, if hell be true, then every man and woman is bound not to fulfil the Divine command of multiplying the race, since by so doing they are aiding to fill the dungeons of hell, and they will, hereafter, have their sons and their daughters cursing the day of their birth, and overwhelming their parents with reproaches for having brought into the world a body, which God was thus enabled to curse with the awful gift of an immortal soul.

We must notice also that God, who is said to love righteousness, can never crush out righteousness in any human soul. There is no one so utterly degraded as to be without one sign of good. Among the lowest and vilest of our population, we find beautiful instances of kindly feeling and generous help. Can any woman be more degraded than she who only values her womanhood as a means of gain, who drinks, fights, and steals? Let those who have been among such women say if they have not been cheered sometimes by a very ray of the light of God, when the most degraded has shown kindness to an equally degraded sister, and when the very gains of sin have been purified by being poured into the lap of a suffering and dying companion. Shall love and devotion, however feeble, unselfishness and sympathy, however transitory in their action, shall these stars of heaven be quenched in the blackness of the pit of hell? If it be so, then, verily, God is not the "righteous Lord who loveth righteousness."

But we cannot leave out of our impeachment of hell that it injures man, as much as it degrades his conceptions of God. It cultivates selfishness and fear, two of his basest passions. There has scarcely perhaps been born into the world this century a purer and more loving soul than that of the late John Keble, the author of the "Christian Year." Yet what a terrible effect this belief had on him; he must cling to his belief in hell, because otherwise he would have no certainty of heaven:

> "But where is then the stay of contrite hearts?
> Of old they leaned on Thy eternal word;
> But with the sinner's fear their hope departs,
> Fast linked as Thy great name to Thee, O Lord;
>
> That Name by which Thy faithful hope is past,
> That we should endless be, for joy or woe;—
> *And if the treasures of Thy wrath could waste,*
> *Thy lovers must their promised heaven forego.*"

That is to say in plain English: "I cannot give up the

certainty of hell for others, because if I do I shall have no certainty of heaven for myself; and I would rather know that millions of my brethren should be tormented for ever, than remain doubtful about my own everlasting enjoyment." Surely a loving heart would say, instead, "O God, let us all die and remain unconscious for ever, rather than that one soul should suffer everlastingly." The terrible selfishness of the Christian belief degrades the noblest soul; the horror of hell makes men lose their self-control, and think only of their personal safety, just as we see men run wild sometimes at a shipwreck, when the gain of a minute means life. The belief in hell fosters religious pride and hatred, for all religious people think that they themselves at least are sure of heaven. If then they are going to rejoice through all eternity over the sufferings of the lost, why should they treat them with kindness or consideration here? Thus hell becomes the mother of persecution; for the heretic, the enemy of the Lord, there is no mercy and no forgiveness. Then the saints persuade themselves that true charity obliges them to persecute, for suffering may either save the heretic himself by forcing him to believe, or may at least scare others from sharing his heresy, and so preserve them from eternal fire. And they are right, if hell is true. Any means are justifiable which may save man from that horrible doom; surely we should not hesitate to knock a man down, if by so doing we preserved him from throwing himself over a precipice.

Belief in hell takes all beauty from virtue; who cares for obedience only rendered through fear? No true love of good is wrought in man by the fear of hell, and outward respectability is of little worth when the heart and the desires are unpurified. We may add that the fear of hell is a very slight practical restraint; no man thinks himself really bad enough for hell, and it is so far off that every one intends to repent at the last and so escape it. Far more restraining is the proclamation of the stern truth that, in the popular sense of the word, there is no such thing as the "forgiveness of sins;" that as a man sows, so shall he reap, and that broken laws avenge themselves without exception.

Belief in hell stifles all inquiry into truth by setting a premium on one form of belief, and by forbidding another under frightful penalties. "If it be true, as it is true, that all who do not believe this shall perish everlastingly, then, I ask, *is it not worth while to believe?*" So says a clergyman of the Church of England. Thus he presses his people to accept the dogma of the Deity of Jesus, not because it is true, but because it is dangerous to deny it. And this difficulty meets us every day. If we urge inquiry, we are told "it is dangerous;" if we suggest a difficulty, we are told "it is safer to believe;" and so this doctrine of hell chains down men's faculties and palsies their intellects, and they dare not seek for truth at all, lest he who is Truth should cast them into hell for it.

It may perhaps be said by many that I have attacked this dogma with undue vehemence, and with excessive warmth. I attack it thus, because I know the harm that it is doing, because it saddens the righteous heart and clouds the face of God. Only those who have realised hell, and realising it, have believed in it, know the awful shadow with which it darkens the world. There are many who laugh at it, but they have not felt its power, and they forget that a dogma which is only ludicrous to them is weighing heavily on many a tender heart aud sensitive brain. Hell drives many mad: to others it is a life-long horror. It pales the sunlight with its lurid flames; it blackens the earth with the smoke of its torment; it makes the Devil an actual presence; it transforms God into an enemy, eternity into an awful doom. It takes the spring out of all pleasures; it poisons all enjoyments; it spreads gloom over life, and enshrouds the tomb in horror unspeakable. Only those who have felt the anguish of this nightmare know what it is to wake up into the sunlight, and find it is only a disordered dream of the darkness; they only know the glorious liberty of heart and soul, with which they lift up smiling faces to meet the smile of God, when they can say from the depths of their glad hearts, "I believe that God is Light, and in Him is no darkness at all; I believe that all mankind is safe, cradled in the everlasting arms."

ON INSPIRATION.

THERE is a certain amount of difficulty in defining the word Inspiration: it is used in so many different senses by the various schools of religious thought, that it is almost necessary to know the theological opinions of the speaker before being quite sure of his meaning when he talks of a book as being inspired. In the halcyon days of the Church, when faith was strong and reason weak, when priests had but to proclaim and laymen but to assent, Inspiration had a distinct and a very definite meaning. An inspired man spoke the very words of God: the Bible was perfect from the "In the beginning" of Genesis to the "Amen" of Revelation: it was perfect in science, perfect in history, perfect in doctrine, perfect in morals. In that diamond no flaw was to be seen; it sparkled with a spotless purity, reflecting back in many-coloured radiance the pure white light of God. But when the chemistry of modern science came forward to test this diamond, a murmuring arose, low at first, but irrepressible. It was scrutinised through the microscope of criticism, and cracks and flaws were discovered in every direction; then, instead of being enshrined on the altar, encircled by candles, it was brought out into the searching sunlight, and the naked eye could see its imperfections. Then it was tested anew, and some bold men were heard to whisper, "It is no diamond at all, God formed in ages past; it is nothing but paste, manufactured by man;" and the news passed from mouth to mouth, until the whisper swelled into a cry, and many voices echoed, "This is no diamond at all." And so things are to-day; the battle rages still; some maintain their jewel is perfect as ever, and that the flaws are in the eyes that look at it; some reluctantly allow that it is imperfect, but still consider it a diamond; others resolutely assert that, though valuable for its antiquity and its beauty, it is really nothing but paste.

To take first the really orthodox theory of inspiration, generally styled the "plenary" or "verbal" inspiration of the Bible. It was well defined centuries since by Athenagoras; according to him the inspired writers "uttered the things that were wrought in them when the Divine Spirit moved them, the Spirit using them as a flute-player would blow into the flute." The same idea has been uttered in powerful poetry by a writer of our own day:—

> "Then thro' the mid complaint of my confession,
> Then thro' the pang and passion of my prayer,
> Leaps with a start the shock of His possession,
> Thrills me and touches, and the Lord is there.
>
> Scarcely I catch the words of His revealing,
> Hardly I hear Him, dimly understand;
> Only the power that is within me pealing,
> Lives on my lips and beckons to my hand."

The idea is exactly the same as that of the Pagan prophetesses: they became literally possesssed by a spirit, who used their lips to declare his own thoughts; so orthodox Christians believe that it is no longer Moses or Isaiah or Paul that speaks, but the Spirit of the Father that speaks in them. This theory is held by all strictly orthodox believers; this and this only is from their lips, inspiration; hard pressed on the subject they will allow that the Spirit inspires all good thoughts "in a sense," but they will be very careful in declaring that this is only inspiration in a secondary sense, an inspiration which differs in kind as well as in degree from the inspiration of the writers of the Bible. By this mechanical theory, so to speak, it is manifest that all possibility of error is excluded; thus, when Matthew quotes from the Old Testament an utterly irrelevant historical reference—"when Israel was a child, then I loved him and *called my son out of Egypt*," as a prophecy of the alleged flight of Jesus into Egypt, and his subsequent return from that country into Palestine—we find Dr. Wordsworth, Right Reverend Father in God, and Bishop of Lincoln, gravely telling us that "the Holy Spirit here declares what had been in His own mind when He uttered these words by Hosea. And who shall venture to say that he knows the mind of the Spirit better than the Spirit Himself?" Dr. Pusey again, standing valiantly, after the manner of the man, to every Church dogma, however it may be against logic, against common sense, against reason, or against charity, makes a very reasonable inquiry of those who believe in an outward and supernatural inspiration, and yet object to the term verbal. "How," he asks, "can thought be conveyed to a man's mind except through words?" The learned doctor's remark is indeed a very pertinent one, as addressed to all those who believe in an exterior revelation. Thoughts which are communicated from without can only become known to man through the medium of words: even his own thoughts only become appreciable to him when they are sufficiently distinct to be clothed in words (of course not necessarily *spoken* words); and we can only exclude from this rule such thoughts as may be presented to the mind through mental sight or hearing: *e.g.*, music might probably be composed mentally by imagining the *sounds*, or mechanical contrivances invented by imagining the *objects;* but any argument, any story, which is capable of reproduction in writing, must be thought out in words. A moment's thought renders this obvious; if a man is arguing with a Frenchman in his own language, he must, to render his arguments clear and powerful, *think* in French. Now, if the Bible be inspired so as to insure accuracy, how can this be done except through words; for many of the facts recorded must, from the necessity of the case, have been unknown to the writers. Suppose for a moment that the Biblical account of the creation of the world were true, no man in that case could possibly have thought it out for himself. Only two theories can reasonably be held regarding this record: one, that it is true, which implies necessarily that it is literally true and verbally inspired, since the knowledge could only have come from the Creator, and, being communicated must have come in the form of words, which words being God's, must be literally true; the other, that it ranks with other ancient cosmogonies, and is simply the thought of some old writer, giving his idea as to the origin of the world around him. I select the account of the Creation as a crucial test of the verbal theory of inspiration, because any other account in the Bible that I can think of has a human actor in it, and it might be maintained—however unlikely the hypothesis—that a report was related or written down by one who had been present at the incident reported, and the inspiration of the final writer may be said to consist in re-writing the previous record which he may be directed to incorporate in his own work. But no one witnessed the creation of the world, save the Creator, or, at the most, He and His angels, and the account given of it must, if true, be word for word divine; or, if false—as it is—must be nothing more than human fancy. We must push this argument one step further. If the account was communicated only to the man's *mind*, in words rising internally to the inward ear alone, how could the man distinguish between these divine thoughts rising in his mind, and his own human thoughts rising in exactly the same manner? Thoughts rise in our minds, we know not how; we only become conscious of them when they are there, and, as far as we can judge, they are produced quite naturally according to certain laws. But how is it possible for us to distinguish whence these thoughts come? There they are, ours, not another's—ours as the child is the father's and mother's, the product of their own beings. If my thought is not mine, but God's, how am I to know this? it is produced within me as my own, and the source of one thought is not distinguishable from that of another. Thus, those who believe in the accuracy of the Bible are step by step driven to allow that not only are words necessary, but *spoken* words; if the Bible be supernaturally inspired at all, then must God have spoken not only in human words but also in human voice; if the Bible be supernaturally inspired at all, it must be verbally inspired, and be literally accurate about every subject on which it treats.

Unfortunately for the maintainers of verbal inspiration, their theory is splendidly adapted for being brought before the bar of inexorable fact. It is worth while to remark, in passing, that the infallibility of the Bible has only remained unchallenged where ignorance has reigned supreme; as soon as men began to read history and to study nature, they also began to question scriptural accuracy, and to defy scriptural authority. Infallibility can only live in twilight: so far, every infallibility has fallen before advancing knowledge, save only the infallibility of Nature, which is the infallibility of God Himself. Protestants consider Roman Catholics fools, in that they are not able to see that the Pope cannot be infallible, because one Pope has cursed what another Pope has blessed. They can see in the case of others that contradiction destroys infallibility, but they cannot see the force of the same argument when applied to their own pope, the Bible. Strong in their "invincible ignorance," they bring us a divinely-inspired book; "good," we answer; "then is your book absolutely true, and it will square with all known truth in science and history, and will, of course, never be self-contradictory." The first important question which arises in our minds as we open so instructive a book as a revelation from on high, refers naturally to the Great Inspirer. The Bible contains, as might indeed be reasonably expected, many statements as to the nature of God, and we inquire of it, in the first place, the character of its Author. May we hope to see Him in this world? "Yes," answers Exodus. "Moses in days gone by spoke to God face to face, and seventy-four Israelites saw Him, and eat and drank in His presence." We have scarcely taken in this answer when we hear the same voice proceed: "No; for God said thou canst not see my face, for there shall no man see me and live; while John declares that no man hath seen Him, and Paul, that no man neither hath nor can see Him." Is He Almighty? "Yes," says Jesus. "With God all things are possible." "No," retorts Judges; "for He could not drive out the inhabitants of the valley, *because* they had chariots of iron." Is He just? "Yes," answers Ezekiel. "The son shall not bear the iniquity of the father; the soul that sinneth *it* shall die." "No," says Exodus. "The Lord declares that He visits the iniquity of the fathers upon the children." Is He impartial? "Yes," answers Peter. "God is no respecter of persons." "No;" says Romans, "for God loved Jacob and hated Esau before they were born, that His purpose of *election* might stand." Is He truthful? "Yes; it is impossible for God to lie," says Hebrews. "No," says God of Himself, in Ezekiel. "I, the Lord, have deceived that prophet." Is He loving? "Yes," sings the Psalmist. "He is loving unto every man, and His tender mercy is over all His works." "No," growls Jeremiah. "He will not pity, nor spare, nor have mercy on them." Is he easily pacified when offended? "Yes," says the Psalmist. "His wrath endureth but the twinkling of an eye." "No," says Jeremiah. "Ye have kindled a fire in His anger that shall burn for ever." Unable to discover anything reliable about God, doubtful whether he be just or unjust, partial or impartial, true or false, loving or fierce, placable or implacable, we come to the conclusion that at all events we had better be friends with Him, and surely the book which reveals His will to us will at least tell us in what way He desires us to approach Him. Does He accept sacrifice? "Yes," says Genesis: "Noah sacrificed and God smelled a sweet savour;" and Samuel tells us how God was prevailed on to take away a famine by the sacrifice of seven men, hanged up before the Lord. In our fear we long to escape from Him altogether, and ask if this be possible? "Yes," says Genesis. "Adam and his wife hid from Him in the trees, and He had to go down from His heaven to see if some evil deeds were rightly reported to Him." "No," says Solomon. "You cannot hide from Him, for His eyes are in every place." So we throw up in despair all hope of finding out anything reliable about Him, and proceed to search for some trustworthy history. We try to find out how man was made. One account tells us that he was made male and female, even in the image of God Himself; another that God made man alone, and subsequently formed a woman for him out of one of his own ribs. Then we find in one chapter that the beasts were all made, and, lastly, that God made "His masterpiece, man." In another chapter we are told that God having made man thought it not good to leave him by himself, and proceeded to make every beast and fowl, saying that he would make Adam a help-meet for him; on bringing them to Adam, however, none was found worthy to mate with him, so woman was tried as a last experiment. As we read on we find evident marks of confusion; double, or even treble, accounts of the same incident, as, for instance, the denying a wife and its consequences. Then we see Moses fearing Pharaoh's wrath, and flying out of Egypt to avoid the king's wrath, and not venturing to return until after his death, and are therefore surprised to learn from Hebrews that he forsook Egypt by faith, *not fearing* the wrath of the king. Then we come across numberless contradictions in Kings and Chronicles, in prophecy and history. Ezekiel prophecies that Nebuchadnezzar shall conquer Tyrus, and destroy it and *take all its riches;* and a few chapters afterwards it is recorded that he did accordingly attack Tyrus but failed, and that as he got *no wages* for this attack he should have Egypt for his failure. In the New Testament the contradictions are endless; Joseph, the husband of Mary, had two fathers, Jacob and Heli; Salah is in the same predicament, for although the son of Canaan, Arphaxad begat him. When John was cast into prison, Jesus *began* to preach, although He had been preaching and gaining disciples while John was still at large. Jesus sent the Twelve to preach, telling them to take a staff, and yet bidding them to take none. He eat the Passover with His disciples, although He was crucified before that feast. He had one title on his cross, but it is verbally inspired in four different ways. He rose with many variations of date and time, and ascended the same evening, although He subsequently went into Galilee and remained on earth for forty days. He sent word to His disciples to meet Him in Galilee, and yet suddenly appeared among them as they sat quietly together the same evening at Jerusalem. Stephen's history contradicts our Old Testament. When Paul is converted, his companions hear a voice, although another account says that they heard none at all. After his conversion he goes in and out at Jerusalem with the Apostles, although, strangely enough, he sees none of them, except Peter and James. But one might spend pages in noting these inconsistencies, while even one of them destroys the verbal inspiration theory. From these contradictions I maintain that one of two things must follow, either the Bible is not an inspired book, or else inspiration is consistent with much error, as I shall presently show.

I am quite ready to allow that the Bible *is* inspired, and I therefore lay down as my first canon of inspiration, that:

"Inspiration does not prevent inaccuracy."

I turn to the second class of orthodox inspirationists, who, while allowing that verbal inspiration is proved impossible by many trivial inconsistencies, yet affirm that God's overruling power ensures substantial accuracy, and that its history and science are perfectly true and are to be relied on. To test this assertion, we—after noting that Bible history is, as has been remarked above, continually self-contradictory—turn to other histories and compare the Bible with them. We notice first that many important Biblical occurrences are quite ignored by "profane" historians. We are surprised to see that while the Babylonish captivity left marks on Israel which are plainly seen, Egypt left no trace on Israel's names or customs, and Israel no trace on Egypt's monuments. The doctrine of angels comes not from heaven, but slips into Jewish theology from the Persian; while immortality is brought to light neither by Hebrew prophet nor by the Gospel of Jesus, but by the people among whom the Jews resided during the Babylonish captivity. The Jewish Scriptures which precede the captivity know of nothing beyond the grave; the Jewish Scriptures after the captivity are radient with the light of a life to come; to these Jesus adds nothing of joy or hope. The very central doctrine of Christianity—the Godhead of Jesus—is nothing but a repetition of an idea of Greek philosophy borrowed by early Christian writers, and is to be found in Plato and Philo as clearly as in the fourth Gospel. Science contradicts the Bible as much as does history; geology laughs at its puny periods of creation; astronomy destroys its heavens, and asks why this little world took a week in making, while the sun and moon and the countless stars were rapidly turned out in twelve hours; natural history wonders why the kangaroos did not stay in Asia after the Deluge, instead of undertaking the long sea voyage to far Australia, and enquires how the Mexicans, and Peruvians, and others, crossed the wide ocean to settle in America; archæology presents its human bones from ancient caves, and asks how they got there, if only six thousand years have passed since Adam and Eve stood alone in Eden, gazing out on the unpeopled earth; the Pyramids point at the negro type distinct and clear, and ask how it comes that it was so rapidly developed at first, and yet has remained stationary ever since. At last, science gets weary of slaying a foe so puny, and goes on its way with a smile on its grand, still face, leaving the Bible to teach its science to whom it lists. Evidence so weighty crushes all life out of this second theory of inspiration, and gives us a second rule to guide us in our search:

"Inspiration does not prevent ignorance and error."

We may pass on to the third class of inspirationists, those who believe that the Bible is not given to man to teach him either history or science, but only to reveal to him what he could not discover by the use of his natural faculties—*e.g.*, the duties of morality and the nature of God. I must note here the subtilty of this retreat. Driven by inexorable fact to allow the Bible to be fallible in everything in which we can test its assertions, they, by a clever strategic movement, remove their defence to a post more difficult to attack. They maintain that the Bible is infallible in points where no cannonade of facts can be brought to bear on it. What is this but to say, that although we can prove the Bible to be fallible on every point capable of proof, we are still blindly to believe it to be infallible where demonstrated error is, from the nature of the case, impossible? As regards the nature of God, we have already seen that the Bible ascribes to him virtue and vice indifferently. We turn to morality, and here our first great difficulty meets us, for when we point to a thing and say, "that is profoundly immoral," our opponents retort, "it is perfectly moral." Only the progress of humanity can prove which of us is in the right, though here, too, we have one great fact on our side, and that is, the conscience in man; already men would rather die than imitate the actions of Old Testament saints who did that which was "right in the eyes of Jehovah;" and presently they will be bold enough to reject in words that which they already reject in deeds. Few would put the Bible freely into the hands of a child, any more than they would give freely to the young the unpurged editions of Swift and Sterne; and I imagine that the most pious parents would scarcely see with unmingled pleasure their son and daughter of fifteen and sixteen studying together the histories and laws of the Pentateuch. But taking the Bible as a rule of life, are we to copy its saints and its laws? For instance, is it right for a man to marry his half-sister, as did the great ancestor of the Jews, Abraham, the friend of God?—a union, by the way, which is forbidden by Jewish law, although said to be the source of their race. Is the lie of the Egyptian midwives right, because Jehovah blessed them for it, even as Jael is pronounced blessed by Deborah, the prophetess, for her accursed treachery and murder? Is the robbery of the Egyptians right, because commanded by Jehovah? Are the old cruel laws of witchcraft right, because Jehovah doomed the witch to death? Are the ordeals of the Middle Ages right, because derived from the laws of Jehovah? Is human sacrifice right, because attempted by Abraham, enjoined by Moses, practised by Jephthah, efficacious in turning away God's wrath when Saul's seven sons were offered up? Is murder right because Phineas wrought atonement by it, and Moses sent his murderers throughout the camp to stay God's anger by slaying their brethren? Is it right that the persons of women captives should be the prey of the conquerors, because the Jews were commanded by Jehovah to save alive the virgins and keep them for themselves, except the sixty-four reserved for himself? Is the man after God's own heart a worthy model for imitation? Are Jehu's lying and slaughter right, because right in the eyes of Jehovah? Is Hosea's marriage commendable, because commanded by Jehovah? or are the signs of Jeremiah and Ezekiel the less childish and indecent because they are prefaced with, "thus saith Jehovah?" Far be it from me to detract from the glorious morality of portions of the Bible; but if the whole book be inspired and infallible in its moral teaching, then, of course, one moral lesson is as important as another, and we have no right to pick and choose where the whole is divine. The harsher part of the Old Testament morality has burnt its mark into the world, and may be traced through history by the groans of suffering men and women, by burning witches and tortured enemies of the Lord, by flaming cities and blood-stained fields. If murder and rapine, treachery and lies, robbery and violence, were commanded long ago by Almighty God; if things are right and wrong only by virtue of His command, then who can say that they may not be right once more, when used in the cause of the Church, and how are we to know that Moses speaks in God's name when he commands them, and Torquemada only in his own? But even Christians are beginning to feel ashamed of some of the exploits of the "Old Testament Saints," and to try and explain away some of the harsher features; we even hear sometimes a wicked whisper about "imperfect light," &c. Good heavens! what blasphemy! Imperfect light can mean nothing less than imperfect God, if He is responsible for the morality of these writings.

So, from our study of the Bible we deduce another canon by which we may judge of inspiration:

"Inspiration does not prevent moral error."

There is a fourth class of inspirationists, the last which clings to the skirts of orthodoxy, which is always endeavouring to plant one foot on the rocks of science, while it balances the other over the quicksands of orthodox supernaturalism. The Broad Church school here takes one wide step away from orthodoxy, by allowing that the inspiration of the Bible differs only in degree and not in kind from the inspiration common to all mankind. They recognise the great fact that the inspiring Spirit of God is the source whence flow all good and noble deeds, and they point out that the Bible itself refers all good and all knowledge to that one Spirit, and that He breathes mechanical skill into Bezaleel and Aholiab, strength into Samson's arms, wisdom into Solomon, as much as He breathes the ecstacy of the prophet into Isaiah, faith into Paul, and love into John. They recognise the old legends as authentic, but would maintain as stoutly that He spoke to Newton through the falling of an apple, as that He spoke of old to Elijah by fire, or to the wise men by a star. This school try and remove the moral difficulties of the Old Testament by regarding the history recorded in it as a history which is specially intended to unveil the working of God through all history, and so to gradually reveal God as He makes Himself known to the world; thus the grosser parts are regarded as wholly attributable to the ignorance of men, and they delight to see the divine light breaking slowly through the thick clouds of human error and prejudice, and to trace in the Bible the gradual evolution of a nobler faith and a purer morality. They regard the miracles of Jesus as a manifestation that God underlies Nature and works ever therein: they believe God to be specially manifested in Jewish history, in order that men may understand that He presides over all nations and rules over all peoples. To Maurice the Bible is the explainer of all earth's problems, the unveiler of God, the Bread of Life. There is, on the whole, little to object to in the Broad Church view of inspiration, although liberal thinkers regret that, as a party, they stop half way, and are still trammelled by the half-broken chains of orthodoxy. For instance, they usually regard the direct revelation of morality as closed by Jesus and His immediate followers, although they allow that God has not deserted His world, nor confined His inspiration within the covers of a book. To them, however, the Bible is still *the* inspired book, standing apart by itself, differing from all other sacred books. From their views of inspiration, which contains so much that is true, we deduce a fourth rule:

"Inspiration is not confined to written words about God."

From a criticism of the book, which is held by orthodox Christians, to be specially inspired, we have then gained some idea of what inspiration does *not* do. It does not prevent inaccuracy, ignorance, error, nor is it confined to any written book. Inspiration, then, cannot be an overwhelming influence, crushing the human faculties and bearing along the subject of it on a flood which he can neither direct nor resist. It is a breathing—gentle and gradual—of pure thoughts into impure hearts, tender thoughts into fierce hearts, forgiving thoughts into revengeful hearts. David calls home his banished son, and he learns that, "even as a father pitieth his children, so is the Lord merciful unto them that fear Him." Paul wishes himself accursed if it may save his brethren, and from his own self-sacrificing love he learns that "God will have all men to be saved, and to come to the knowledge of the truth." Thus inspiration is breathed into the man's heart. "I love and forgive, weak as I am; what must be the depth of the love and forgiveness of God?" David's fierce revenge finds an echo in his writings; for man writes, and not God: he defaces God by ascribing to Him the passions surging only in his own burning Eastern heart: then, as the Spirit moves him to forgiveness, his song is of mercy; for he feels that his Maker must be better than himself. That part of the Bible is inspired, I do not deny, in the sense that all good thoughts are the result of inspiration, but only as we share the inspiration of the Bible can we distinguish between the noble and the base in it, between the eternal and that which is fast passing away. But as we do not expect to find that inspiration, now-a-days, guards men from much error, both of word and deed, so we should not expect to find it otherwise in days gone by; nor should we wonder that the man who spoke of God as showing His tender fatherhood by punishing and correcting, could so sink down into hard thoughts of that loving Father as to say that it was a fearful thing to fall into His hands. These contradictions meet us in every man; they are the highest and the lowest moments of the human soul. Only as we are inspired to love and patience in our conduct towards men will our words be inspired when we speak of God.

Having thus seen what inspiration does not do, we must glance at what it really is. It is, perhaps, natural that we, rejecting, as we do, with somewhat of vehemence, the idea of supernatural revelation, should oftentimes be accused of denying all revelation and disbelieving all inspiration. But even as we are not atheists, although we deny the Godhead of Jesus, so are we not unbelievers in inspiration because we refuse to bend our necks beneath the yoke of an inspired Bible. For we believe in a God too mighty and too universal to be wrapped in swaddling clothes or buried in a cave, and we believe in an inspiration too mighty and too universal to belong only to one nation and to one age. As the air is as free and as refreshing to us as it was to Isaiah, to Jesus, or to Paul, so does the spiritual air of God's Spirit breathe so softly and as refreshingly on our brows as on theirs. We have eyes to see and ears to hear quite as much as they had in Judea long ago. "If God be omnipresent and omniactive, this inspiration is no miracle, but a regular mode of God's action on conscious Spirit, as gravitation on unconscious matter. It is not a rare condescension of God, but a universal uplifting of man. To obtain a knowledge of duty, a man is not sent away outside of himself to ancient documents for the only rule of faith and practice; the Word is very nigh him, even in his heart, and by this word he is to try all documents whatever. . . . Wisdom, Righteousness, and Love are the Spirit of God in the soul of man; wherever these are, and just in proportion to their power, there is inspiration from God. . . . Inspiration is . . . the in-come of God to the soul, in the form of Truth through the Reason, of Right through the Conscience, of Love and Faith through the Affections and Religious Element. . . . A man would be looked on as mad who should claim miraculous inspiration for Newton, as they have been who denied it in the case of Moses. But no candid man will doubt that, humanly speaking, it was a more difficult thing to write the Principia than to write the Decalogue. Man must have a nature most sadly anomalous if, unassisted, he is able to accomplish all the triumphs of modern science, and yet cannot discover the plainest and most important principles of Religion and Morality without a miraculous inspiration; and still more so if, being able to discover by God's natural aid these chief and most important principles, he needs a miraculous inspiration to disclose minor details."* Thus we believe that inspiration from God is the birthright of humanity, and to be an heir of God it needs only to be a son of man. Earth's treasures are highly priced and hard to win, but God's blessings are, like the rain and the sunshine, showered on all-comers.

"'Tis only heaven is *given* away;
'Tis only God may be had for the asking;
No price is set on the lavish summer;
June may be had by the poorest comer."

If inspiration were indeed that which it is thought to be by the orthodox Christians, surely we ought to be able to distinguish its sayings from those of the uninspired. If inspiration be confined to the Christian Bible, how is it that the inspired thoughts were in many cases spoken out to the world hundreds of years before they fell from the lips of an inspired Jew? It seems a somewhat uncalled for miraculous interference for a man to be supernaturally inspired to inform the world of some moral truth which had been well known for hundreds of years to a large portion of the race. Or is it that a great moral truth bears within

* Theodore Parker.

itself so little evidence of its royal birth, that it cannot be accepted as ruler by divine right over men until its proclamation is signed by some duly accredited messenger of the Most High? Then, indeed, must God be "more cognizable by the senses than by the soul;" and then "the eye or the ear is a truer and quicker percipient of Deity than the Spirit which came forth from Him."* Was Paul inspired when he wished himself accursed for his brethren's sake, but Kwan-yin uninspired, when she said, "Never will I seek nor receive private individual salvation; never enter into final peace alone?" If Jesus and the prophets were inspired when they placed mercy above sacrifice, was Manu uninspired in saying that a man "will fall very low if he performs ceremonial acts only, and fails to discharge his moral duties"? Was Jesus inspired when he taught that the whole law was comprehended in one saying, namely, "Thou shalt love thy neighbour as thyself?" and yet was Confucius uninspired when, in answer to the question, "What one word would serve as a rule to one's whole life?" he said, "Reciprocity; what you do not wish done to yourself, do not to others." Or take the Talmud and study it, and then judge from what uninspired source Jesus drew much of His highest teaching. "Whoso looketh on the wife of another with a lustful eye, is considered as if he had committed adultery."—(Kalah.) "With what measure we mete, we shall be measured again."—(Johanan.) "What thou wouldst not like to be done to thyself, do not to others; this is the fundamental law."—(Hillel.) "If he be admonished to take the splinter out of his eye, he would answer, Take the beam out of thine own."—(Tarphon.) "Imitate God in His goodness. Be towards thy fellow-creatures as He is towards the whole creation. Clothe the naked; heal the sick; comfort the afflicted; be a brother to the children of thy Father." The whole parable of the houses built on the rock and on the sand is taken out of the Talmud, and such instances of quotation might be indefinitely multiplied. What do they all prove? That there is no inspiration in the Bible? by no means. But surely that inspiration is not confined to the Bible, but is spread over the world; that much in all "sacred books" is the outcome of inspired minds at their highest, although we find the same books containing gross and low thoughts. We should always remember that although the Bible is more

* W. R. Greg.

specially a revelation to us of the Western nations than are the Vedas and the Zend-Avesta, that it is only so because it is better suited to our modes of thought, and because it has been one of the agents in our education. The reverence with which we may regard the Bible as bound up with many sacred memories, and as the chosen teacher of many of our greatest minds and purest characters, is rightly directed in other nations to their own sacred books. The books are really all on a level, with much good and much bad in them all; but as the Hebrew was inspired to proclaim that "the Lord thy God is one Lord" to the Hebrews, so was the Hindoo inspired to proclaim to Hindoos, "There is only one Deity, the great Soul." Either all are inspired, or none are. They stand on the same footing. And we rejoice to believe that one Spirit breathes in all, and that His inspiration is ours to-day. "The Father worketh hitherto," although men fancy He is resting in an eternal Sabbath. The orthodox tells us that, in rejecting the rule of morality laid down for us in the Bible, and in trusting ourselves to this inspiration of the free Spirit of God, our faith and our morality will alike be shifting and unstable. But we reck not of their warnings; our faith and our morality are only shifting in this sense, that, as we grow holier, and purer, and wiser, our conception of God and of righteousness will rise and expand with our growth. It was a golden saying of one of God's noblest sons that "no man knoweth the Father save the Son:" to know God we must resemble Him, as we see in the child the likeness of the parent. But in trusting ourselves to the guidance of the Spirit of God, we are not building the house of our faith on the shifting sand; rather are we "dwelling in a city that hath foundations, whose builder and maker is God." Wisely was it sung of old, "Except the Lord build the house, their labour is but lost that build it." Vain are all efforts of priestly coercion; vain all toils of inspired books; vain the utter sacrifice of reason and conscience; their labour is but lost when they strive to build a temple of human faith, strong enough to bear the long strain of time, or the earthquake-shock of grief. God only, by the patient guiding of His love, by the direct inspiration of His Spirit, can lay, stone by stone, and timber by timber, that priceless fabric of trust and love, which shall outlive all attacks and all changes, and shall stand in the human soul as long as His own Eternity endures.

ON THE RELIGIOUS EDUCATION OF CHILDREN.

IN every transition-stage of the world's history the question of education naturally comes to the front. So much depends on the first impressions of childhood, on the first training of the tender shoot, that it has always been acknowledged, from Solomon to Forster, that to "train up a child in the way he should go" is among the most important duties of fathers and citizens. To the individual, to the family, to the State, the education of the rising generation is a question of primary importance. Plato began the education of the citizens of his ideal Republic from the very hour of their birth; the nursing child was taken from the mother lest injudicious treatment should mar, in the slightest degree, the perfection of the future warrior. On this point modern and ancient wisdom clasp hands, and place the education of the child among the most important duties of the State. The battle at present raging between the advocates of "secular" and "religious" education—to use the cant of the day—is a most natural and righteous recognition of the vast interests at stake when Church or State claims the right of training the sons and daughters of England. No one has yet attempted to explain why it should be "irreligious" to teach writing, or history, or geography; or why it should "destroy a child's soul" to improve his mental faculties. It is among the "mysteries" of the faith, why it is better for our poor to leave them to grow up in both moral and intellectual darkness, than to dissipate the intellectual darkness by some few rays of knowledge, and to leave the moral training to other hands. If we left a starving man to die because we could only give him bread, and were unable to afford cheese in addition, all would unite in declaiming at our folly: but "religious" people would rather that our street Arabs grew up both heathens and brutes, than that we should improve their minds without Christianizing their souls. Better let a lad grow up a thief and a drunkard, than turn him into an artizan and a free-thinker. There can scarcely be a better proof of the unreasonableness of Christian doctrine, than the Christian fear of sharpening mental faculties, without binding them down, at the same time, in the chains of dogma. Only a religion founded on reason can dare to train children's minds to the utmost, and then leave them free to use all the power and keenness acquired by that training on the investigation of any religious doctrine presented to them. We, who have written Tekel on the Christian faith, share in the opinion of the Christian clergy, that man's carnal reason is a terrible foe to the Christian revelation; but here we begin to differ from them, for while they regard this reason as a child of the devil, to be scourged and chained down, we do homage to it as to the fairest offspring of the Divine Spirit, the brightest earthly reflection of His glory, and the nearest image of His "Person"; we would cherish it, tend it, nourish it, as our Father's noblest gift to humanity, as our surest guide and best counsellor, as the ear which hears His voice, and the eye which sees Him, as the sharpest weapon against superstition, the ultimate arbiter on earth between right and wrong. To us, then, education is ranged on the side of God; we welcome it freely and gladly, because all truth, all light, all knowledge, are foes of falsehood, of darkness, of ignorance. If we mistake error for truth a brighter light will set us right, and we only wish to be taught truth, not to be proved right.

Most liberal thinkers agree in recognizing the fact that the duties of the State in the matter of education must, in the nature of things, be purely "secular:" that is to say, that while the State insists that the future citizen shall be taught at least the elements of learning, so as to fit him or her for fulfilling the duties of that citizenship, it has no right to insist on impressing on the mind of its pupil any set of religious dogmas or any form of religious creed. The abdication by the State of the pretended right of enforcing on its citizens any special form of religion, is not at all identical with the opposition by the State to religious teaching; it is merely a development of the very wise maxim of the great Jewish Teacher, to render the things of Cæsar to Cæsar, and the things of God to God. To teach reading, writing, honesty, regard for law, these things are Cæsar's duties; to teach religious dogma, creed, or article, is entirely the province of the teachers who claim to hold the truth of God.

But my object now is not to draw the line between the duties of Church and State, of school and home; nor do I wish to enter the lists of sectarian controversy, to break a lance in favour of a new religious dogma. The question is rather this: "What are the limits of the religious education which it is wise to impose on the young? Is any dogmatic teaching to be a part of their moral training, and is the dogmatism against which we have rebelled to be revived in a new form? Are the fetters which we are breaking for ourselves to be welded together again for the young limbs of our children? Are they to be fed on the husks which have starved our own religious aspirations, and which we have analysed, and rejected as unfit to sustain our moral and mental vigour? On the other hand, are our children to grow up without any religious teaching at all, without a ray of that sunshine which is to most of us the very source of our gladness, and the renewal of our strength?"

I think the best way of deciding this question is to notice the gradual development of the childish body and mind. Nature's indications are a sure guide-post, and we cannot go very far wrong in following her hints. I am now on ground with which mothers are familiar, though perhaps few men have watched young children with sufficient attention to be able to note their gradual development. The first instincts of a baby are purely personal: the "not-I" is for it non-existent: food, warmth, cleanliness, comprise all its needs and all our duties to it. The next stage is when the infant becomes conscious of the existence of something outside itself: when, vaguely and indistinctly, but yet decidedly, it shows signs of observing the things around it: to cultivate observation, to attract attention, slowly to guide it into distinguishing one object from another, are the next steps in its education. The child soon succeeds in distinguishing forms, and learns to attach different sounds to different shapes: it is also taught to avoid some things and to play with others: it awakes to the knowledge that while some objects give pleasure, others give pain: so far as material things go, it learns to choose the good and to avoid the evil. This power is only gained by experience, and is therefore acquired but gradually, and after a time, side by side with it, runs another lesson; slowly and gradually there appears a dawning appreciation of "right" and "wrong." This appreciation is not, however, at first an appreciation of any intrinsic rightness or wrongness in any given action; it is simply a recognition on the child's part that some of its acts meet with approval, others with disapproval, from its elders. The standard of its seniors is unquestioningly accepted by the child. The moral sense awakes, but is completely guided in its first efforts by the hand of the child's teacher, as completely as the first efforts to walk are directed by the mother. Thus it comes to pass that the conscience of the child is but the reflex of the conscience of its parents or guardians: "right" and "wrong" in a child's vocabulary are in the earliest stages equivalent to "reward" and "punishment;" its final court of appeal in cases of morality is the judgment of the parent.* It is perhaps scarcely accurate to call this motive power in the child a *moral* sense at all; still, this recognition of some thing which is immaterial and intangible, and which is yet to be the guide of its actions, is a great step forward from the simple consciousness of outer and material objects, and is truly the dawn of that moral sense which becomes in men and women the test of right and wrong. So far we have considered the growing faculties of the child as regards physical and moral development, and I particularly wish to remark that the moral sense appears long before any "religious" tendency can be noted. There is, however, another

* The moral sense does show itself, however, in very young children, in a higher form than this; for we may often observe in a young child an instinctive sense of shame at having done wrong. But the moral sense is awakened and educated by the parents' approval and disapproval. This may be proved, I think, by the fact that a child brought up among thieves and evil-livers will accept their morality as a matter of course, and will steal and lie habitually, without attaching to either act any idea of wrong. The moral sense is inherent in man, and is in no way *given* by the parent; but I think that it is first aroused and put into action by the parent; the parent accustoms the child to regard certain actions as right and wrong; this appeals to the moral sense in the child, and the child very rapidly is ashamed of wrong, as wrong, and not simply from dread of punishment. I would be understood to mean, in the text, that the wish for reward is the first response of the child to the idea of an inherent distinction between different actions; this feeling rapidly developes into the true moral sense, which regards right as right, and wrong as wrong.

I append this note at the suggestion of a valued friend, who feared that the inference might be drawn from the text that the moral sense was implanted by the parent instead of being, as it is, the gift of God.

side of the complete human character which is very important, but which is slow in showing itself in any healthy child; I mean what may be called the *spiritual* sense, in distinction from the moral; the sense which is the crowning grace of humanity, the sense which belongs wholly to the immortal part of man: the outstretched hands of the human spirit groping after the Eternal Spirit; the yearning after that all-pervading Power which men call God. I know well that in many precociously-pious children this spiritual sense is forced into a premature and unwholesome maturity; by means of a spiritual hot-house the summer-fruit of piety may be obtained in the spring-time of the childish heart. The imitative instinct of childhood quickly reproduces the sentiments around it, and set phrases which meet with admiration flow glibly from baby-lips. But this strongly developed religious feeling in a child is both unnatural and harmful, and can never, because it is unreal, produce any lasting good effect. Yet is it none the less true that, at an early age, differing much in different children, the "spiritual sense" does show signs of awakening; that children soon begin to wonder about things around them, and to ask questions which can only find their true answer in the name of God. How to meet these questions, how to train this growing sentiment without crushing it on the one hand, and without unduly stimulating it on the other, is a source of deep anxiety to many a mother's heart in the present day. They are unable to tell their children the stories which satisfied their own childish cravings: no longer can they hold up before the eager faces the picture of the manger at Bethlehem, or dim the bright eyes with the story of the cross on Calvary; no longer can they fold the little hands in prayer to the child of Nazareth, or hush the hasty tongue with the reminder of the obedience of the Virgin's son. To a certain extent this is a loss. A child quickly seizes the concrete; the idea of the child Jesus or the man Jesus is readily grasped by a child's intellect; the God of the Old Testament, the "magnified man," is also, though more dimly, understood. These conceptions of the childhood of humanity suit the childhood of the individual, and it is far more difficult for the child to realize the idea of God when he is divested of these materialistic garments. Yet I speak from experience when I say that it is by no means impossible to train a child into the simplest and happiest feelings as regards the Supreme Being, without degrading the Divine into the human. By one name we can speak of God by which He will be readily welcomed to the child's heart, and that is the name of the Father. Most children are keenly alive to natural beauties, and are quick to observe birds, and flowers, and sunshine; at times they will ask how these things come there, and then it is well to tell them that they are the works of God. Thus the child's first notions of the existence of a Power he cannot see or feel will come to him clothed in the things he loves, and will be free from any suggestion of fear.* Even those who regard God from the stand-point of Pantheism may use natural objects so as to train the child into a fearless and happy recognition of the constant working of the Spirit of Nature, and so guard the young mind against that shrinking from, and terror of God, which popular Christianity is so apt to induce. The lad or girl who grows up with even the habit of regarding God as the calm and mighty motive-power of the forces of Nature, changeless, infinite, absolutely trustworthy, will be slow to accept in later life the crude conceptions which incarnate the creative power in a virgin's womb, and ascribe caprice, injustice, and cruelty to the mighty Spirit of the Universe.

There is a deep truth in the idea of Pantheism, that "Nature is an apparition of the Deity, God in a mask;" that "He is the light of the morning, the beauty of the noon, and the strength of the sun. . . He is the One, the All. . . The soul of all; more moving than motion, more stable than rest; fairer than beauty, and stronger than strength. The power of Nature is God. . . He is the All; the Reality of all phenomena." The child fed on this food will have scarcely anything to unlearn, even when he begins to believe that God is something more than Nature; "the created All is the symbol of God," and he will pass easily and naturally on from seeing God in Nature to see Him in a higher form.

Of course, as a Theist, I should myself go much further than this: I should speak of all natural glory as but the reflection of the Deity, or as the robe in which He veils His infinite beauty; I should bid my children rejoice in all

* The ordinary shrinking of a child from the idea of a Presence which he cannot see, but which sees him, will not be felt by children whose only ideas about God are that He is the Father from whose hand come all beautiful things. In any home where the parents' thoughts of God are free from doubt and mistrust, the children's thoughts will be the same; religion, in their eyes, will be synonymous with happiness, for God and good will be convertible terms.

happiness as in the gift of a Father who delights in sharing His joy with His creatures; I should point out that the pain caused by ignorance of, or by breaking natural laws, is God's way of teaching men obedience for their own ultimate good: in the freedom and fulness of Nature's gifts I should teach them to see the equal love of God for all; through marking that in Nature's visible kingdom no end can be gained without labour and without using certain laws, they should learn that in the invisible kingdom they need not expect to find favouritism, nor think to share the fruits of victory without patient toil. To all who believe in a God who is also the Father of Spirits such teaching as this comes easily; as they themselves learn of God only through His works, so they naturally teach their children to seek Him in the same way.

The questions, so familiar to every mother, "Can God see me?" "Where is God?" can only be met with the simple assertion that God sees all, and is everywhere. For there are many childish questions which it is wisest to meet with statements which are above the grasp of the childish mind. These statements may be simply given to the child as statements which it is too young either to question or to understand. Nothing is gained by trying to smooth down spiritual subjects to the level of a child's capacity; the time will come later when the child must meet and answer for itself all great spiritual questions; the parent's care should be to remove all hindrances from the child's path of inquiry, but not to give it cut-and-dried answers to every possible question; religion, to be worth anything, must be a personal matter, and each must find it out for himself; the wise parent will endeavour to save the child from the pain of unlearning, by giving but little formal religious teaching; he cannot fight the battle for his child, but he can prevent his being crippled by a fancied armour which will stifle rather than protect him; he can give a few wide principles to direct him, without weighing him down with guide-books.

But even the most general ideas of God should not be forced on a childish mind; they should come, so to speak, by chance; they should be presented in answer to some demand of the child's heart; they should be inculcated by stray words and passing remarks; they should form the atmosphere surrounding the child habitually, and not be a sudden "wind of doctrine." Of course all this is far more troublesome than to teach a child a catechism or a creed, but it is a far higher training. Dogma, *i.e.*, conviction petrified by authority, should be utterly excluded from the religious education of children; a few great axiomatic truths may be laid down, but even in these primary truths dogmatism should be avoided. The parent should always take care to make it apparent that he is stating his own convictions, but is not enforcing them on the child by his authority. So far as the child is capable of appreciating them, the reasons for the religious conviction should be presented along with the conviction itself. Thus the child will see, as he grows older, that religion cannot be learned by rote, that it is not shut up in a book, or contained in creeds; he will appreciate the all-important fact that free inquiry is the only air in which truth can breathe; that one man's faith cannot justly be imposed on another, and that every individual soul has the privilege and the responsibility of forming his own religion, and must either hear God with his own ears, or else not hear Him at all.

We have noticed that the moral sense awakes before the religious (I must state my repugnance to these terms, although I use them for the sake of clearness; but morality *is* religion, although religion is more than morality, and the so-called religion which is not morality is worthless and hateful). There remains then to consider what we will call the second side of religion, although it is by far its most important side. True religion consists not only in feelings towards God, but also in duties towards men: the first, noble and blessed as they are, should, in every healthy religion, give place to the second; for a morally good man who does not believe in God at all, is in a far higher state of being than the man who believes in God and is selfish, cruel or unjust. Error in faith is forgiveable; error in life is fatal. The good man shall surely see God, although, for a time, his eyes be holden; the evil man, though he hold the noblest faith yet known, shall never taste the joy of God, until he turns from sin, and struggles after holiness. Faith first, and then morality, is the war-cry of the churches; morality above all, and let faith follow in good time, is the watch-word of Theism; so, among us, the principal part of the religious training of our children should be morality; religious feeling may be over-strained, or give rise to self-deception; religious talk may be morbid and unreal; religious faith may be erring, and must be imperfect; but morality is a rock which can never be shaken, a guide which can never mislead. Whether we are right or wrong in our belief about God, whether we are immortal spirits or perishable organizations, yet purity is nobler than vice, courage than cowardice, truth than falsehood, love than hate. Let us, then, teach our children morality above all things. Let us teach them to love good for its own sake, without thought of reward, and they will remain good, even if, in after life, they should, alas! lose all hope of immortality and all faith in God. A child's natural instinct is towards good; a tale of heroism, of self-sacrifice, of generosity, will bring the eager blood flushing up to a child's face and wake a quick response and a desire of emulation. It is therefore well to place in children's hands tales of noble deeds in days gone by. Nothing is easier than to train a child into feeling a desire to be good for the sake of being so. There is something so attractive in goodness, that I have found it more effectual to hold up the nobility of courage and unselfishness before the child's eyes, than to descend to punishment for the corresponding faults. If a child is in the habit of regarding all wrong as something low and degrading, he quickly shrinks from it; all mothers know the instinctive ambition of children to be something superior and admirable, and this instinct is most useful in inculcating virtue. Later in life nothing ruins a young man like discovering that morality and religion are often divorced, and that the foremost professors of religion are less delicately honourable and trustworthy than high-minded "worldly men;" on the other hand, nothing will have so beneficial an effect on men and women entering life, as to see that those who are most joyful in their faith towards God, lead the purest and most blameless lives. "Do good, be good" is, as has been well said, the golden rule of life; "do good, be good" must be the law impressed on our children's hearts. Whatever "eclipse of faith" may await England, whatever darkness of most hopeless scepticism, whatever depth of uttermost despair of God, there is not only the hope, but the certainty of the resurrection of religion, if we all hold fast through the driving storm to the sheet-anchor of pure morality, to most faithful discharge of all duty towards man, to love, and tenderness, and charity, and patience. Morality never faileth; but, whether there be dogmas, they shall fail; whether there be creeds, they shall cease; whether there be churches, they shall crumble away; but morality shall abide for evermore and endure as long as the endless circle of Nature revolves around the Eternal Throne.

NATURAL RELIGION

VERSUS

REVEALED RELIGION.

ONE is almost ashamed to repeat so trite an aphorism as the well-worn saying that "history repeats itself." But in studying the course taken by the advocates of what is called "revealed religion," in seeing their disdain of "mere nature," their scornful repudiation of the idea that any poor natural product can come into competition with their special article, hall-stamped by heaven itself, I feel irresistibly compelled to glance backwards down the long vista of history, and there I see the conflict of the present day raging fierce and long. I see the same serried ranks of orthodoxy marshalled by bishops and priests, arrayed in all the splendour of prescriptive right, armed with mighty weapons of authority and thunderbolts of Church anathemas. Their war-cry is the same as that which rings in our ears to-day; "revelation" is inscribed on their banners and "infallible authority" is the watchword of their camp. The Church is facing nature for the first time, and is setting her revealed science against natural science. "Mere Nature" is temporarily getting the worst of it, and Galileo, Nature's champion, is sorely pressed by "revealed truth." I hear scornful taunts at his presumption in attacking revealed science by his pretended natural facts. Had they not God's Own account of His creation, and did he pretend to know more about the matter than God Himself? Was he present when God created the world, that he spoke so positively about its shape? Could he declare, of his own personal knowledge, that it was sent hurtling through space in the ridiculous manner he talked about, and could he, by the evidence of his own eye-sight, declare that God was mistaken when He revealed to man how He "laid the foundation of the earth that it never should move at any time?" But if he was only reasoning from the wee bit of earth he knew, was he not speaking of things he had not seen, being vainly puffed-up in his fleshly mind? Was it probable, *à priori*, that God would allow mankind to be deceived for thousands of years on so important a matter; would in fact—God forgive it!—deceive man Himself by revealing through His holy prophets an account of His creation which was utterly untrue; nay, further, would carry on the delusion for century after century, by working miracles in support of it—for what but a miracle could make men unconscious of the fact that they were being hurried through space at so tremendous a rate? Surely very little reverence, or rather no reverence at all, was needed to allow that God the Holy Ghost, who inspired the Bible, knew better than we did how He made the world. But, the theologian proceeds, he must remind his audience that, under the specious pretext of investigating the creation, this man, this pseudo-scientist, was in reality blaspheming the Creator, by contradicting His revealed word, and thus "making Him a liar." It was all very well to talk about *natural* science; but he would ask this presuming speculator, what was the use of God revealing science to us if man's natural faculties were sufficient to discover it for himself? They had sufficient proofs of the absurdities of science into which reason, unenlightened by revelation, had betrayed men in past ages. The idea of the Hindoo, that the world rested on an elephant and the elephant on a tortoise, was a sad proof of the incapacity of the acutest natural intellect to discover scientific truth without the aid of revelation. Reason had its place, and a very noble place, in science; but it must always bow before revelation, and not presume to set its puny guesses against a "thus saith the Lord." Let reason, then, pursue its way with belief, not unbelief, for its guide. What could reason, with all its vaunted powers, tell us of the long-past creation of the world? Eye hath not seen those things of ages past, but God hath revealed them to us by His Spirit. A darkness that might be felt would enshroud the origin of the world were it not for the magnificent revelation of Moses, that "in six days God created the heaven and the earth." He might urge how our conceptions of God were enlarged and elevated, and what a deep awe filled the adoring heart on contemplating the revealed truth, that this wonderful earth with its varied beauty, and the heavens above with their countless stars, were all called forth out of nothing within the space of one short week by the creative fiat of the Almighty. What could this pseudo-science give them in exchange for such a revelation as that? Was it probable, further, that God would have become incarnate for the sake of a world that was only one out of many revolving round the sun? How irreverent to regard the theatre of that awful sacrifice as aught less than the centre of the universe, the cynosure of angelic eyes, gazing from their thrones in the heaven above! Galileo might say that his heresy does not affect the primary truths of our holy faith; but this is only one of the evasions natural to evil-doers—and it is unnecessary to remark that intellectual error is invariably the offspring of moral guilt—for consider how much is involved in his theory. The inspiration of Scripture receives its death-blow; for if fallible in one point, we have no reason to conclude it to be infallible in others. If there is one fact revealed to us more clearly than another in Holy Scripture, it is this one of the steadfastness of our world, which we are distinctly told, "cannot be moved." It is plainly revealed to us that the earth was created and fixed firmly on its foundations; that then there was formed over it the vast vault of heaven, in which were set the stars, and in this vault was prepared "the course" for the sun, spoken of, as you will remember, in the 19th Psalm, where holy David reveals to us that in the heavens God has made a tabernacle for the sun, which "goeth forth from the uttermost part of the heaven, and runneth about unto the end of it again." Language has no definiteness of meaning if this inspired declaration can be translated into a statement that the sun remains stationary and is encircled by a revolving earth. This great revealed truth cannot be contradicted by any true science. God's works cannot contradict His word; and if for a moment they appear mutually irreconcileable, we may be sure that our ignorance is to blame, and that a deeper knowledge will ultimately remove the apparent inconsistency. But it is yet more important to observe that some of the cardinal doctrines of the Church are assailed by this novel teaching. How could our blessed Redeemer, after accomplishing the work of our salvation, ascend from a revolving earth? Whither did He go? North, south, east, or west? For, if I understand aright this new heresy, the space above us at one time is below us at another, and thus Jesus might be actually descending at His glorious Ascension. Where, too, is that Right Hand of God to which He went, in this new universe without top or bottom? How can we hope to rise and meet Him in the air at His return, according to the most sure promise given to us through the blessed Paul, if He comes we know not from what direction? How can the lightning of His coming shine at once all round a globe to herald His approach, or how can the people at the other side of the world see the sign of the Son of Man in the heavens? But I cannot bring myself to accumulate these blasphemies; all must see that the most glorious truths of the Bible are bound up with its science, and must stand or fall together. And if this is so, and this so-called natural science is to be allowed to undermine the revealed science, what have we got to rely upon in this world or in the next? With the absolute truth of the Bible stands or falls our faith in God and our hope of immortality; on the truth of revelation hinges all morality, and they who deny to-day the truth of revealed science will tamper to-morrow with the truth of revealed history, of revealed morality, of revealed religion. Shall we, then, condescend to accept natural science instead of revealed; shall we, the teachers of revelation, condescend to abandon revealed science, and become the mere teachers of nature?

Thunders of applause greeted the right reverend theologian as he concluded—he happened to be a bishop, the direct ancestor in regular apostolical succession of a late prelate who inherited among other valuable qualities the very argument which closed the speech above quoted—and Galileo, the foolish believer in facts and the heretical student of mere nature, turned away with a sigh from trying to convince them, and contented himself with the *fact* he knew, and which must surely announce itself in the long run. *E pur si muove!* Fear not, noble martyr of science: facts alter not to suit theologies: many a one may fall crushed and vanquished before the Juggernaut-car of the Church, but "God does not die with His children, nor truth with its martyrs;" the *natural* is the divine, for Nature is only "God in a mask." So, looking down at that first great battle-field between nature and revelation I see the serried ranks break up and fly, and the excommunicated student become the prophet of the future, Galileo the seer, the revealer of the truth of God.

It is eternally true that nature must triumph in the long run. Theories are very imposing, doubtless, but when they are erected on a misconception the inexorable fact is sure to assert itself sooner or later, and with pitiless serenity level the magnificent fabric with the dust. It is this which gives to scientific men so grave and calm an attitude; theologians wrangle fiercely and bitterly because they wrangle about *opinions*, and one man's say is as good as another's where both deal in intangibles; but the man of science, when absolutely sure of his ground, *can afford to wait*, because the fact he has discovered remains unshaken, however it be assailed, and it will, in time, assert itself. When nature and revelation then come into contact, revelation must go to the wall; no outcry can save it; it is doomed; as well try and dam the rising Thames with a feather, as seek to bolster up a theology whose main dogmas are being slowly undermined by natural science. Of course no one nowadays (at least among educated people, for Zadkiel's Almanac I believe still protests on Biblical grounds against the heresy of the motion of the earth) dreams of maintaining Bible, *i.e.*, revealed, science against natural science; it is agreed on all hands that on points where science speaks with certainty *the words of the Bible must be explained so as to accord with the dictum of nature; i.e.*, it is allowed—though the admission is wrapped up in thick folds of circumlocution—that science must mould revelation, and not revelation science. The desperate attempts to force the first chapter of Genesis into some faint resemblance to the ascertained results of geological investigations are a powerful testimony to the conscious weakness of revealed science and to the feeling on the part of all intelligent theologians that the testimony graven with an iron pen on the rocks cannot be contradicted or refuted. In fact so successfully has science asserted its own pre-eminence in its own domain that many defenders of the Bible assert loudly, to cover their strategic movement to the rear, that revelation was not intended to teach science, and that scientific mistakes were only to be expected in a book given to mankind by the great Origin of all scientific law. They are freely welcome to find out any reasons they like for the errors in revealed science; all that concerns us is that their revelation should get out of the way of advancing science, and should no longer interpose its puny anathemas to silence inquiry into facts, or to fetter free research and free discussion.

But I challenge revelation further than this, and assert that when the dictates of natural *religion* are in opposition to those of revealed *religion*, then the natural must again triumph over the revealed. Christianity has so long successfully impressed on human hearts the revelation that natural impulses are in themselves sinful, that in "the flesh dwelleth no good thing," that man is a fallen creature, thoroughly corrupt and instinctively evil, that it has come to pass that even those who would be liberal if they dared, shrink back when it comes to casting away their revelation-crutches, and ask wildly *what* they can trust to if they give up the Bible. Their teachers tell them that if they let this go they will wander compassless on the waves of a pathless ocean; and so determinedly do they fix their eyes on the foaming waters, striving to discern there the trace of a pathway and only seeing the broken reflections of the waving torches in their hands, that they do not raise their heads and gaze upwards at the everlasting stars, the silent natural guides of the bewildered mariner. "Trust to mere nature!" exclaim the priesthood, and their flocks fall back aghast, clutching their revelation to their bosom and crying out: "What indeed is there to rely on if this be taken from us?" Only God. "Mere" God indeed, who is a very feeble support after the bolstering up of creeds and dogmas, of Churches and Bibles. As the sunshine dazzles eyes accustomed to the darkness, as the fresh wind makes shiver an invalid from a heated room, so does the light of God dazzle those who live amid the candles of the Churches, and the breath of His inspiration blows cold on feeble souls. But the light and the air invigorate and strengthen, and nature is a surer medicine than the nostrums of the quack physician.

"Mere" God is, in very truth, all that we Theists have to offer the world in exchange for the certainties of its Bibles, Korans, Vedas, and all other revelations whatsoever. On points where they each speak with certainty, our lips are dumb. About much they assert, we confess our ignorance. Where they know, we only think or hope. Where they possess all the clearness of a sign-post, our eyes can only study the mistiness of a valley before the rising sun has dispelled the wreathing clouds. They proclaim immortality, and are quite *au fait* as to the particulars of our future life. They differ in details, it is true, as to whether we live in a jewelled city, where the dust is gold-dust and the gates pearls, and spend our time in attending Sacred Harmonic Societies with an archangelic Costa directing perpetual oratorios, or whether we lie in rose-embowered arbours with delights unlimited, albeit unintellectual; but if we take them one at a time they are most satisfactory in the absolute information afforded by each. But we, we can only whisper—and the lips of some of us quiver too much to speak—"I believe in the life everlasting." We do not pretend to *know* anything about it; the belief is intuitive, but is not demonstrable; it is a hope and a trust, not an absolute knowledge. We entertain a reasonable hope of immortality; we argue its likelihood from considerations of the justice and the love which, as we believe, rule the universe; we, many of us—as I freely confess I do myself—believe in it with a firmness of conviction absolutely immovable; but challenged to *prove* it, we cannot answer. "Here," the revelationists triumphantly exclaim, "is *our* advantage; we foretell with absolute certainty a future life, and can give you all particulars about it." Then follows a confused jumble of harps and houris, of pasture-field and hunting-grounds; we seek for certainty and find none. All that they agree in, *i.e.*, *a* future life, we find imprinted on our own hearts, a dictate of natural religion; all they differ in is contained in their several revelations, and as they all contradict each other about the revealed details, we gain nothing from them. Nature whispers to us that there is a life to come; revelation babbles a number of contradictory particulars, marring the majesty of the simple promise, and adding nothing reliable to the sum of human knowledge. And the subject of immortality is a fair specimen of what is taught respectively by nature and by revelation; what is common to all creeds is natural, what is different in each is revealed. It is so with respect to God. The idea of God belongs to all creeds alike; it is the foundation-stone of natural religion; confusion begins when revelation steps in to change the musical whisper of Nature into a categorical description worthy of "Mangnall's Questions." Triune, solitary, dual, numberless, whatever He is revealed to be in the world's varied sacred books, His nature is understood, catalogued, dogmatised on; each revelation claims to be His own account of Himself; but each contradicts its fellows; on one point only they all agree, and that is the point confessed by natural religion—"God is."

From these facts I deduce two conclusions: first, that

revelation does not come to us with such a certainty of its truth as to enable us to trust it fearlessly and without reserve; second, that revelation is quite superfluous, since natural religion gives us every thing we need.

I. Revelation gives an uncertain sound. There are certain books in the world which claim to stand on a higher ground than all others. They claim to be special revelations of the will of God and the destiny of man. Now surely one of the first requisites of a Divine revelation is that it should be undoubtedly of Divine origin. But about all these books, except the Koran of Mahomet, hangs much obscurity both as regards their origin and their authorship. "Believers" urge that were the proofs undoubted there would be no room for faith and no merit in believing. They conceive it, then, to be a worthy employment for the Supreme Intelligence to set traps for His creatures; and, there being certain facts of the greatest importance, undiscoverable by their natural faculties, He proceeds to reveal these facts, but envelopes them in such wrappings of mystery, such garments of absurdity, that those of His creatures whom he has dowered with intellects and gifted with subtle brains, are forced to reject the whole as incredible and unreasonable. That God should give a revelation, but should not substantiate it, that He should speak, but in tones unintelligible, that His noblest gifts of reason should prove an insuperable bar to accepting his manifestation, are surely statements incredible, are surely statements utterly irreconcileable with all reverent ideas of the love and wisdom of Almighty God. Further, the believers in the various revelations all claim for their several oracles the supreme position of *the* exponent of the Will of God, and each rejects the sacred books of other nations as spurious productions, without any Divine authority. As these revelations are mutually destructive, it is evident that only one of them, *at the most*, can be Divine, and the next point of the inquiry is to distinguish which this is. We, of the Western nations, at once put aside the Hindoo Vedas, or the Zendavesta, on certain solid grounds; we reject their claims to be inspired books because they contain error; their mistaken science, their legendary history, their miraculous stories, stamp them, in our impartial eyes, as the work of fallible men; the nineteenth century looks down on these ancient writings as the instructed and cultured man smiles at the crude fancies and imaginative conceits of the child. But when the generality of Christians turn to the Bible they lay aside all ordinary criticism and all common-sense. Its science may be absurd; but excuses are found for it. Its history may be false, but it is twisted into truth. Its supernatural marvels may be flagrantly absurd; but they are nevertheless believed in. Men who laugh at the visions of the "blessed Margaret" of Paray-le-Monial assent to the devil-drowning of the swine of Gadara; and those who would scorn to investigate the tale of the miraculous spring at Lourdes, find no difficulty in believing the story of the angel-moved waters of Bethesda's pool. A book which contains miracles is usually put aside as unreliable. There is no good reason for excepting the Bible from this general rule. Miracles are absolutely incredible, and discredit at once any book in which they occur. They are found in all revelations, but never in nature, they are plentiful in man's writings, but they never deface the orderly pages of the great book of God, written by His own Hand on the earth, and the stars, and the sun. Powers? Yes, beyond our grasping, but Powers moving in stately order and changeless consistency. Marvels? Yes, beyond our imagining, but marvels evolved by immutable laws. Revelation is incredible, not only because it fails to bring proof of its truth, but because the proofs abound of its falsehood; it claims to be Divine, and we reject it because we test it by what we know of His undoubted works, for men can write books of Him and call them His revelations, but the frame of nature can only be the work of that mighty Power which man calls God. Revelation depicts Him as changeable, nature as immutable; revelation tells us of perfection marred, nature of imperfection improving; revelation speaks of a Trinity, nature of one mighty central Force; revelation relates interferences, miracles, nature unbroken sequences, inviolable law. If we accept revelation we must believe in a God Who made man upright but could not keep him so; Who heard in his far-off heaven the wailing of His earth and came down to see if things were as bad as was reported; Who had a face which brought death, but Whose hinder parts were visible to man; Who commanded and accepted human sacrifice; Who was jealous, revengeful, capricious, vain; Who tempted one king and then punished him for yielding, hardened the heart of another and then punished him for not yielding, deceived a third and thereby drew him to his death. But nature does not so outrage our morality and trample on our hearts; only we learn of a power and wisdom unspeakable, "mightily and sweetly ordering all things," and our hearts tell of a Father and a Friend, infinitely loving, and trustworthy, and good. The God of Nature and the God of Revelation are as opposed as Ormuzd and Ahriman, as darkness and light; the Bible and the universe are not writ by the same hand.

II. Revelation then being so utterly untrustworthy, it is satisfactory to discover, secondly, that it is perfectly superfluous.

All man needs for his guidance in this world he can gain through the use of his natural faculties, and the right guidance of his conduct in this world must, in all reasonableness, be the best preparation for whatever lies beyond the grave. Revelationists assure us that without their books we should have no rules of morality, and that without the Bible man's moral obligations would be unknown. Their theory is that only through revelation can man know right from wrong. Using the word "revelation" in a different sense most Theists would agree with them, and would allow that man's perception of duty is a ray which falls on him from the Righteousness of God, and that man's morality is due to the illumination of the inspiring Father of Light. Personally, I believe that God does teach morality to man, and is, in very deed, the Inspirer of all gracious and noble thoughts and acts. I believe that the source of all morality in man is the Universal Spirit dwelling in the spirits He has formed, and moving them to righteousness, and, as they answer to His whispers by active well-doing—speaking ever in louder and clearer accents. I believe also that the most obedient followers of that inner voice gain clearer and loftier views of duty and of the Holiest, and thus become true prophets of God, revealers of His will to their fellows. And this *is* revelation in a very real sense; it is God revealing Himself by the natural working of moral laws, even as all science is a true revelation, and is God revealing Himself by the natural working of physical laws. For laws are modes of action, and modes of action reveal the nature and character of the actor, so that every law, physical and moral, which is discovered by truth-seekers and proclaimed to the world is a direct and trustworthy revelation of God Himself. But when Theists speak thus of "revelation" using the word as rightfully applicable to all discoveries and all nobly written religious or scientific books, it is manifest that the word has entirely changed its signification, and is applied to "natural" and not "supernatural" results. We believe in God working through natural faculties in a natural way, while the revelationists believe in some non-natural communication, made no one knows how, no one knows where, no one knows to whom.

Where opposing theories are concerned an ounce of fact outweighs pounds of assertion; and so against the statement of Christians, that morality is derived only from the Bible and is undiscoverable by "man's natural faculties," I quote the morality of natural religion, unassisted by what they claim as their special "revelation."

Buddha, as he lived 700 years before Christ, can hardly be said to have drawn his morality from that of Jesus or even to have derived any indirect benefit from Christian teaching, and yet I have been gravely told by a Church of England clergyman—who ought to have known better—that forgiveness of injuries and charity were purely Christian virtues. This heathen Buddha, lighted only by natural reason and a pure heart, teaches: "a man who foolishly does me wrong I will return to him the protection of my ungrudging love; the more evil comes from him the more good shall go from me;" among principal virtues are: "to repress lust and banish desire; to be strong without being rash; to bear insult without anger; to move in the world without setting the heart on it; to investigate a matter to the very bottom; to save men by converting them; to be the same in heart and life." "Let a man overcome evil by good, anger by love, the greedy by liberality, the liar by truth. For hatred does not cease by hatred at any time; hatred ceases by love; this is an old rule." He inculcates purity, charity, self-sacrifice, courtesy, and earnestly recommends personal search after truth: "do not believe in guesses—in assuming something at hap-hazard as a starting-point—reckoning your two and your three and your four before you have fixed your number one. Do not believe in the truth of that to which you have become attached by habit, as every nation believes in the superiority of its own dress and ornaments and language. Do not believe merely because you have heard, but when of your own consciousness you know a thing to be evil abstain from it. Methinks these sayings of Buddha are unsurpassed by any revealed teaching, and contain quite as noble and lofty a morality as the Sermon on the Mount, "natural" as they are.

Plato, also, teaches a noble morality and soars into ideas about the Divine Nature as pure and elevated as any which are to be found in the Bible. The summary of his teaching, quoted by Mr. Lake in a pamphlet of Mr. Scott's series, is a glorious testimony to the worth of natural religion. "It is better to die than to sin. It is better to suffer wrong than to do it. The true happiness of man consists in being united to God, and his only misery in being separated from Him. There is one God, and we ought to love and serve Him, and to endeavour to resemble Him in holiness and righteousness." Plato saw also the great truth that suffering is not the result of an evil power, but is a necessary training to good, and he anticipates the very words of Paul—if indeed Paul does not quote from Plato—that "to the just man all things work together for good, whether in life or death." Plato lived 400 years before Christ, and yet in the face of such teaching as his and Buddha's,—and they are only two out of many—Christians fling at us the taunt that we, rejectors of the Bible, draw all our morality from it, and that without this one revelation the world would lie in moral darkness, ignorant of truth and righteousness and God. But the light of God's revealing shines still upon the world, even as the sunlight streams upon it steadfastly as of old; "it is not given to a few men in the infancy of mankind to monopolise inspiration and to bar God out of the soul. . . . Wherever a heart beats with love, where Faith and Reason utter their oracles, there also is God, as formerly in the heart of seers and prophets."*

It is a favourite threat of the priesthood to any inquiring spirit: "If you give up Christianity you give up all certainty; rationalism speaks with no certain sound; no two rationalists think alike; the word rationalism covers everything outside Christianity, from Unitarianism to the blankest atheism;" and many a timid soul starts back, feeling that if this is true it is better to rest where it is, and inquire no more. To such—and I meet many such—I would suggest one very simple thought: does "Christianity" give any more certainty than rationalism? Just try asking your mentor, "*whose* Christianity am I to accept?" He will stammer out, "Oh, the teaching of the Bible, of course." But persevere: "As explained by whom? for all claim to found their Christianity on the Bible: am I to accept the

* Theodore Parker.

defined logical Christianity of Pius IX., defiant of history, of science, of common sense, or shall I sit under Spurgeon, the denunciator, and flee from the scarlet woman and the cup of her fascinations : shall I believe the Christianity of Dean Stanley, instinct with his own gracious, kindly spirit, cultured and polished, pure and loving, or shall I fly from it as a sweet but insidious poison, as I am exhorted to do by Dr. Pusey, who rails at his 'variegated language which destroys all definiteness of meaning.' For pity's sake, good father, label for me the various bottles of Christian medicine, that I may know which is healing to the soul, which may be touched with caution, as for external application, and which are rank poison." All the priest will find to answer is, that "under sad diversities of opinion there are certain saving truths common to all forms of Christianity," but he will object to particularise what they are, and at this stage will wax angry and refuse to argue with anyone who shows a spirit so carping and so conceited. There is the same diversity in rationalism as in Christianity, because human nature is diverse, but there is also one bond between all freethinkers, one "great saving truth" of rationalism, one article of faith, and that is, that "free inquiry is the right of every human soul;" diverse in much, we all agree in this, and so strong is this bond that we readily welcome *any* thinker, however we disagree with his thoughts, provided only that he think themhonestly and allow to all the liberty of holding their own opinions also. We are bound together in one common hatred of Dogmatism, one common love of liberty of thought and speech.

It is probably a puzzle to good and unlearned Christians whence men, unenlightened by revelation, drew and still draw their morality. We answer, "from mere Nature, and that because Nature and not revelation is the true basis of all morality." We have seen the untrustworthiness of all so-called revelations; but when we fall back on Nature we are on firm ground. Theists start in their search after God from their well-known axiom : "If there be a God at all He must be at least as good as His highest creature;" and they argue that what is highest and noblest and most lovable in man *must* be below, but cannot be above, the height and the nobleness and the loveableness of God. "Of all impossible thing, the most impossible must surely be that a man should dream something of the Good and the Noble, and that it should prove at last that his Creator was less good and less noble than he had dreamed."* "The ground on which our belief in God rests is Man. Man, parent of Bibles and Churches, inspirer of all good thoughts and good deeds. Man, the master-piece of God's work on earth. Man, the text-book of all spiritual knowledge. Neither miraculous or infallible, Man is nevertheless the only trustworthy record of the Divine mind in things pertaining to God. Man's reason, conscience, and affections are the only true revelation of his Maker."† And as we believe that we may glean some hints of the Glory and Beauty of our Creator from the glory and beauty of human excellence, so we believe that to each man, as he lives up to the highest he can perceive, will surely be unveiled fresh heights of righteousness, fresh possibilities of moral growth. To all men alike, good and evil, is laid open Nature's revelation of morality, as exemplified in the highest human lives; and these noble lives receive ever the heavenly hall-mark by the instinctive response from every human breast that they "are very good." To those only who live up to the good they see, does God give the further inner revelation, which leads them higher and higher in morality, quickening their moral faculties, and making more sensitive and delicate their moral susceptibilities. We cannot, as revelationists do, chalk out all the whole range of moral perfection: we "walk by faith and not by sight:" step by step only is the path unveiled to us, and only as we surmount one peak do we gain sight of the peak beyond: the distant prospect is shrouded from our gaze, and we are too fully occupied in doing the work which is given us to do in this world, to be for ever peering into and brooding over the world beyond the grave. We have light enough to do our Father's work here; when he calls us yonder it will be time enough to ask Him to unveil our new sphere of labour and to cause His sun to rise on it. Wayward children fret after some fancied happiness and miss the work and the pleasure lying at their feet, and so petulant men and women cry out that "man that is born of woman . . . is full of misery," and wail for a revelation to ensure some happier life: they seem to forget that if this world is full of misery *they* are put here to mend it and not to cry over it, and that it is our shame and our condemnation that in God's fair world so much sin and unhappiness are found. If men would try to read nature instead of revelation, if they would study natural

* Frances Power Cobbe. † Rev. Charles Voysey.

laws and leave revealed laws, if they would follow human morality instead of ecclesiastical morality, then there might be some chance of real improvement for the race, and some hope that the Divine Voice in Nature might be heard above the babble of the Churches.

And Nature is enough for us, gives us all the light we want and all that we, as yet, are fitted to receive. Were it possible that God should now reveal Himself to us as He is, the Being of Whose Nature we can form no conception, I believe that we should remain as ignorant as we are at present, from the want of faculties to receive that revelation: the Divine language might sound in our ears, but it would be as unintelligible as the roar of the thunder-clap, or the moan of the earthquake, or the whisper of the wind to the leaves of the cedar-tree. God *is* slowly revealing Himself by His works, by the course of events, by the progress of Humanity: if He has never spoken from Heaven in human language, He is daily speaking in the world around us to all who have ears to hear, and as Nature in its varied forms is His only revelation of Himself, so the mind and the heart alone can perceive His presence and catch the whispers of His mysterious voice.

Never yet has been broken
  The silence eternal:
Never yet has been spoken
  In accents supernal
    God's Thought of Himself.

We are groping in blindness
  Who yearn to behold Him:
But in wisdom and kindness
  In darkness He folds Him
    Till the soul learns to see.

So the veil is unriven
  That hides the All-Holy,
And no token is given
  That satisfies wholly
    The cravings of man.

But, unhasting, advances
  The march of the ages,
To truth-seekers' glances
  Unrolling the pages
    Of God's revelation.

Impatience unheeding,
  Time, slowly revolving,
Unresting, unspeeding,
  Is ever evolving
    Fresh truths about God.

Human speech has not broken
  The stillness supernal :
Yet ever is spoken
  Through silence eternal,
    With growing distinctness
    God's Thought of Himself.

ON THE NATURE AND THE EXISTENCE OF GOD.

IT is impossible for those who study the deeper religious problems of our time to stave off much longer the question which lies at the root of them all, "What do you believe in regard to God?" We may controvert Christian doctrines, one after another; point by point we may be driven from the various beliefs of our churches; reason may force us to see contradictions where we had imagined harmony, and may open our eyes to flaws where we had dreamed of perfection; we resign all idea of a revelation; we seek for God in Nature only; we renounce for ever the hope (which glorified our former creed into such alluring beauty) that at some future time we should verily "see" God, that "our eyes should behold the King in his beauty" in that fairy "land which is very far off." But every step we take onwards towards a more reasonable faith and a surer light of Truth leads us nearer and nearer to the problem of problems, "What is THAT which men call God?" Not till theologians have thoroughly grappled with this question have they any just claim to be called religious guides; from each of those whom we honour as our leading thinkers we have a right to a distinct answer to this question, and the very object of the present paper is to provoke discussion on this point.

Men are apt to turn aside somewhat impatiently from an argument about the Nature and Existence of the Deity, because they consider that the question is a metaphysical one which leads nowhere; a problem the resolution of which is beyond our faculties, and the study of which is at once useless and dangerous; they forget that action is ruled by thought, and that our ideas about God are therefore of vast practical importance. On our answer to the question propounded above depends our whole conception of the nature and origin of evil, and of the sanctions of morality; on our idea of God turns our opinion on the much-disputed question of prayer, and, in fact, our whole attitude of mind towards life, here and hereafter. Does morality consist in obedience to the will of a perfectly moral Being, and are we to aim at righteousness of life *because* in so doing we please God? Or are we to lead noble lives because nobility of life is desirable for itself alone, and because it spreads happiness around us and satisfies the desires of our own nature? Is our mental attitude to be that of kneeling or standing? Are our eyes to be fixed on heaven or on earth? Is prayer to God reasonable and helpful, the natural cry of a child for help from a Father in Heaven? Or is it, on the other hand, a useless appeal to an unknown and irresponsible force? Is the mainspring of our actions to be the idea of duty to God, or a sense of the necessity of bringing our being into harmony with the laws of the universe? It appears to me that these questions are of such grave and vital moment that no apology is needed for drawing attention to them; and because of their importance to mankind I challenge the leaders of the religious and non-religious world alike, the Christians, Theists, Pantheists, and those who take no specific name, duly to test the views they severally hold. In this battle the simple foot soldier may touch with his lance the shield of the knight, and the insignificance of the challenger does not exempt the general from the duty of lifting the gauntlet flung down at his feet. Little care I for personal defeat, if the issue of the conflict should enthrone more firmly the radiant figure of Truth. One fault, however, I am anxious to avoid, and that is the fault of ambiguity. The orthodox and the free-thinking alike do a good deal of useless fighting from sheer misunderstanding of each other's standpoint in the controversy. It appears, then, to be indispensable in the prosecution of the following inquiry that the meaning of the terms used should be unmistakably distinct. I begin, therefore, by defining the technical forms of expression to be employed in my argument; the definitions may be good or bad, that is not material; all that is needed is that the sense in which the various terms are used should be clearly understood. When men fight only for the sake of discovering truth, definiteness of expression is specially incumbent on them; and, as has been eloquently said, "the strugglers being sincere, truth may give laurels to the victor and the vanquished: laurels to the victor in that he hath upheld the truth, laurels still welcome to the vanquished, whose defeat crowns him with a truth he knew not of before.

The definitions that appear to me to be absolutely necessary are as follows:—

Matter is used to express that which is tangible. *Spirit* (or *spiritual*) is used to express those intangible forces whose existence we become aware of only through the effects they produce.

Substance is used to express that which exists in itself and by itself, and the conception of which does not imply the conception of anything preceding it.

God is used to represent exclusively that Being invested by the orthodox with certain physical, intellectual, and moral attributes.

Particular attention must be paid to this last definition, because the term "atheist" is often flung unjustly at any thinker who ventures to criticise *the popular and traditional idea* of God; and different schools, Theistic and non-Theistic, with but too much facility, bandy about this vague epithet in mutual reproach.

As an instance of this uncharitable and unfair use of ugly names, all schools agree in calling the late Mr. Austin Holyoake an "atheist," and he accepted the name himself, although he distinctly stated (as we find in a printed report of a discussion held at the Victoria Institute) that he did not deny the possibility of the existence of God, but only denied the possibility of the existence of that God in whom the orthodox exhorted him to believe. It is well thus to protest beforehand against this name being bandied about, because it carries with it, at present, so much popular prejudice, that it prevents all possibility of candid and free discussion. It is simply a convenient stone to fling at the head of an opponent whose arguments one cannot meet, a certain way of raising a tumult which will drown his voice; and, if it have any serious meaning at all, it might fairly be used, as I shall presently show, against the most orthodox pillar of the orthodox faith.

It is manifest to all who will take the trouble to think steadily, that there can be only one eternal and underived substance, and that matter and spirit must therefore only be varying manifestations of this one substance. The distinction made between matter and spirit is then simply made for the sake of convenience and clearness, just as we may distinguish perception from judgment, both of which, however, are alike processes of thought. Matter is, in its constituent elements, the same as spirit; existence is *one*, however manifold in its phenomena; life is one, however multiform in its evolution. As the heat of the coal differs from the coal itself, so do memory, perception, judgment, emotion, and will, differ from the brain which is the instrument of thought. But nevertheless they are all equally products of the one sole substance, varying only in their conditions. It may be taken for granted that against this preliminary point of the argument will be raised the party-cry of "rank materialism," because "materialism" is a doctrine of which the general public has an undefined horror. But I am bold to say that if by matter is meant that which is above defined as substance, then no reasoning person can help being a materialist. The orthodox are very fond of arguing back to what they call the Great First Cause. "God is a spirit," they say, "and from him is derived the spiritual part of man." Well and good; they have traced back a part of the universe to a point at which they conceive that only one universal essence is possible, that which they call God, and which is spirit only. But I then invite their consideration to the presence of something which they do not regard as spirit, *i.e.*, matter. I follow their own plan of argument step by step: I trace matter, as they traced spirit, back and back, till I reach a point beyond which I cannot go, one only existence, substance or essence; am I therefore to believe that God is matter only? But we have already found it asserted by Theists that he is spirit only, and we cannot believe two contradictories, however logical the road which led us to them; so we must acknowledge two substances, eternally existent side by side; if existence be dual, then, however absurd the hypothesis, there must be two First Causes. It is not I who am responsible for an idea so anomalous. The orthodox escape from this dilemma by an assumption, thus: "God, to whom is to be traced back all spirit, *created* matter." Why, am I not equally justified in assuming, if I please, that matter created spirit? Why should I be logical in one argument and illogical in another? If we come to assumptions, have not I as much right to my assumption as my neighbour has to his? Why may he predicate creation of one half of the universe, and I not predicate it of the other half? If the assumptions be taken into consideration at all, then I contend that mine is the more reasonable of the two, since it is possible to imagine matter as existing without mind, while it is utterly impossible to conceive of mind existing without matter. We all know how a stone looks, and we are in the habit of regarding that as lifeless matter; but who has any distinct idea of a mind *pur et simple?* No clear conception of it is possible to human faculties; we can only conceive of mind as it is found *in* an organisation; intelligence has no appreciable existence except as residing in the brain and as manifested in results. The lines of spirit and matter are not one, say the orthodox; they run backwards side by side; why then, in following the course of these two parallel lines, should I suddenly bend one into the other? and on what principle of selection shall I choose the one I am to curve? I must really decline to use logic just as far as it supports the orthodox idea of God, and arbitrarily throw it down the moment it conflicts with that idea. I find myself then compelled to believe that one only substance exists in all around me; that the universe is eternal, or at least eternal so far as our faculties are concerned, since we cannot, as some one has quaintly put it, "get to the outside of everywhere;" that a Deity cannot be conceived of as apart from the universe, pre-existent to the universe, post-existent to the universe; that the Worker and the Work are inextricably interwoven, and in some sense eternally and indissolubly combined. Having got so far, we will proceed to examine into the possibility of proving the existence of that one essence popularly called by the name of *God*, under the conditions strictly defined by the orthodox. Having demonstrated, as I hope to do, that the orthodox idea of God is unreasonable and absurd, we will endeavour to discover whether *any* idea of God, worthy to be called an idea, is attainable in the present state of our faculties.

The orthodox believers in God are divided into two camps, one of which maintains that the existence of God is as demonstrable as any mathematical proposition, while the other asserts that his existence is not demonstrable to the intellect. I select Dr. McCann, a man of considerable reputation, as the representative of the former of these two opposing schools of thought, and give the Doctor's position in his own words:—"The purpose of the following paper is to prove the fallacy of all such assumptions" (*i.e.*, that the existence of God is an insoluble problem), "by showing that we are no more at liberty to deny His being, than we are to deny any demonstration of Euclid. He would be thought unworthy of refutation who should assert that any two angles of a triangle are together greater than two right angles. We would content ourselves by saying, 'The man is mad'—mathematically, at least—and pass on. If it can be shown that we affirm the existence of Deity for the very same reasons as we affirm the truth of any geometric proposition; if it can be shown that the former is as capable of demonstration as the latter—then it necessarily follows that if we are justified in calling the man a fool who denies the latter, we are also justified in calling him a fool who says there is no God, and in refusing to answer him according to his folly." Which course is a very convenient one when you meet with an awkward opponent whom you cannot silence by sentiment and declamation. Again: "In conclusion, we believe it to be very important to be able to prove that if the mathematician be justified in asserting that the three angles of a triangle are equal to two right angles, the Christian is equally justified in asserting, not only that he is compelled to believe in God, but that he *knows* Him (*sic*). And that he who denies the existence of the Deity is as unworthy of serious refutation as is he who denies a mathematical demonstration." ('A Demonstration of the Existence of God,' a lecture delivered at the Victoria Institute, 1870, pp. 1 and 11.) Dr. McCann proves his very startling thesis by laying down as axioms six statements, which, however luminous to the Christian traditionalist, are obscure to the sceptical intellect. He seems to be conscious of this defect in his so-called axioms, for he proceeds to prove each of them elaborately, forgetting that the simple statement of an axiom should carry direct conviction—that it needs only to be understood in order to be accepted. However, let this pass: our teacher, having stated and "proved" his axioms, proceeds to draw his conclusions from them; and as his foundations are unsound, it is scarcely to be wondered at that his superstructure should be insecure. I know of no way so effectual to defeat an adversary as to beg all the questions raised, assume every point in dispute, call assumptions axioms, and then proceed to reason from them. It is really not worth while to criticise Dr. McCann in detail, his lecture being nothing but a mass of fallacies and unproved assertions. Christian courtesy allows him to call those who dissent from his assumptions "fools;" and as these terms of abuse are not considered admissible by those whom he assails as unbelievers, there is a slight difficulty in "answering" Dr. McCann "according to his" deserts. I content myself with suggesting that they who wish to learn how pretended reasoning may pass for solid argument, how inconsequent statements may pass for logic, had better study this lecture. For my own part, I confess that my "folly" is not, as yet, of a sufficiently pronounced type to enable me to accept Dr. McCann's conclusions.

The best representation I can select of the second orthodox party, those who admit that the existence of God is not demonstrable, is the late Dean Mansel. In his 'Limits of Religious Thought,' the Bampton Lectures for 1867, he takes up a perfectly unassailable position. The peculiarity of this position, however, is that he, the pillar of orthodoxy, the famed defender of the faith against German infidelity and all forms of rationalism, regards God from exactly the same point as does a well-known modern "atheist." I have almost hesitated sometimes which writer to quote from, so identical are they in thought. Probably neither Dean Mansel nor Mr. Bradlaugh would thank me for bracketing their names; but I am forced to confess that the arguments used by the one to prove the endless absurdities into which we fall when we try to comprehend the nature of God, are exactly the same arguments that are used by the other to prove that God, as believed in by the orthodox, cannot exist. I quote, however, exclusively from the Dean, because it is at once novel and agreeable to find oneself sheltered by Mother Church at the exact moment when one is questioning her very foundations; and also because the Dean's name carries with it so orthodox an odour that his authority will tell where the same words from any of those who are outside the pale of orthodoxy would be regarded with suspicion. Nevertheless, I wish to state plainly that a more "atheistical" book than these Bampton Lectures—at least, in the earlier part of it—I have never read; and had its title-page borne the name of any well-known Free-thinker, it would have been received in the religious world with a storm of indignation.

The first definition laid down by the orthodox as a characteristic of God is that he is an Infinite Being. "There is but one living and true God . . . of *infinite* power, &c." (Article of Religion, 1.) It has been said that *infinite* only means *indefinite*, but I must protest against this weakening of a well-defined theological term. The term

Infinite has always been understood to mean far more than indefinite; it means literally *boundless:* the infinite has *no* limitations, *no* possible restrictions, *no* "circumference." People who do not think about the meaning of the words they use speak very freely and familiarly of the "infinitude" of God, as though the term implied no inconsistency. Deny that God is infinite and you are at once called an atheist, but press your opponent into a definition of the term and you will generally find that he does not know what he is talking about. Dean Mansel points out, with his accurate habit of mind, all that this attribute of God implies, and it would be well if those who "believe in an infinite God" would try and realise what they express. Half the battle of freethought will be won when people attach a definite meaning to the terms they use. The Infinite has no bounds; then the finite cannot exist. Why? Because in the very act of acknowledging any existence beside the Infinite One you limit the Infinite. By saying, "This is not God" you at once make him finite, because you set a bound to his nature; you distinguish between him and something else, and by the very act you limit him; that *which is not he* is as a rock which checks the waves of the ocean; in that spot a limit is found, and in finding a limit the Infinite is destroyed. The orthodox may retort, "this is only a matter of terms;" but it is well to force them into realising the dogmas which they thrust on our acceptance under such awful penalties for rejection. *I* know what "an infinite God" implies, and, as apart from the universe, I feel compelled to deny the possibility of his existence; surely it is fair that the orthodox should also know what the words they use mean on this head, and give up the term if they cling to a "personal" God, distinct from "creation."—Further—and here I quote Dean Mansel—the "Infinite" must be conceived as containing within itself the sum, not only of all actual, but of all possible modes of being. . . . If any possible mode can be denied of it . . . it is capable of becoming more than it now is, and such a capability is a limitation." (The hiatus refers to the "absolute" being of God, which it is better to consider separately.) "An unrealised possibility is necessarily (a relation and) a limit." Thus is orthodoxy crushed by the powerful logic of its own champion. God is infinite; then, in that case, everything that exists is God; all phenomena are modes of the Divine Being; there is literally nothing which is not God. Will the orthodox accept this position? It lands them, it is true, in the most extreme Pantheism, but what of that? They believe in an "infinite God" and they are therefore necessarily Pantheists. If they object to this, they must give up the idea that their God is infinite at all; there is no half-way position open to them; he is infinite or finite, which?

Again, God is "before all things," he is the only Absolute Being, dependent on nothing outside himself; all that is *not* God is relative; that is to say, that God exists alone and is not necessarily related to anything else. The orthodox even believe that God did, at some former period (which is not a period, they say, because time then was not —however, at that hazy "time" he did), exist alone, *i.e.*, as what is called an *Absolute* Being: this conception is necessary for all who, in any sense, believe in a *Creator*.

> "Thou, in Thy far eternity,
> Didst live and love alone."

So sings a Christian minstrel; and one of the arguments put forward for a Trinity is that a plurality of persons is necessary in order that God may be able to love at the "time" when he was alone. Into this point, however, I do not now enter. But what does this "Absolute" imply? A simple impossibility of creation, just as does the Infinite; for creation implies that the relative is brought into existence, and thus the Absolute is destroyed. "Here again the Pantheistic hypothesis seems forced upon us. We can think of creation only as a change in the condition of that which already exists, and thus the creature is conceivable only as a phenomenal mode of the being of the Creator." Thus once more looms up the dreaded spectre of Pantheism, "the dreary desolation of a Pantheistic wilderness;" and who is the Moses who has led us into this desert? It is a leader of orthodoxy, a dignitary of the Church; it is Dean Mansel who stretches out his hand to the universe and says, "This is thy God, O Israel."

The two highest attributes of God land us, then, in the most thorough Pantheism; further, before remarking on the other divine attributes, I would challenge the reader to pause and try to realise this infinite and absolute being. "That a man can be conscious of the infinite is, then, a supposition which, in the very terms in which it is expressed, annihilates itself. . . . The infinite, if it is to be conceived at all, must be conceived as potentially everything and actually nothing ; for if there is anything in general which it cannot become, it is thereby limited ; and if there is anything in particular which it actually is, it is thereby excluded from being any other thing. But again, it must also be conceived as actually everything and potentially nothing ; for an unrealised potentiality is likewise a limitation. If the infinite can be" (in the future) "that which it is not" (in the present) "it is by that very possibility marked out as incomplete and capable of a higher perfection. If it is actually everything, it possesses no characteristic feature by which it can be distinguished from anything else and discerned as an object of consciousness." I think, then, that we must be content, on the showing of Dr. Mansel, to allow that God is, in his own nature—from this point of view—quite beyond the grasp of our faculties ; *as regards us he does not exist*, since he is indistinguishable and undiscernable. Well might the Church exclaim "Save me from my friends !" when a dean acknowledges that her God is a self-contradictory phantom ; oddly enough, however, the Church likes it, and accepts this fatal championship. I might have put this argument wholly in my own words, for the subject is familiar to every one who has tried to gain a distinct idea of the Being who is called "God," but I have preferred to back my own opinions with the authority of so orthodox a man as Dean Mansel, trusting that by so doing the orthodox may be forced to see where logic carries them. All who are interested in this subject should study his lectures carefully ; there is really no difficulty in following them, if the student will take the trouble of mastering once for all the terms he employs. The book was lent to me years ago by a clergyman, and did more than any other book I know to make me what is called an "infidel ;" it proves to demonstration the impossibility of our having any logical, reasonable, and definite idea of God, and the utter hopelessness of trying to realise his existence. It seems necessary here to make a short digression to explain, for the benefit of those who have not read the book from which I have been quoting, how Dean Mansel escaped becoming an "atheist." It is a curious fact that the last part of this book is as remarkable for its assumptions, as is the earlier portion for its pitiless logic. When he ought in all reason to say, "we can know nothing and therefore can believe nothing," he says instead, "we can know nothing and therefore let us take Revelation for granted." An atheistic reasoner suddenly startles us by becoming a devout Christian; the apparent enemy of the faithful is "transformed into an angel of light." The existence of God "is inconceivable by the reason," and, therefore, "the only ground that can be taken for accepting one representation of it rather than another is, that one is revealed and the other not revealed." It is the acknowledgment of a previously formed *determination* to believe at any cost; it is a wail of helplessness; the very apotheosis of despair. We cannot have history, so let us believe a fairy-tale; we can discover nothing, so let us assume anything; we cannot find truth, so let us take the first myth that comes to hand. Here I feel compelled to part company with the Dean, and to leave him to believe in, to adore, and to love that which he has himself designated as indistinguishable and undiscernable; it may be an act of faith but it is a crucifixion of intellect; it may be a satisfaction to the yearnings of the heart, but it dethrones reason and tramples it in the dust.

We proceed in our study of the attributes of God. He is represented as the Supreme Will, the Supreme Intelligence, the Supreme Love.

As the Supreme Will. What do we mean by "will?" Surely, in the usual sense of the word, a will implies the power and the act of choosing. Two paths are open to us, and we *will* to walk in one rather than in the other. But can we think of power of choice in connection with God? Of two courses open to us one must needs be better than the other, else they would be indistinguishable and be only one; perfection implies that the higher course will always be taken; what then becomes of the power of choice? *We* choose because we are imperfect; we do not know everything which bears on the matter on which we are about to exercise our will; if we knew everything we should inevitably be driven in one direction, that which is the *best possible course.* The greater the knowledge, the more circumscribed the will; the nobler the nature, the more impossible the lower course. Spinoza points out most clearly that the Divinity *could not* have made things otherwise than they are made, because any change in his action would imply a change in his nature; God, above all, must be bound by necessity. If we believe in a God at all we must surely ascribe to him perfection of wisdom and perfection of goodness; we are then forced to conceive of him—

however strange it may sound to those who believe, not only without seeing but also without thinking— as without will, because he must always necessarily pursue the course which is wisest and best.

As the Supreme Intelligence. Again, the first question is, what do we mean by *intelligence?* In the usual sense of the word intelligence implies the exercise of the various intellectual faculties, and gathers up into one word the ideas of perception, comparison, memory, judgment, and so on. The very enumeration of these faculties is sufficient to show how utterly inappropriate they are when thought of in connection with God. Does God perceive what he did not know before? Does he compare one fact with another? Does he draw conclusions from this correlation of perceptions, and thus judge what is best? Does he remember, as we remember, long past events? Perfect wisdom excludes from the idea of *God* all that is called intelligence in *man;* it involves unchangeableness, complete stillness; it implies a knowledge of all that is knowable; it includes an acquaintance with every fact, an acquaintance which has never been less in the past, and can never be more in the future. The reception at any time of a new thought or a new idea is impossible to perfection, for if it could ever be added to in the future it is necessarily something less than perfect in the past.

As the Supreme Love. We come here to the darkest problem of existence. Love, Ruler of the world permeated through and through with pain, and sorrow, and sin? Love, mainspring of a nature whose cruelty is sometimes appalling? Love? Think of the "martyrdom of man!" Love? Follow the History of the Church! Love? Study the annals of the slave-trade! Love? Walk the courts and alleys of our towns! It is of no use to try and explain away these things, or cover them up with a veil of silence; it is better to look them fairly in the face, and test our creeds by inexorable facts. It is foolish to keep a tender spot which may not be handled; for a spot which gives pain when it is touched implies the presence of disease: wiser far is it to press firmly against it, and, if danger lurk there, to use the probe or the knife. We have no right to pick out all that is noblest and fairest in man, to project these qualities into space, and to call them God. We only thus create an ideal figure, a purified, ennobled, "magnified" Man. We have no right to shut our eyes to the sad *revers* *de la médaille*, and leave out of our conceptions of the Creator the larger half of his creation. If we are to discover the Worker from his works we must not pick and choose amid those works; we must take them as they are, "good" and "bad." If we only want an ideal, let us by all means make one, and call it *God*, if thus we can reach it better, but if we want a true induction we must take *all* facts into account. If God is to be considered as the author of the universe, and we are to learn of him through his works, then we must make room in our conceptions of him for the avalanche and the earthquake, for the tiger's tooth and the serpent's fang, as well as for the tenderness of woman and the strength of man, the radiant glory of the sunshine on the golden harvest, and the gentle lapping of the summer waves on the gleaming shingled beach.*

The Nature of God, what is it? Infinite and Absolute, he evades our touch; without human will, without human intelligence, without human love, where can his faculties—the very word is a misnomer—find a meeting-place with ours? Is he everything or nothing? one or many? *We know not. We know nothing.* Such is the conclusion into which we are driven by orthodoxy, with its pretended faith, which is credulity, with its pretended proofs, which are presumptions. It defines and maps out the perfections of Deity, and they dissolve when we try to grasp them; nowhere do these ideas hold water for a moment; nowhere is this position defensible. Orthodoxy drives thinkers into atheism; weary of its contradictions they cry, "there is *no* God"; orthodoxy's leading thinker lands us himself in

* "I know it is usual for the orthodox when vindicating the moral character of their God to say:—'All the Evil that exists is of *man;* All that God has done is only *good.*' But granting (which facts do not substantiate) that man is the only author of the sorrow and the wrong that abound in the world, it is difficult to see how the Creator can be free from imputation. Did not God, according to orthodoxy, plan all things with an infallible perception that the events foreseen must occur? Was not this accurate prescience based upon the inflexibility of God's Eternal purposes? As, then, the purposes, in the order of nature, at least preceded the prescience and formed the groundwork of it, man has become extensively the instrument of doing mischief in the world simply because the God of the Christian Church did not choose to prevent man from being bad. In other words, man is as he is by the ordained design of God, and, therefore, God is responsible for all the suffering, shame, and error, spread by human agency.—So that the Christian apology for God in connection with the spectacle of evil falls to pieces."—*Note by the Editor.*

atheism. No logical, impartial mind can escape from unbelief through the trap-door opened by Dean Mansel: he has taught us reason, and we cannot suppress reason. The "serpent intellect"—as the Bishop of Peterborough calls it—has twined itself firmly round the tree of knowledge, and in that type we do not see, with the Hebrew, the face of death, but, with the older faiths, we reverence it as the symbol of life.

There is another fact, an historical one, still on the destructive side, which appears to me to be of the gravest importance, and that is the gradual attenuation of the idea of God before the growing light of true knowledge. To the savage everything is divine; he hears one God's voice in the clap of the thunder, another's in the roar of the earthquake, he sees a divinity in the trees, a deity smiles at him from the clear depths of the river and the lake; every natural phenomenon is the abode of a god; every event is controlled by a god; divine volition is at the root of every incident. To him the rule of the gods is a stern reality; if he offends them they turn the forces of nature against him; the flood, the famine, the pestilence, are the ministers of the avenging anger of the gods. As civilisation advances, the deities lessen in number, the divine powers become concentrated more and more in one Being, and God rules over the whole earth, maketh the clouds his chariot, and reigns above the waterfloods as a king. Physical phenomena are still his agents, working his will among the children of men; he rains great hailstones out of heaven on his enemies, he slays their flocks and desolates their lands, but his chosen are safe under his protection, even although danger hem them in on every side; "thou shalt not be afraid for any terror by night, nor for the arrow that flieth by day; for the pestilence that walketh in darkness; nor for the sickness that destroyeth in the noon-day. A thousand shall fall besides thee, and ten thousand at thy right hand; but it shall not come nigh thee. . . . He shall defend thee under his wings, and thou shalt be safe under his feathers." (Ps. xci., Prayer-Book.) Experience contradicted this theory rather roughly, and it gave way slowly before the logic of facts; it is, however, still more or less prevalent among ourselves, as we see when the siege of Paris is proclaimed as a judgment on Parisian irreligion, and when the whole nation falls on its knees to acknowledge the cattle-plague as the deserved punishment of its sins! The next step forward was to separate the physical from the moral, and to allow that physical suffering came independently of moral guilt or righteousness: the men crushed under the fallen tower of Siloam were not thereby proved to be more sinful than their countrymen. The birth of science rang the death-knell of an arbitrary and constantly interposing Supreme Power. The theory of God as a miracle worker was dissipated; henceforth if God ruled at all it must be as *in* nature and not from *outside* of nature; he no longer imposed laws on something exterior to himself, the laws could only be the necessary expression of his own being. Laws were, further, found to be immutable in their working, changing not in accordance with prayer, but ever true to a hair's breadth in their action. Slowly, but surely, prayer to God for the alteration of physical phenomena is being found to be simply a well-meant superstition; nature swerves not for our pleading, nor falters in her path for our most passionate supplication. The "reign of law" in physical matters is becoming acknowledged even by theologians. As step by step the knowledge of *the natural* advances, so step by step does the belief in *the supernatural* recede; as the kingdom of science extends, so the kingdom of miraculous interference gradually disappears. The effects which of old were thought to be caused by the direct action of God are now seen to be caused by the uniform and calculable working of certain laws—laws which, when discovered, it is the part of wisdom implicitly to obey. Things which we used to pray for, we now work and wait for, and if we fail we do not ask God to add his strength to ours, but we sit down and lay our plans more carefully. How is this to end? Is the future to be like the past, and is science finally to obliterate the conception of a personal God? It is a question which ought to be pondered in the light of history. Hitherto the supernatural has always been the makeweight of human ignorance; is it, in truth, this and nothing else?

I am forced, with some reluctance, to apply the whole of the above reasoning to every school of thought, whether nominally Christian or non-Christian, which regards God as a "magnified man." The same stern logic cuts every way and destroys alike the Trinitarian and the Unitarian hypothesis, wherever the idea of God is that of a Creator, standing, as it were, outside his creation. The liberal thinker, whatever his present position, seems driven infallibly to the above conclusions, as soon as he sets himself to realise his idea of his God. The Deity must of necessity be that one and only substance out of which all things are evolved under the uncreated conditions and eternal laws of the universe; he must be, as Theodore Parker somewhat oddly puts it, "the materiality of matter, as well as the spirituality of spirit;" *i.e.*, these must both be products of this one substance: a truth which is readily accepted as soon as spirit and matter are seen to be but different modes of one essence. Thus we identify substance with the all-comprehending and vivifying force of nature, and in so doing we simply reduce to a physical impossibility the existence of the Being described by the orthodox as a God possessing the attributes of personality. The Deity becomes identified with nature, co-extensive with the universe; but the *God* of the orthodox no longer exists; we may change the signification of God, and use the word to express a different idea, but we can no longer mean by it a Personal Being in the orthodox sense, possessing an individuality which divides him from the rest of the universe. I say that I use these arguments "with some reluctance," because many who have fought and are fighting nobly and bravely in the army of freethought, and to whom all free-thinkers owe much honour, seem to cling to an idea of the Deity, which, however beautiful and poetical, is not logically defensible, and in striking at the orthodox notion of God, one necessarily strikes also at all idea of a "Personal" Deity. There are some Theists who have only cut out the Son and the Holy Ghost from the Triune Jehovah, and have concentrated the Deity in the Person of the Father; they have returned to the old Hebrew idea of God, the Creator, the Sustainer, only widening it into regarding God as the Friend and Father of all his creatures, and not of the Jewish nation only. There is much that is noble and attractive in this idea, and it will possibly serve as a religion of transition to break the shock of the change from the supernatural to the natural. It is reached entirely by a process of *giving up;* Christian notions are dropped one after another, and the God who is believed in is *the residuum.* This Theistic school has not gained its idea of God from any general survey of nature or from any philosophical induction from facts; it has gained it only by stripping off from an idea already in the mind everything which is degrading and revolting in the dogmas of Trinitarianism. It starts, as I have noticed elsewhere, from a very noble axiom: "If there be a God at all he must be at least as good as his highest creatures," and thus is instantly swept away the Augustinian idea of a God,—that monster invented by theological dialectics; but still the same axiom makes God in the image of man, and never succeeds in getting outside a human representation of the Divinity. It *starts* from this axiom, and the axiom is prefaced by an "if." It assumes God, and then argues fairly enough what his character must be. And this "if" is the very point on which the argument of this paper turns.

"If there be a God" all the rest follows, but *is there a God at all* in the sense in which the word is generally used? And thus I come to the second part of my problem; having seen that the orthodox "idea of God is unreasonable and absurd, is there any idea of God, worthy to be called an idea, which is attainable in the present state of our faculties?" (P. 10.)

The argument from design does not seem to me to be a satisfactory one; it either goes too far or not far enough. Why in arguing from the evidences of adaptation should we assume that they are planned by a mind? It is quite as easy to conceive of matter as self-existent, with inherent vital laws moulding it into varying phenomena, as to conceive of any intelligent *mind* directly modelling matter, so that the "heavens declare the glory of God, and the firmament showeth his handy-work." It is, I know, customary to sneer at the idea of beautiful forms existing without a conscious designer, to parallel the adaptations of this world to the adaptations in machinery, and then triumphantly to inquire, "if skill be inferred from the one, why ascribe the other to chance?" We do not believe in *chance;* the steady action of law is not chance; the exquisite crystals which form themselves under certain conditions are not a "*fortuitous* concourse of atoms:" the only question is whether the laws which we all allow to govern nature are immanent in nature, or the outcome of an intelligent mind. If there be a law-maker, is *he* self-existent, or does he, in turn, as has been asked again and again by Positivist, Secularist, and Atheist, require a maker? If we think for a moment of the vast mind implied in the existence of a Creator of the universe, is it possible to believe that such a mind is the result of chance? If man's mind imply a master-mind, how much more that of God? Of course the question seems an absurd one, but it is quite as pertinent as the question about a world-maker. We *must* come to a stop somewhere, and it is quite as logical to stop at one point as at another. The argument from design would be valuable if we could prove, *à priori*, as Mr. Gillespie attempted to do,* the existence of a Deity; this *being proved* we might then fairly argue deductively to the various apparent signs of mind in the universe. Again, if we allow design we must ask, "how far does design extend?" If some phenomena are designed, why not *all?* And if not all, on what principle can we separate that which is designed from that which is not? If intellect and love reveal a design, what is revealed by brutality and hate? If the latter are not the result of design, how did they become introduced into the universe? I repeat that this argument implies either too much or too little.

There is but one argument that appears to me to have any real weight, and that is the argument from instinct. Man has faculties which appear, at present, as though they were not born of the intellect, and it seems to me to be unphilosophical to exclude this class of facts from our survey of nature. The nature of man has in it certain sentiments and emotions which, reasonably or unreasonably, sway him powerfully and continually; they are, in fact, his strongest motive powers, overwhelming the reasoning faculties with resistless strength; true, they need discipline and controlling, but they do not need to be, and they cannot be, destroyed. The sentiments of love, of reverence, of worship, are not, as yet, reducible to logical processes; they are intuitions, spontaneous emotions, incomprehensible to the keen and cold intellect. They may be laughed at or denied, but they still exist in spite of all; they avenge themselves, when they are not taken into account, by ruining the best laid plans, and they are continually bursting the cords with which reason strives to tie them down. I do not for a moment pretend to deny that these "intuitions" will, as our knowledge of psychology increases, be reducible to strict laws; we call them instincts and intuitions simply because we are unable to trace them to their source, and this vague expression covers the vagueness of our ideas. Therefore, intuition is not to be accepted as a trustworthy guide, but it may suggest an hypothesis, and this hypothesis must then be submitted to the stern verification of observed facts. We are not as yet able to say to what the instinct in

* "The Necessary Existence of Deity."

man to worship points, or what reality answers to his yearning. Increased knowledge will, we may hope, reveal to us* where there lies the true satisfaction of this instinct: so long as the yearning is only an "instinct" it cannot pretend to be logically defensible, or claim to lay down any rule of faith. But still I think it well to point out that this instinct exists in man, and exists most strongly in some of the noblest souls.

Of all the various sentiments which are thus at present "intuitional," none is so powerful, none so overmastering as this instinct to worship, this sentiment of religion. It is as natural for man to worship as to eat. He will do it, be it reasonable or unreasonable. Just as the baby crams everything into his mouth, so does man persist in worshipping something. It may be said that the baby's instinct does not prove that he is right in trying to devour a match-box; true, but it proves the existence of something *eatable;* so fetish-worship, polytheism, theism, do not prove that man has worshipped rightly, but do they not prove the existence of something *worshipable?* The argument does not, of course, pretend to amount to a demonstration; it is nothing more than the suggestion of an analogy. Are we to find that the supply is correlated to the demand throughout nature, and yet believe that this hitherto invariable system is suddenly altered when we reach the spiritual part of man? I do not deny that this instinct is hereditary, and that it is fostered by habit. The idea of reverence for God is transmitted from parent to child; it is educated into an abnormal development, and thus almost indefinitely strengthened; but yet it does appear to me that the bent to worship is an integral part of man's nature. This instinct has also sometimes been considered to have its root in the feeling that one's individual self is but a "part of a stupendous

* "Is there in man any such Instinct? May not the general tendency to worship a Deity, everywhere be the result of the influence gained by Priests over the mind by the play of the mysterious Unknown and Hereafter upon susceptible imaginations? Besides, what are we to say of the immense number of philosophical Buddhists and Brahmins, for whose comfort or moral guidance the idea of a God or a hereafter is felt to be quite unnecessary? They cannot comprehend it, and consequently acts of worship to God would be deemed by them fanatical. It is traditionalists who either do not think at all, or think only within a narrow, creed-bound circle, that are most devoted to worshipping Deity; and if so, may not the whole history of *worship* have its origin in superstition and priestcraft! In that case, the theory of an instinct of worship falls to the ground."—*Note by the Editor.*

whole;" that the so-called religious feeling which is evoked by a grand view or a bright starlight night is only the realisation of personal insignificance, and the reverence which rises in the soul in the presence of the mighty universe of which we form a part. Whatever the root and the significance of this instinct, there can be no doubt of its strength; there is nothing rouses men's passions as does theology; for religion men rush on death more readily and joyfully than for any other cause; religious fanaticism is the most fatal, the most terrible power in the world. In studying history I also see the upward tendency of the race, and note that current which Mr. Matthew Arnold has called "that stream of tendency, not ourselves, which makes for righteousness." Of course, if there be a conscious God, this tendency is a proof of his moral character, since it would be the outcome of his laws; but here again an argument which would be valuable were the existence of God already proved, falls blunted from the iron wall of the unknown. The same tendency upwards would naturally exist in any "realm of law," although the law were an unconscious force. For righteousness is nothing more than obedience to law, and where there is obedience to law, Nature's mighty forces lend their strength to man, and progress is secured. Only by obedience to law can advance be made, and this rule applies, of course, to morality as well as to physics. Physical righteousness is obedience to physical laws; moral righteousness is obedience to moral laws: just as physical laws are discovered by the observation of natural phenomena, so must moral laws be discovered by the observation of social phenomena. That which increases the general happiness is right; that which tends to destroy the general happiness is wrong. Utility is the test of morality. But a law must not be drawn from a single fact or phenomenon; facts must be carefully collated, and the general laws of morality drawn from a generalisation of facts. But this subject is too large to enter upon here, and it is only hinted at in order to note that, although there is a moral tendency apparent in the course of events, it is rather a rash assumption to take it for granted that the power in question is a conscious one: it *may* be, and that, I think, is all we can justly and reasonably say.

Again, as regards Love. I have protested above against the easiness which talks glibly of the Supreme Love while shutting its eyes to the supreme agony of the world. But here, in putting forward what may be said on the other side of the question, I must remark that there is a possible explanation for sorrow and sin which is consistent with love. Given immortality of man and beast, and the future gain may then outweigh the present loss. But we are bound to remember that we can only have a *hope* of immortality; we have no demonstration of it, and this is, therefore, only an assumption by which we escape from a difficulty. We ought to be ready to acknowledge, also, that there *is* love in nature, although there is cruelty too; there *is* the sunshine as well as the storm, and we must not fix our eyes on the darkness alone and deny the light. In mother-love, in the love of friends, loyal through all doubt, true in spite of danger and difficulty, strongest when most sorely tried, we see gleams of so divine, so unearthly a beauty, that our hearts whisper to us of an universal heart pulsating throughout nature, which, at these rare moments, we cannot believe to be a dream. But there seems, also, to be a vague idea that love and other virtues could not exist unless derived from *the* Love, &c. It is true that we do conceive certain ideals of virtue which we personify, and to which we apply various terms implying affection; we speak of a love of Truth, devotion to Freedom, and so on. These ideals have, however, a purely subjective existence; they are not objective realities; there is nothing answering to these conceptions in the outside world, nor do we pretend to believe in their individuality. But when we gather up all our ideals, our noblest longings, and bind them into one vast ideal figure, which we call by the name of God, then we at once attribute to it an objective existence, and complain of coldness and hardness if its reality is questioned, and we demand to know if we can love an abstraction? The noblest souls *do* love abstractions, and live in their beauty and die for their sake.

There appears, also, to be a possibility of a mind in Nature, although we have seen that intelligence is, strictly speaking, impossible. There cannot be perception, memory, comparison, or judgment; but may there not be a perfect mind, unchanging, calm, and still? Our faculties fail us when we try to estimate the Deity, and we are betrayed into contradictions and absurdities; but does it therefore follow that He IS not? It seems to me that to deny his existence is to overstep the boundaries of our thought-power almost as much as to try and define it. We pretend to know the Unknown if we declare Him to be the Unknowable. Unknowable to us at present, yes! Unknowable for ever, in other possible stages of existence?—We have reached a region into which we cannot penetrate; here all human faculties fail us; we bow our heads on "the threshold of the unknown."

> And the ear of man cannot hear, and the eye of man cannot see;
> But if we could see and hear, this Vision—were it not He?

Thus sings Alfred Tennyson, the poet of metaphysics: "*if* we could see and hear"; alas! it is always an "if."

We come back to the opening of this essay: what is the practical result of our ideas about the Divinity, and how do these ideas affect the daily working life? What conclusions are we to draw from the undeniable fact that, even if there be a "personal God," his nature and existence are beyond our faculties, that "clouds and darkness are round about him," that he is veiled in eternal silence and reveals himself not to men? Surely the obvious inference is that, if he does really exist, he desires to conceal himself from the inhabitants of our world. I repeat, that if the Deity exist, he does not wish us to know of his existence. There may be, in the very nature of things, an impossibility of his revealing himself to men; we may have no faculties with which to apprehend him; can we reveal the stars and the rippling expanse of ocean to the sightless limpet on the rock? Whether this be so or not, certain is it that the Deity does *not* reveal himself; either he cannot or he will not. And the reason—I am granting for the moment, for argument's sake, his personal existence—is not far to seek; it is blazed upon the face of history. For what has been the result of theology upon the whole? It has turned men's eyes from earth, to fix them on heaven; it has bid them be careless of the temporal, while luring them to grasp at the eternal; it has induced multitudes to lavish fervent sentiment upon a conception framed by Priests of an incomprehensible God, while diverting their strength from the plain duties which Humanity has before it; it has taught them to live for the world to come, when they should live for the world around them; it has made earth's wrongs endurable with the hope of the glory to be revealed. Wisely indeed would the Deity hide himself, when even a phantom of him has wrought such fatal mischief; and never will real and steady progress be secured until men acquiesce in this beneficent law of their nature, which draws a stern circle of the "limits of Religious

Thought" and bids them concentrate their attention on the work they have to do in this world, instead of being "for ever peering into and brooding over the world beyond the grave."

"*What is to be our conception of morality, is it to base itself on obedience to God, or is it to be sought for itself and its effects?*" When we admit that God is beyond our knowing, morality becomes at once necessarily grounded on utility, or the natural adaptation of certain feelings and actions to promote the general welfare of society. As no revelation is given to us as one "infallible standard of right and wrong," we must form our morality for ourselves from thought and from experience. For example, our moral nature, as educated under the highest civilisation, tells us that lying is wrong;* with this hypothesis in our minds we study facts, and discover that lying causes mistrust, anarchy, and ruin; thence we lay down as a moral law, "Lie not at all." The science of morality must be content to grow like other sciences; first an hypothesis, round which to group our facts, then from the collected and collated facts reasoning up to a solid law. Scientific morality has this great advantage over revealed, that it stands on firm, unassailable ground; new facts will alter its details, but can never touch its method; like all other sciences, it is at once positive and progressive.

"*Is our mental attitude to be kneeling or standing?*" When we admit that the Deity is veiled from us, how can we pray? When we see that that law is inexorable, of what use to protest against its absolute sway? When we feel that all, including ourselves, are but modes of Being which is one and universal, and in which we "live and move," how shall we pray to that which is close to us as our own souls, part of our very selves, inseparable from our thoughts, sharing our consciousness? As well talk aloud to ourselves as pray to the universal Essence. Children *cry* for what they want; men and women *work* for it. There are two points of view from which we may regard prayer: from the one it is a piece of childishness only, from the other it is sheer impertinence. Regarding Nature's mighty order, her grand, silent, unvarying march,—the importunity which frets against her changeless progress is a mark of the most extreme childishness of

* All men do not think lying wrong, *e.g.*, Thugs and old Spartans. Therefore it is not our *moral nature* that intuitively tells us thus, but our moral nature as instructed by the moral ideas prevailing in the society in which we happen to be living.—*Note by the Editor.*

mind; it shows that complete irreverence of spirit which cannot conceive the idea of a greatness before which the individual existence is as nothing, and that infantile conceit which imagines that its own plans and playthings rival in importance the struggles of nations and the interests of distant worlds. Regarding Nature's laws as wiser than our own whims, the idea which finds its outlet in prayer is a gross impertinence; who are we that we should take it on ourselves to remind Nature of her work, God of his duty? Is there any impertinence so extreme as the prayer which "pleads" with the Deity? There is only one kind of "prayer" which is reasonable, and that is the deep, silent, adoration of the greatness and beauty and order around us, as revealed in the realms of non-rational life and in Humanity; as we bow our heads before the laws of the universe and mould our lives into obedience to their voice, we find a strong, calm peace steal over our hearts, a perfect trust in the ultimate triumph of the right, a quiet determination to "make our lives sublime." Before our own high ideals, before those lives which show us "how high the tides of divine life have risen in the human world," we stand with hushed voice and veiled face; from them we draw strength to emulate, and even dare struggle to excel. The contemplation of the ideal is true prayer; it inspires, it strengthens, it ennobles. The other part of prayer is work: from contemplation to labour, from the forest to the street. Study Nature's laws, conform to them, work in harmony with them, and work becomes a prayer and a thanksgiving, an adoration of the universal wisdom, and a true obedience to the universal law.

Is the mainspring of our actions to be the idea of duty to God, or the of loyalty to law and to man's well-being?" We cannot serve God in any real sense; we are awed before the Unknown, but we cannot *serve* it. For the Mighty, for the Incomprehensible, what can we do? But we can serve man, ay, and he needs our service; service of brain and hand, service untiring and unceasing, service through life and unto death. The race to which we belong (our own familes and kinsfolk, and then the community at large) has the first claim on our allegiance, a claim from which nothing can release us until death drops a veil over our work.

Surely I may claim that my subject is not an unpractical one, and that our ideas of the Nature and Existence of God influence our lives in a very real way. If I have substituted a different basis of morality for that on which it now stands, if I have suggested a different theory of prayer, and offered a different motive for duty, surely these changes affect the whole of human life And if one by one these theories ate denied by the orthodox, and they reject them because they sever human life from that which is called revealed religion, is not my position justified, that the ideas we hold of God are the ruling forces of our lives? that it is of primary importance to the welfare of mankind that a false theory on this point should be destroyed and a more reasonable faith accepted?

Will any one exclaim, "You are taking all beauty out of human life, all hope, all warmth, all inspiration; you give us cold duty for filial obedience, and inexorable law in the place of God?" All beauty from life? Is there, then, no beauty in the idea of forming part of the great life of the universe, no beauty in conscious harmony with Nature, no beauty in faithful service, no beauty in ideals of every virtue? "All hope?" Why, I give you more than hope, I give you certainty: if I bid you labour for this world, it is with the knowledge that this world will repay you a thousand-fold, because society will grow purer, freedom more settled, law more honoured, life more full and glad. What is your hope? A heaven in the clouds. I point to a heaven attainable on earth. "All warmth?" What! You serve warmly a God unknown and invisible, in a sense the projected shadow of your own imaginings, and can only serve coldly your brother whom you see at your side? There is no warmth in brightening the lot of the sad, in reforming abuses, in establishing equal justice for rich and poor? You find warmth in the church, but none in the home? Warmth in imagining the cloud-glories of heaven, but none in creating substantial glories on earth? "All inspiration?" If you want inspiration to feeling, to sentiment, perhaps you had better keep to your Bible and your creeds; if you want inspiration to work, go and walk through the east of London, or the back streets of Manchester. You are inspired to tenderness as you gaze at the wounds of Jesus, dead in Judæa long ago, and find no inspiration in the wounds of men and women dying in the England of to-day? You "have tears to shed for him," but none for the sufferer at your doors? His passion arouses your sympathies, but you see no pathos in the passion of the poor? Duty is colder than "filial obedience?" What do you mean by filial obedience? Obedience to your ideal of goodness and love, is it not so? Then how is duty cold? I offer you ideals for your homage: here is Truth for your Mistress, to whose exaltation you shall devote your intellect; here is Freedom for your General, for whose triumph you shall fight; here is Love for your Inspirer, who shall influence your every thought; here is Man for your Master—not in heaven but on earth—to whose service you shall consecrate every faculty of your being. Inexorable law in the place of God? Yes: a stern certainty that you shall not waste your life, yet gather a rich reward at the close; that you shall not sow misery, yet reap gladness; that you shall not be selfish, yet be crowned with love, nor shall you sin, yet find safety in repentance. True, our creed *is* a stern one, stern with the beautiful sternness of Nature. But if we be in the right, look to yourselves: laws do not check their action for your ignorance; fire will not cease to scorch, because "you did not know."

We know nothing beyond Nature; we judge of the future by the present and the past; we are content to work now, and let the work to come wait until it appears as the work to do; we find that our faculties are sufficient for fulfilling the tasks within our reach, and we cannot waste time and strength in gazing into impenetrable darkness. We must needs fight against superstitions, because they hinder the advancement of the race, but we will not fall into the error of opponents and try to define the Undefinable.

EUTHANASIA.

"I HAVE already related to you with what care they look after their sick, so that nothing is left undone which may contribute either to their health or ease. And as for those who are afflicted with incurable disorders, they use all possible means of cherishing them, and of making their lives as comfortable as possible; they visit them often, and take great pains to make their time pass easily. But if any have torturing, lingering pain, without hope of recovery or ease, the priests and magistrates repair to them and exhort them, since they are unable to proceed with the business of life, are become a burden to themselves and all about them, and have in reality outlived themselves, they should no longer cherish a rooted disease, but choose to die since they cannot but live in great misery; being persuaded, if they thus deliver themselves from torture, or allow others to do it, they shall be happy after death. Since they forfeit none of the pleasures, but only the troubles of life by this, they think they not only act reasonably, but consistently with religion; for they follow the advice of their priests, the expounders of God's will. Those who are wrought upon by these persuasions, either starve themselves or take laudanum. But no one is compelled to end his life thus; and if they cannot be persuaded to it, the former care and attendance on it is continued. And though they esteem a voluntary death, when chosen on such authority, to be very honourable, on the contrary, if any one commit suicide without the concurrence of the priest and senate, they honour not the body with a decent funeral, but throw into a ditch.*

In pleading for the morality of Euthanasia, it seems not unwise to show that so thoroughly religious a man as Sir

* Memoirs. A translation of the Utopia, &c., of Sir Thomas Moore, Lord High Chancellor of England. By A. Cayley the Younger, pp. 102, 103. (Edition of 1808.)

Thomas Moore deemed that practice so consonant with a sound morality as to make it one of the customs of his ideal state, and to place it under the sanction of the priesthood. As a devout Roman Catholic, the great Chancellor would naturally imagine that any beneficial innovation would be sure to obtain the support of the priesthood; and although we may differ from him on this head, since our daily experience teaches *us* that the priest may be counted upon as the steady opponent of all reform, it is yet not uninstructive to note that the deep religious feeling which distinguished this truly good man, did not shrink from this idea of euthanasia as from a breach of morality, nor did he apparently dream that any opposition would (or could) be offered to it on religious grounds. The last sentence of the extract is specially important; in discussiug the morality of euthanasia we are not discussing the moral lawfulness or unlawfulness of suicide in general; we may protest against suicide, and yet uphold euthanasia, and we may even protest against the one and uphold the other, on exactly the same principle, as we shall see further on. As the greater includes the less, those who consider that a man has a right to choose whether he will live or not, and who therefore regard *all* suicide as lawful, will, of course, approve of euthanasia; but it is by no means necessary to hold this doctrine because we contend for the other. *On the general question of the morality of suicide, this paper expresses no opinion whatever.* This is not the point, and we do not deal with it here. This essay is simply and solely directed to prove that there are circumstances under which a human being has a moral right to hasten the inevitable approach of death. The subject is one which is surrounded by a thick fog of popular prejudice, and the arguments in its favour are generally dismissed unheard. I would therefore crave the reader's generous patience, while laying before him the reasons which dispose many religious and social reformers to regard it as of importance that euthanasia should be legalised.

In the fourth Edition of an essay on Euthanasia, by P. D. Williams, jun.,—an essay which powerfully sums up what is to be said for and against the practice in question, and which treats the whole subject exhaustively—we find the proposition for which we contend laid down in the following explicit terms:

"That in all cases of hopeless and painful illness, it

should be the recognised duty of the medical attendant, whenever so desired by the patient, to administer chloroform, or such other anæsthetic as may by-and-by supersede chloroform, so as to destroy consciousness at once, and to put the sufferer to a quick and painless death; all needful precautions being adopted to prevent any abuse of such duty; and means being taken to establish, beyond the possibility of doubt or question, that the remedy was applied at the express wish of the patient."

It is very important, at the outset, to lay down clearly the limitations of the proposed medical reform. It is, sometimes, thoughtlessly stated that the supporters of euthanasia propose to put to death all persons suffering from incurable disorders; no assertion can be more inaccurate or more calculated to mislead. We propose only, that where an incurable disorder is accompanied with extreme pain—pain, which nothing can alleviate except death—pain, which only grows worse as the inevitable doom approaches—pain, which drives almost to madness, and which must end in the intensified torture in the death agony—that pain should be at once soothed by the administration of an anæsthetic, which should not only produce unconsciousness, but should be sufficiently powerful to end a life, in which the renewal of consciousness can only be simultaneous with the renewal of pain. So long as life has some sweetness left in it, so long the offered mercy is not needed; euthanasia is a relief from unendurable agony, not an enforced extinguisher of a still desired existence. Besides, no one proposes to make it obligatory on anybody; it is only urged that where the patient asks for the mercy of a speedy death, instead of a protracted one, his prayer may be granted without any danger of the penalties of murder or manslaughter being inflicted on the doctors and nurses in attendance. I will lay before the reader a case which is within my own knowledge,—and which can be probably supplemented by the sad experience of almost every individual,—in which the legality of euthanasia would have been a boon equally to the sufferer and to her family. A widow lady was suffering from cancer in the breast, and as the case was too far advanced for the ordinary remedy of the knife, and as the leading London surgeons refused to risk an operation which might hasten, but could not retard, death, she resolved, for the sake of her orphan children, to allow a medical practitioner to perform a terrible operation, whereby he hoped to prolong her life for some years. Its details are too painful to enter into unnecessarily; it will suffice to say that it was performed by means of quick-lime, and that the use of chloroform was impossible. When the operation, which extended over days, was but half over, the sufferer's strength gave way, and the doctor was compelled to acknowledge that even a prolongation of life was impossible, and that to complete the operation could only hasten death. So the patient had to linger on in almost unimaginable torture, knowing that the pain could only end in death, seeing her relatives worn out by watching, and agonised at the sight of her sufferings, and yet compelled to live on from hour to hour, till at last the anguish culminated in death. Is it possible for any one to believe that it would have been wrong to have hastened the inevitable end, and thus to have shortened the agony of the sufferer herself, and to have also spared her nurses months of subsequent ill-health. It is in such cases as this that euthanasia would be useful. It is, however, probable that all will agree that the benefit conferred by the legalisation of euthanasia would, in many instances, be very great; but many feel that the objections to it, on moral grounds, are so weighty, that no physical benefit could countervail the moral wrong. These objections, so far as I can gather them, are as follows:—

Life is the gift of God, and is therefore sacred, and must only be taken back by the giver of life.*

Euthanasia is an interference with the course of nature, and is therefore an act of rebellion against God.

Pain is a spiritual remedial agent inflicted by God, and should therefore be patiently endured.

Life is the gift of God, and is therefore sacred, and must only be taken back by the Giver of life. This objection is one of those high-sounding phrases which impose on the careless and thoughtless hearer, by catching up a form of words which is generally accepted as an unquestionable axiom, and by hanging thereupon an unfair corollary. The ordinary man or woman, on hearing this assertion, would probably answer—"Life sacred? Yes, of course; on the sacredness of life depends the safety of society; anything which tampers with this principle must be both wrong and dangerous." And yet, such is the inconsistency of the

* We, of course, here, have no concern with theological questions touching the existence or non-existence of Deity, and express no opinion about them.

thoughtless, that, five minutes afterwards, the same person will glow with passionate admiration at some noble deed, in which the sacredness of life has been cast to the winds at the call of honour or of humanity, or will utter words of indignant contempt at the baseness which counted life more sacred than duty or principle. That life is sacred is an undeniable proposition; every natural gift is sacred, *i.e.*, is valuable, and is not to be lightly destroyed; life, as summing up all natural gifts, and as containing within itself all possibilities of usefulness and happiness, is the most sacred physical possession which we own. But it is *not* the most sacred thing on earth. Martyrs slain for the sake of principles which they could not truthfully deny; patriots who have died for their country; heroes who have sacrificed themselves for others' good;—the very flower and glory of humanity rise up in a vast crowd to protest that conscience, honour, love, self-devotion, are more precious to the race than is the life of the individual. Life is sacred, but it may be laid down in a noble cause; life is sacred, but it must bend before the holier sacredness of principle; life which, though sacred, can be destroyed, is as nothing before the indestructable ideals which claim from every noble soul the sacrifice of personal happiness, of personal greatness, yea, of personal life.*

It will be conceded, then, on all hands, that the proposition that life is sacred must be accepted with many limitations: the proposition, in fact, amounts only to this, that life must not be voluntarily laid down without grave and sufficient cause. What we have to consider is, whether there are present, in any proposed euthanasia, such conditions as overbear considerations for the *acknowledged* sanctity of life. We contend that in the cases in which it is proposed that death should be hastened, these conditions do exist.

We will not touch here on the question of the endurance of pain as a duty, for we will examine that further on. But is it a matter of no importance that a sufferer should condemn his attendants to a prolonged drain on their health

* The word "life" is here used in the sense of "personal existence in this world." It is, of course, not intended to be asserted that life is really destructible, but only that personal existence, or identity, may be destroyed. And further, no opinion is given on the possibility of life otherwhere than on this globe; nothing is spoken of except life on earth, under the conditions of human existence.

and strength, in order to cling to a life which is useless to others, and a burden to himself? The nurse who tends, perhaps for weeks, a bed of agony, for which there is no cure but death—whose senses are strained by intense watchfulness — whose nerves are racked by witnessing torture which she is powerless to alleviate—is, by her self-devotion, sowing in her own constitution the seeds of ill-health—that is to say, she is deliberately shortening her own life. We have seen that we have a right to shorten life in obedience to a call of duty, and it will at once be said that the nurse is obeying such a call. But has the nurse a right to sacrifice her own life—and an injury to health is a sacrifice of life —for an obviously unequivalent advantage? We are apt to forget, because the injury is partially veiled to us, that we touch the sacredness of life whenever we touch health: every case of over-work, of over-strain, of over-exertion, is, so to speak, a modified case of euthanasia. To poison the spring of life is as real a tampering with the sacredness of life as it is to check its course. The nurse is really committing a slow euthanasia. Either the patient or the nurse must commit an heroic suicide for the sake of the other—which shall it be? Shall the life be sacrificed, which is torture to its possessor, useless to society, and whose bounds are already clearly marked? or shall a strong and healthy life, with all its future possibilities, be undermined and sacrificed *in addition to that which is already doomed?* But, granting that the sublime generosity of the nurse stays not to balance the gain with the loss, but counts herself as nothing in the face of a human need, then surely it is time to urge then to permit this self-sacrifice is an error, and *that to accept it* is a crime. If it be granted that the throwing away of life for a manifestly unequivalent gain is wrong, that we ought not to blind ourselves to the fact, that to sacrifice a healthy life in order to lengthen by a few short weeks a doomed life, is a grave moral error, however much it may be redeemed in the individual by the glory of a noble self-devotion. Allowing to the full the honour due to the heroism of the nurse, what are we to say to the patient who accepts the sacrifice? What are we to think of the morality of a human being who, in order to preserve the miserable remnant of life left to him, allows another to shorten life? If we honour the man who sacrifices himself to defend his family, or risks his own life to save theirs, we must surely blame him who, on the contrary, sacrifices those he ought to value most, in order to prolong his own now useless existence. The measure of our admiration for the one, must be the measure of our pity for the weakness and selfishness of the other. If it be true that the man who dies for his dear ones on the battlefield is a hero, he who voluntarily dies for them on his bed of sickness is a hero no less brave. But it is urged that *life is the gift of God, and must only be taken back by the Giver of life.* I suppose that in any sense in which it can be supposed true that life is the gift of God, it *can* only be taken back by the giver—that is to say, that just as life is produced in accordance with certain laws, so it can only be destroyed in accordance with certain other laws. Life is not the direct gift of a superior power: it is the gift of man to man and animal to animal, produced by the voluntary agent, and not by God, under physical conditions, on the fulfilment of which *alone* the production of life depends. The physical conditions must be observed if we desire to produce life, and so must they be if we desire to destroy life. In both cases man is the voluntary agent, in both law is the means of his action. If life-giving is God's doing, then life-destroying is his doing too. But this is not what is intended by the proposers of this aphorism. If they will pardon me for translating their somewhat vague proposition into more precise language, they say that they find themselves in possession of a certain thing called life, which must have come from *somewhere*; and as in popular language the unknown is always the divine, it must have come from God: therefore this life must only be taken from them by a cause that also proceeds from *somewhere*—*i.e.*, from an unknown cause—*i.e.*, from the Divine will. Chloroform comes from a visible agent, from the doctor or nurse, or at least from a bottle, which can be taken up or left alone at our own choice. If we swallow this, the cause of death is known, and is evidently not divine; but if we go into a house where scarlet fever is raging, although we are in that case voluntarily running the chance of taking poison quite as truly as if we swallow a dose of chloroform, yet if we die from the infection, we can imagine the illness to be sent from God. Wherever we think the element of chance comes in, there we are able to imagine that God rules directly. We quite overlook the fact that there is no such thing as chance. There is only our ignorance of law, not a break in natural order. If our constitution be susceptible of the particular poison to which we expose it, we take the disease. If we knew the laws of infection as accurately as we know the laws affecting chloroform, we should be able to foresee with like certainty the inevitable consequence; and our ignorance does not make the action of either set of laws less unchangeable or more divine. But in the "happy-go-lucky" style of thought peculiar to ignorance, the Christian disregards the fact that infection is ruled by definite laws, and believes that health and sickness are the direct expressions of the will of his God, and not the invariable consequence of obscure but probably discoverable antecedents; so he boldly goes into the back slums of London to nurse a family stricken down with fever, and knowingly and deliberately runs "the chance" of infection—*i.e.*, knowingly and deliberately runs the chance of taking poison, or rather of having poison poured into his frame. This he does, trusting that the nobility of his motive will make the act right in God's sight. Is it more noble to relieve the sufferings of strangers, than to relieve the sufferings of his family? or is it more heroic to die of voluntarily-contracted fever, than of voluntarily-taken chloroform?

The argument that *life must only be taken back by the life-giver*, would, if thoroughly carried out, entirely prevent all dangerous operations. In the treatment of some diseases there are operations that will either kill or cure: the disease must certainly be fatal if left alone; while the proposed operation may save life, it may equally destroy it, and thus may take life some time before the giver of life wanted to take it back. Evidently, then, such operations should not be performed, since there is risked so grave an interference with the desires of the life-giver. Again, doctors act very wrongly when they allow certain soothing medicines to be taken when all hope is gone, which they refuse so long as a chance of recovery remains: what right have they to *compel* the life-giver to follow out his apparent intentions? In some cases of painful disease, it is now usual to produce partial or total unconsciousness by the injection of morphia, or by the use of some other anæsthetic. Thus, I have known a patient subjected to this kind of treatment, when dying from a tumour in the æsophagus; he was consequently for some weeks before his death, kept in a state of almost complete unconsciousness, for if he were allowed to become conscious, his agony was so unendurable as to drive him wild. He was thus, although breathing, practically dead for weeks before his death. We cannot but wonder, in view of such a case as his, what it is that people mean when they talk of "life." Life includes, surely, not only the involuntary animal functions, such as the movements of heart and lungs; but consciousness, thought, feeling, emotion. Of the various constituents of human life, surely those are not the most "sacred" which we share with the brute, however necessary these may be as the basis on which the rest are built. It is thought, then, that we may rightfully destroy all that constitutes the beauty and nobility of human life, we may kill thought, slay consciousness, deaden emotion, stop feeling, we may do all this, and leave lying on the bed before us a breathing figure, from which we have taken all the nobler possibilities of life; but we may not touch the purely animal existence; we may rightly check the action of the nerves and the brain, but we must not dare to outrage the Deity by checking the action of the heart and the lungs.

We ask, then, for the legalisation of euthanasia, because it is in accordance with the highest morality yet known, that which teaches the duty of self sacrifice for the greater good of others, because it is sanctioned in principle by every service performed at personal danger and injury, and because it is already partially practised by modern improvements in medical science.

Euthanasia is an interference with the course of nature, and its herefore an act of rebellion against God. In considering this objection, we are placed in difficulty by not being told what sense our opponents attach to the word "nature"; and we are obliged once more to ask pardon for forcing these vague and high-flown arguments into a humiliating precision of meaning. Nature, in the widest sense of the word, includes all natural laws: and in this sense it is of course impossible to interfere with nature at all. We live, and move, and have our being *in* nature; and we can no more get outside it than we can get outside everything. With this nature we cannot interfere: we can study its laws, and learn how to balance one law against another, so as to modify results; but this can only be done by and through nature itself. The "interference with the course of nature" which is intended in the above objection does not of course mean this impossible proceeding; and it can then only mean an interference with things which would proceed in one course without human agency meddling with them, but which are susceptible of being turned into another course by human agency. If interference with nature's course be a rebellion against God, we are rebelling against God every day of our lives. Every achievement of civilisation is an interference with nature. Every artificial comfort we enjoy is an improvement on nature. "Everybody professes to approve and admire many great triumphs of art over nature: the junction by bridges of shores which nature had made separate, the draining of nature's marshes, the excavation of her wells, the dragging to light of what she has buried at immense depths in the earth, the turning away of her thunderbolts by lightning-rods, of her inundations by embankments, of her ocean by breakwaters. But to commend these and similar feats, is to acknowledge that the ways of nature are to be conquered, not obeyed; that her powers are often towards man in the position of enemies, from whom he must wrest, by force and ingenuity, what little he can for his own use, and deserves to be applauded when that little is rather more than might be expected from his physical weakness in comparison to those gigantic powers. All praise of civilisation, or art, or contrivance, is so much dispraise of nature; an admission of imperfection, which it is man's business, and merit, to be always endeavouring to correct or mitigate.* It is difficult to understand how anyone, contemplating the course of nature, can regard it as the expression of a Divine will, which man has no right to improve upon. Natural law is essentially unreasoning and unmoral: gigantic forces clash around us on every side unintelligent, and unvarying in their action. With equal impassiveness these blind forces produce vast benefits and work vast catastrophes. The benefits are ours, if we are able to grasp them; but nature troubles itself not, whether we take them or leave them alone. The catastrophes may rightly be averted, if we can avert them; but nature stays not its grinding wheel for our moans. Even allowing that a Supreme Intelligence gave these forces their being, it is manifest that he never intended man to be their plaything, or to do them homage; for man is dowered with reason to calculate, and with genius to foresee; and into man's hands is given the realm of nature (in this world) to cultivate, to govern, to improve. So long as men believed that a god wielded the thunderbolt, so long would a lightning-conductor be an outrage on Jove; so long as a god guided each force

* "Essay on Nature," by John Stuart Mill.

of nature, so long would it be impiety to resist, or to endeavour to regulate the divine volitions. Only as experience gradually proved that no evil consequences followed each amendment of nature, were natural forces withdrawn, one by one, from the sphere of the unknown and the divine. Now, even pain, that used to be God's scourge, is soothed by chloroform, and death alone is left for nature to inflict, with what lingering agony it may. But why should death, any more than other ills, be left entirely to the clumsy, unassisted processes of nature?—why, after struggling against nature all our lives, should we let it reign unopposed in death? There are some natural evils that we cannot avert. Pain and death are of these; but we can dull pain by dulling feeling, and we can ease by shortening its pangs. Nature kills by slow and protracted torture; we can defy it by choosing a rapid and painless end. It is only the remains of the old superstition that makes men think that to take life is the special prerogative of the gods. With marvellous inconsistency, however, the opponents of euthanasia do not scruple to "interfere with the course of nature" on the one hand, while they forbid us to interfere on the other. It is right to prolong pain by art, although it is wrong to shorten it. When a person is smitten down with some fearful and incurable disease, they do not leave him to nature; on the contrary, they check and thwart nature in every possible way; they cherish the life that nature has blasted; they nourish the strength that nature is undermining; they delay each process of decay which nature sows in the disordered frame; they contest every inch of ground with nature to preserve life; and then, when life means torture, and we ask permission to step in and quench it, they cry out that we are interfering with nature. If they would leave nature to itself, the disease would generally kill with tolerable rapidity; but they will not do this. They will only admit the force of their own argument when it tells on the side of what they choose to consider right. "Against nature" is the cry with which many a modern improvement has been howled at; and it will continue to be raised, until it is generally acknowledged that happiness, and not nature, is the true guide to morality, and until men recognises that nature is to be harnessed to his car of triumph, and to bend its mighty forces to fulfil the human will.

Pain is a spiritual remedial agent, inflicted by God, and should therefore be patiently endured. Does anyone, except a self-torturing ascetic, endure any pain which he can get rid of? This might be deemed a sufficient answer to this objection, for common sense always bids us avoid all possible pain, and daily experience tells us that people invariably evade pain, wherever such evasion is possible. The objection ought to run: "pain is a spiritual remedial agent, inflicted by God, which is to be got rid of as soon as possible, but ought to be patiently endured when unavoidable." Pain *as* pain has no recommendations, spiritual or otherwise; nor is there the smallest merit in a voluntary and needless submission to pain. As to its remedial and educational advantages, it as often as not sours the temper and hardens the heart; if a person endures great physical or mental pain with unruffled patience, and comes out of it with uninjured tenderness and sweetness, we may rest assured that we have come across a rare and beautiful nature of exceptional strength. As a general rule, pain, especially if it be mental, hardens and roughens the character. The use of anæsthetics is utterly indefensible, if physical pain is to be regarded as a special tool whereby God cultivates the human soul. If God is directly acting on the sufferer's body, and is educating his soul by racking his nerves, by what right does the doctor step between with his impious anæsthetic, and by reducing the patient to unconsciousness, deprive God of his pupil, and man of his lesson? If pain be a sacred ark, over which hovers the divine glory, surely it must be a sinful act to touch the holy thing. We may be inflicting incalculable spiritual damage by frustrating the divine plan of education, which was corporeal agony as a spiritual agent. Therefore, if this argument be good for anything at all, we must from henceforth eschew all anæsthetics, we must take no steps to alleviate human agony, we must not venture to interfere with this beneficent agent, but must leave nature to torture us it will. But *we* utterly deny that the unneccessary endurance of pain is even a merit, much less a duty; on the contrary, we believe that it is our duty to war against pain as much as possible, to alleviate it wherever we cannot stop it entirely; and, where continuous and frightful agony can only end in death, then to give to the sufferer the relief he craves for, in the sleep which is mercy. "It is a mercy God has taken him," is an expression often heard when the racked frame at last lies quiet, and the writhed features settle slowly into the peaceful smile of the dead. That mercy we plead that man should be allowed to give to man, when human skill and human tenderness have done their best, and when they have left within their reach no greater boon than a speedy and painless death.

We are not aware that any objection, which may not be classed under one or other of these three heads, has been levelled against the proposition that euthanasia should be legalised. It has, indeed, been suggested that to put into a doctor's hands this "power of life and death," would be to offer a dangerous temptation to those who have any special object to gain by putting a troublesome person quietly out of the way. But this objection overlooks the fact that the patient himself must *ask* for the draught, that stringent precautions can be taken to render euthanasia impossible except at the patient's earnestly, or even repeatedly, expressed wish, that any doctor or attendant, neglecting to take these precautions, would then, as now, be liable to all the penalties for murder or for manslaughter; and that an ordinary doctor would no more be ready to face these penalties then, than he is now, although he undoubtedly has now the power of putting the patient to death with but little chance of discovery. Euthanasia would not render murder less dangerous than it is at present, since no one asks that a nurse may be empowered to give a patient a dose which would ensure death, or that she might be allowed to shield herself from punishment on the plea that the patient desired it. If our opponents would take the trouble to find out what we do ask, before they condemn our propositions, it would greatly simplify public discussion, not alone in this case, but in many proposed reforms.

It may be well, also, to point out the wide line of demarcation which separated euthanasia from what is ordinarily called suicide. Euthanasia, like suicide, is a voluntarily chosen death, but there is a radical difference between the motives which prompt the similar act. Those who commit suicide thereby render themselves useless to society for the future; they deprive society of their services, and selfishly evade the duties which ought to fall to their share; therefore, the social feelings rightly condemn suicide as a crime against society. I do not say that under no stress of circumstances is suicide justifiable; that is not the question; but I wish to point out that it is justly regarded as a social offence. But the very motive which restrains from suicide, prompts to euthanasia. The sufferer who knows that he is lost to society, that he can never again serve his fellow-men; who knows, also, that he is depriving society of the services of those who uselessly exhaust themselves for him, and is further injuring it by undermining the health of its healthy members, feels urged by the very social instincts which would prevent him from committing suicide while in health, to yield a last service to society by relieving it from a useless burden. Hence it is that Sir Thomas Moore, in the quotation with which he began this essay, makes the *social authorities* of his ideal state urge euthanasia as the duty of a faithful citizen, while they yet consistently reprobate ordinary suicide as a *lèse-majesté*, a crime against the State. The life of the individual is, in a sense, the property of society. The infant is nurtured, the child is educated, the man is protected by others; and, in return for the life thus given, developed, preserved, society has a right to demand from its members a loyal, self-forgetting devotion to the common weal. To serve humanity, to raise the race from which we spring, to dedicate every talent, every power, every energy, to the improvement of, and to the increase of happiness in, society, this is the duty of each individual man and woman. And, when we have given all we can, when strength is sinking, and life is failing, when pain racks our bodies, and the worse agony of seeing our dear ones suffer in our anguish tortures our enfeebled minds, when the only service we can render man is to relieve him of a useless and injurious burden, then we ask that we may be permitted to die voluntarily and painlessly, and so to crown a noble life with the laurel wreath of a self-sacrificing death.

ON PRAYER.

THE mania for Prayer-meetings has lately been largely on the increase, and the continual efforts being made to

"Move the arm that moves the world,"

naturally draw one's attention strongly to the subject of Prayer; to its reasonableness, propriety, and prospect of success. If Prayer to God be reverent as towards the Deity, if it be consistent with his immutability, with his fore-knowledge, with his wisdom, and with every kind of trust in his goodness—if it be also, as regards man, permissible by science, and approved by experience, then there can be no doubt at all that it should be sedulously practised, and should be of universal obligation. But if it be at once use-less and absurd, if it be forbidden by reason and frowned at by common sense, if it weaken man and be irreverent towards the Being to whom it is said to be addressed, then it will be well for all who practise it to reconsider their posi-tion, and at least to endeavour to give some solid reason for persisting in a course which is condemned by the intellect and is unneeded by the heart.

The practice of Prayer is generally founded upon the supposed position held by man—first, as a creature towards his Creator, and secondly, as a child towards his Father in heaven. In its first aspect, it is a simple act of homage from the inferior to the superior, parallel to the courtesy shown by the subject to the monarch; it is an acknowledg-ment of dependence, and a sign of gratitude for the gifts which are supposed to be freely given by God to man—gifts which man has done nothing to deserve, but which come from the free bounty of the giver. Putting aside the whole question of God as Creator, which is not the point at issue, we might argue that, since he brought us into this world without our request, and even without our consent, he is in duty bound to see that we have all things necessary for our life and happiness in the world in which he has thus placed us. We might argue that the "blessings" said to be bestowed upon us, such as food, clothing, &c., can only be called "given" by a fiction, for that they are won by our own hard toil, and are never "gifts from God" in any real sense at all. Further, we might plead that we find "bestowed" upon us many things which are decidedly the reverse of blessings, and that if gratitude be due to God for some things, the contrary of gratitude is due to him for others; and that if praise be his right for the one, blame must be his desert for the second. We should be thus forced into the logical, but somewhat peculiar, frame of mind of the savage, who caresses his fetish when it hears his prayers, and belabours it heartily when it fails to help him. But, taking the position that Prayer is due from man by reason of his creaturehood, it must surely be clear that it cannot be a proper way of manifesting a sense of inferiority to degrade the Being to whom the homage is offered. Yet Prayer is essentially degrading to God, and the character ascribed to him of "a hearer and answerer of Prayer" is a most lowering conception of Deity. For God to hear and to answer Prayer means that Prayer changes his action, making him do that which he would otherwise have abstained from doing; it means that man is wiser than God, and is able to instruct him in his duty; and it means that God is less loving than he ought to be, and will not bestow upon his creature that which is good for him, unless he be importuned into giving it. We are told that God is immutable, "the same yesterday, to-day, and for ever;" "God is not a man that he should lie, nor the son of man that he should repent." If this be true—and surely immutability of purpose must be a necessary characteristic of an all-wise and all-good Being—how can Prayer be anything more than a childish fretting against the inevitable? The Changeless One has planned a certain course of action, and is steadily carrying it out; in passionless serenity he goes upon his way; then man breaks in with his feeble cries and petulant upbraidings, and actually turns God from his purpose, and changes the course of his providence. If Prayer does not do this it does nothing at all; either it changes the mind of God or it does not. If it does, God is at the disposal of man's whim; if it does not, it is perfectly useless, and might just as well be left undone. The parable told by

Christ about the unjust judge (Luke xviii. 1-8) is a most extraordinary representation of God: "Because this widow troubleth me, I will avenge her, lest by her continual coming she weary me. . . . And shall not God avenge his own elect, which cry day and night unto him?" Verily, the picture of the divine justice is not an attractive one! The judge does his duty, not because it *is* his duty, not because the widow needs his aid, not because her cause is a just one, but "lest by her continual coming she weary" him. There is only one moral to be drawn from this, namely, that God will not care for his "elect," because they are "his own;" that he will not guard them, because it is his duty; but that, if they cry day and night to him, he will attend to them, because the continual cry wearies him, and he desires to silence it. In the same way God the immutable changes at the sound of Prayer, not because the change will be better or wiser, but because man's cry "wearies" him, and he will be quiet if he obtains his petition. Surely the idea is as degrading as it can be; it puts God on a level with the unwise human parent, who allows himself to be governed by the clamour of his children, and gives any favour to the spoilt child, if only the child be tiresome enough in its petulant persistence.

Is Prayer consistent with the *foreknowledge* of God? It is one of the attributes ascribed to God that he knows all before it happens, and that the future lies mapped out before him as clearly as does the past. If this be so, is it more reasonable to pray about things in the future than things in the past? No one is so utterly irrational as to pray to God, in so many words, to change the things that are gone, or to alter the record of the past. Yet, is it more rational to ask him to change the things that are coming, and to alter the already-written chart of the future? In reality, man's own eyes being blinded, he deems his God such an one as himself, and where he cannot *see*, he can allow himself to *hope*. But there is no excuse from the inexorable logic which pierces us with one horn or the other of this dilemma, however we may writhe in our efforts to escape them; either God knows the future or he knows it not; if he knows it, it cannot be altered, so it is of no use to pray about it, everything being already fixed; if he knows it not, he is not God, he is no wiser than man. But, then, some Christians argue, he has pre-arranged that he will give this blessing in answer to Prayer, and he foreknows the Prayer as well as its answer. Then, after all, it is pre-determined whether we shall pray or not in any given case, and we have only to follow the course along which we are impelled by an irresistible destiny; so the matter is beyond all discussion, and the power to pray, or not to pray, does not reside in us; if there is a blessing in store for us which needs the arm of Prayer to pluck it from the tree on which it hangs, we shall inevitably pray for it at the right moment, and thus—in his effort to escape from one difficulty—the praying Christian has landed himself in a worse one, for absolute foreknowledge implies complete determinism, and prevents all human responsibility of any kind.

Is Prayer consistent with the *wisdom* of God? After all, what does Prayer mean, boldly stated? It means that man thinks that he knows better than God, and so he tells God that which ought to happen. Is there any self-conceit so intolerable as that which pretends to bow itself in the dust before him who created and who upholds the infinite worlds which make up the universe, and which then sets itself to correct the ordering of him who traced the orbits of the planets, and who measured the rule of suns? Finite wisdom instructing infinite wisdom; mortal reason laying down the course of immortal reason; low intelligence guiding supreme intelligence; man instructing God. All this is implied in the fact of Prayer, and every man who has prayed, and who believes in God, ought to cast himself down in passionate humiliation before the wisdom he has insulted and impugned, and ask pardon for the insolent presumption which dared to lay hands on the helm of the Supreme, and to dream that man could be more wise than God. At least, those who believe in God might be humble enough to acknowledge his superiority to themselves, and if they demand that homage should be paid to him by their brethren, they should also confess him to be wiser and higher than they are themselves.

Is Prayer consistent with *trust in the goodness* of God? Surely Prayer is a distinct refusal to trust, and is a proclamation that we think that we could do better for ourselves than God will do for us. If God be "good and loving to every man," it is manifest that, without any pressure being put upon him, he will do for each the best thing that can possibly be done. The people of Madagascar are wiser, in this matter than the people who throng our churches and our chapels, for they say, addressing the good Spirit, "We need not pray to thee, for thou, without our prayers, wilt give us all things that be good for us;" and then they turn to the evil Spirit, saying, that they must pray to *him*, lest, if they do not, he should work them harm, and send troubles in their way. Prayer implies that God judges all good gifts, and will withhold them unless they are wrung from his reluctant hands; it denies that he loves his creatures, and is good to all. In addition to this, it also implies that we will not trust him to judge what is best for us; on the contrary, we prefer to judge for ourselves, and to have our own way. If a trouble comes, it is prayed against, and God is besought "to remove his heavy hand." What does this mean, except that when God sends sorrow, man clamours for joy, and when God deems it best that his child should weep, the child demands cause for smiles? If people trusted God, as they pretend to trust him—if the phrases of the Sunday were the practice of the week—if men believed that God's ways were higher than man's ways, and his thoughts than their thoughts—then no Prayer would ever ascend from earth to the "Throne of grace," and man would welcome joy and sorrow, peace and care, wealth and poverty, as wise men welcome nature's order, when the rain comes down to swell the seed for the harvest, and the sunshine glows down upon earth to burnish the golden grain.

But, say the praying Christians, even if Prayer be not defensible as homage from the creature to the Creator, in that it lowers our idea of God, it must surely yet be natural as the instinctive cry from the child to the Father in heaven; and then follow arguments drawn from the family and the home, and the need of communion between parent and child. As a matter of fact,—taking the analogy, imperfect as it is—do we find much Prayer, as from child to parent, in the best and the happiest homes; *is not the amount of asking the exact measure of the imperfection of the relationship?* The wiser and the kinder the parent, the less will the child ask for; rather, it learns from experience to trust the older wisdom, and to be contented with the love which is ever giving, unsolicited, all good things. At the most, the simple expression of the child's wish is all that is needed, if the child desire anything of which the parent have not thought; and even this mere statement of a wish is still the result of *imperfection*, *i.e.*, the want of knowledge on the parent's part of the child's mind and heart. In this case there is no pleading, no urging; the single request and single answer suffice; there is nothing which corresponds with the idea of the prophet to pray to God and to "give him no rest" until he grant the petition. In a well-ordered home, the child who persisted in pressing his request would receive a rebuke for his want of trust, and for his conceited self-sufficiency; and yet *this* is the analogy on which Prayer to God is built up, and in this fashion "natural instincts" are dragged in, in order to support supernatural and artificial cravings.

Leaving Prayer, as it affects man's relationship to God, let us look at it as it regards man's relationship to things around him, and ask if it be permitted by our scientific knowledge, and approved by experience and by history. The chief lesson of science is that all things work by law, that we dwell in a realm of law, and that *nothing* goes by chance. All science is built up upon this idea; science is not possible unless this primary rule be correct; science is only the codified experience of the race, the observed sequence of to-day marked down for the guidance of to-morrow, the teaching of the past hived up for the improvement of the future. But all this accumulation and correlation of facts becomes useless if laws can be broken—*i.e.*, if this observed sequence of phenomena can be suddenly broken by the interposition of an unknown and incalculable force, acting spasmodically and guided by no discoverable order of action. Science is impossible if these "providential occurrences" may take place at any moment. A physician, in writing his prescription, selects the drugs which experience has pointed out as the suitable remedy for the disease under which his patient is labouring. These drugs have a certain effect upon the tissues of the human frame, and the physician calculates on this effect being produced; but if Prayer is to come in as a factor, of what use the physician's science? Here is suddenly introduced—to speak figuratively—a new drug of unknown power, and the effect of medicine *plus* Prayer can in no way be calculated upon. The prescription is either efficient or non-efficient; if it be efficient, Prayer is unnecessary, as the cure would take place without it; if it be non-efficient, and Prayer makes up the deficiency, then medical science is not needed, for the impotency of the drugs can always be balanced by the potency of the Prayer. This argument may be used as regards every science. Prayer is put up for a ship which goes to sea. The ship is fitted for the perils it encounters, or it is unfit. If fitted, it arrives safely without Prayer; if, though unfit, it arrives, being guarded by Prayer, then Prayer becomes a factor in the ship-builder's calculations, and sound timbers and strong rivets sink into minor importance. If it be argued that to speak thus is to use Prayer unfairly, because it is our duty to take every proper means to ensure safety, what. is this except to say that, after all, Prayer is only a fiction, and that while we bow our knees to God, and pretend to look to *him* for safety, we are really looking to the strong timbers of the ship-builder, and to the skill of the captain?

Science teaches, also, that all phenomena are the results of preceding phenomena, and that an unbroken sequence of cause and effect stretches back further than our poor thoughts can reach. In stately harmony all Nature moves, evolving link after link of the endless chain, each link bound firmly to its predecessor, and affording, in its turn, the same support to its successor. Prayer is put up in the churches for fair weather; but rain and sunshine do not follow each other by chance, they obey a changeless law. To alter the weather of to-day means to alter the weather of countless yesterdays, which have faded away, one after another, "into the infinite azure of the past." The weather of to-day is the result of all those long-past phases of temperature, and, unless they were altered, no change is possible to-day. The Prayer that goes up in English churches should really run:—"O God, we pray thee to change all that thou hast wrought in the past; we, to-day, in this petty corner of thy world, are discontented with thy ordering; we desire of thee, then, that, to pleasure our fancy, thou wilt unroll the record of the past, and change all its order, remoulding its history to suit our convenience here to-day." It is difficult to say which is the worse, the self-conceit which deems its own petty needs worthy of such complaisance of Deity, or the ignorance which forgets the absurdities implied in the request it makes. But, after all, it is the ignorance which is to blame: these Prayers were written when science was scarcely born; in those days God was the immediate cause of each phenomena, sending rain from heaven when it pleased him, thundering from heaven against his enemies, pouring hailstones from heaven to slay his foes, opening and closing the windows of heaven to punish a wicked king or to pleasure an angry prophet. In those days heaven was very close to earth: so near that when it opened, the dying Stephen could see and recognise the form and features of the Son of Man; so near that, lest man should build a tower which should reach it, God had himself to descend and discomfit the builders. All these things were true to the writers whose words are repeated in English churches in the nineteenth century, and they naturally believed that what God wrought in days of old he could work also among themselves. But knowledge has shattered the fairy fabric which fancy had raised up; astronomy built towers—not of Babel—from which men could gauge the heaven, and find that through illimitable ether worlds innumerable rolled, and that where the throne of God should have been seen, suns and planets sped on their ceaseless rounds. Further and further back, the ancient God who dwelt among men was pressed back, till now, at last, no room is found for spasmodic divine solutions, but Nature's mighty order rolls on uninterrupted, in a silence unbroken by voice and undisturbed by miraculous volitions, bound by a golden chain of inviolable law. The most learned and the most thoughtful Christian people now acknowledge that prayer is out of place in dealing with "natural order;" but surely it is time that they should make their voices heard plainly, so as to erase from the Prayer-book these obsolete notions, born of an ignorance which the world has now outgrown. Few really *believe* in the power of Prayer over the weather, but people go on from the sheer force of habit, repeating, parrot-like, phrases which have lost their meaning, because they are too indolent to exert thought, or too fettered by habit to test the Prayer of the Sunday by the standard of the week. When people begin to *think* of what they repeat so glibly, the battle of Free Thought will have been won.

Many earnest people, however, while recognising the fact that Prayer ought not to be used for rain, fine weather, and the like, yet think that it may be rightly employed to obtain "spiritual benefits." Is not this idea also the product of ignorance? When men knew nothing of natural laws they thought they could gain natural benefits by Prayer; now that people know nothing of "spiritual" laws, they think they can gain "spiritual" benefits by Prayer. In each case the Prayer springs from ignorance. Is it really more reasonable to expect to gain miraculous spiritual strength from Prayer, than to expect to give vigour, by Prayer, to arms enfeebled by fever? Growth, slow and steady, is Nature's law; no sudden leaps are possible; and no Prayer will give that spiritual stature which only develops by continual effort, and by "patient continuance in well-doing." The mind—which is probably what is generally meant by the word "spirit"—has its own laws, according to which it grows and strengthens; it is moulded, formed, developed, as the body is, by the play of the circumstances around it, and by the organisation with which it comes into the world, and which it has inherited from a long race of ancestors. Here, too, inexorable law surrounds all, and in mind, as in matter, the "reign of law" is all-embracing, all-compelling.

Is Prayer approved by experience? It seems necessary here to refer to the experience of some, who say that they have found Prayer strengthen them to meet a trouble which they had dreaded, or to accomplish a duty for which their own ability was insufficient. This appears to be very probable, but the reason is not far to seek, and as the explanation of the increased strength may be purely natural, it seems unnecessary to search for a supernatural cause. Prayer, when earnest and heartfelt, appears to exert a kind of reflex action on the person praying, the petition not piercing heaven, but falling back upon earth. A duty has to be done or a trouble has to be faced; the person affected prays for help, and by the intense concentration of his thoughts, and by the passion of his desire, he naturally gains a strength he had not, when he was less deeply and thoroughly in earnest. Again, the interior conviction that a divine strength is on his side, nerves his heart and braces his courage: the soldier fights with a tenfold courage when he is sure that endurance will make victory a certainty. But all this is no proof that God hears and answers Prayer; if it were so, it would prove also that the Virgin Mother, and all the saints, and Buddha, and Brahma, and Vishnu were alike hearers and answerers of Prayer. In all cases the sincere worshipper gains strength and comfort, and finds the same "answer" to his Prayer. Yet surely no one will contend that *all* these are "Prayer-hearing and Prayer-answering" Gods? This fancied answer is not a proof of the truth of the worshipper's belief, but is only a proof *of his conviction of its truth;* not the soundness of the belief, but the sincerity of the conviction, is proved by the glow and ardour which succeed the act of Prayer. All the dormant energies are aroused; the soul's whole strength is put forth; the worshipper is warmed by the fire struck from his own heart, and is thrilled with the electricity which resides in his own frame. So far, Prayer is found to be answered, just as every strong conviction, however erroneous, is found to confer increased strength and vigour on him who possesses it. But, excepting this, Prayer is *not* proved to be efficacious when tested by experience. How many Prayers have gone up to the Father in heaven from his children overwhelmed in the sea, and drowning in floods, and encircled by fire? How many passionate appeals of patriots and martyrs, of exiles and of slaves? How many cries of anguish from beside the beds of the dying, and the fresh graves of the newly-dead? In vain the wife's wail for the husband, the mother's pleading for the only child; no voice has answered "Weep not;" no command has replied, "Rise up;" the Prayers have fallen back on the breaking heart, poor white-winged birds that have tried to fly towards heaven, but have only sunk back to earth, their breasts bruised and bleeding from striking against the iron bars of a pitiless and relentless fate. So continually has Prayer failed to win an answer, that, in spite of the clearness and the force of the Bible promises in regard to it, Christians have found themselves obliged to limit their extent, and to say that God judges whether or no it will be beneficial for the worshipper to grant the petition, and if the Prayer be a mistaken one he will, in mercy, withhold the implored-for boon. Of course, this prevents Prayer from being ever tested by experience at all, because whenever a Prayer remains unanswered the reply is ready, that "it was not according to the will of God." This means, that we cannot test the value of Prayer in any way; we must accept its worth wholly as a matter of faith; we must pray because we are bidden to do so, and fulfil an useless form which affords no tangible results. In this melancholy position are we landed by an appeal to experience, by which we are challenged to test the value of Prayer.

The answer of history is even yet more emphatic. The Ages of Prayer are the Dark Ages of the world. When learning was crushed out, and superstition was rampant, when wisdom was called witchcraft, and priests ruled Europe, then Prayer was always rising up to God from the countless monasteries where men dwarfed themselves into monks, and from the convents where women shrivelled up into nuns. The sound of the bell that called to Prayer was never silent, and the time that was needed for work was wasted in Prayer, and in the straining to serve God the service of man was neglected and despised.

There is one obvious fact that throws into bright relief the absurdity of Prayer. Two people pray for exactly opposite things; whose Prayers are to be answered? Two armies ask for victory; which is to be crowned? Amongst ourselves, now, the Church is divided into two opposing camps, and while the Ritualists appeal to God for protection, the Evangelical clamour also for his aid. To which is he to bend his ear? which Prayer is he to answer? Both appeal to his promises; both urge that his honour is pledged to them by the word he has given; yet it is simply impossible that he should grant the Prayer of both, because the Prayer of the one is the direct contradiction of the prayer of the other.

Again, none of the believers in Prayer appear to consider, that, if it were true that Prayer is so powerful a weapon—if it were true that by Prayer man can prevail with God—it would then be madness ever to pray at all. To pray would be as dangerous a thing as to put a cavalry sword into the hands of a child just strong enough to lift it, but unable to control it, or to understand the danger of its blows. Who can tell all the results to himself and to others which might flow from a granted Prayer, a Prayer made in all honesty of purpose, but in ignorance and short-sightedness? If Prayers really brought answers it would be most wickedly reckless ever to pray at all, as wickedly reckless as if a man, to quench a moment's thirst, pierced a hole in a reservoir of water which overhung a town.

But, in spite of all arguments, in spite of all that reason can urge and that logic can prove, it is probable that many will still cling to the practice of Prayer, craving for the relief it gives to the feelings of the heart, however much it may be condemned by the judgment of the intellect. They seem to think that they will lose a great inspiration to work if they give up "communion with God," and that they will miss the glow of ardour which they deem they have caught from Prayer. But surely it may fairly be urged on them that no real good can arise from continuing a practice which it is impossible to defend when it is carefully analysed. Prayer is as the artificial stimulant which excites, but does not strengthen, and lends a factitious brightness, which is followed by deeper depression. Those who have prayed most have often stated that "seasons of special blessing" are generally followed by "special temptations of Satan." The reaction follows on the unreal excitation, and the soul that has been flying in heaven grovels upon earth. To the patient who is weak and depressed from long illness, the bright air of the morning seems chill and cold, and he yearns for the warmth of the artificial stimulants to which he has grown accustomed; yet better for him is it to gain health from the morning breezes, and stimulus from the glad clear sunshine, than to yield to the craving which is a relic of his disease. If they who find in communion with God a sweetness which is lacking when they commune with their brethren—if they who cultivate dependence on God would learn the true dependence of man on man—if they who yearn for the invisible would concentrate their energies on the visible—then they would soon find a sweetness in labour which would compensate for the languor of Prayer, and they would learn to draw from the joy of serving men, and from the serene strength of an earnest life, a warmth of inspiration, a passion of fervour, an exhaustless fount of energy, beside which all Prayer-given ardour would seem dull and nerveless, in the glow of which the fancied warmth of God-communion would seem as the pale cold moonshine in the glory of the rising sun.

CONSTRUCTIVE RATIONALISM.

IT is a common complaint against the Rationalistic school of thought that they can destroy but cannot construct; that they tear down, but do not build up; that they are armed only with the axe and with the sword, and not with the trowel and the mason's line. "We have had enough of negations," is a common cry; "give us something positive." Much of this feeling is foolish and unreasonable; the negation of error, where error is supreme, is necessary before the assertion of truth can become possible. Before a piece of ground can be sown with wheat, it must be cleared of the weeds which infest it; before a solid house can be built in the place of a crumbling ruin, the ancient rubbish must be carried off, and the rotten walls must be thoroughly pulled down. Destructive criticism is necessary and wholesome; the heavy battering-ram of science must thunder against the walls of the churches; the swift arrows of logic must rain on the black-robed army; the keen lance-points of irony must pierce through the leather jerkin of superstition. But the destruction of orthodox Christianity being accomplished, there remains for the Rationalist much more to do. He has to frame a code which shall rule in the place of the code of Moses and of Jesus; he has to found a morality which shall replace the morality of the Bible; he has to construct an ideal which shall be as attractive as the ideal of the Churches; he has to proclaim laws which shall supersede revelation: in a word, he has to build up the religion of humanity.

As the Rationalist looks abroad over the contending armies of faith and of reason, he gradually recognises the fact that his new religion, if it is to serve as a bond of union, must stand on stable ground, apart from the warring hosts. Round the idea of God rages the hottest din of the battle. The old, popular, and traditional belief is wounded to the death, and is slowly breathing out its life. The philosophical subtleties of the metaphysician are beyond the grasp of folk busied chiefly with common work. The new school of Theists, believers in a "spiritual personal God," stands on a slippery incline, whereon is no firm foothold. It simply spreads over the abysses of thought a sentimental veil of poetical imaginings, and bows down before a beatified and celestial man, whose image it has sculptured out of the thought-marble of its sublimest aspirations. If the idea of God be thus warred over, thus changing, thus uncertain, it is plain that the new religion cannot find its foundation on this shifting and disputed ground. While theologians are wrangling about God, plain men are looking wistfully over the shattered idols to find the ideal to which they can cling. The new religion, then, studying the varying phases of the God-idea, seizes on its one permanent element, its idealised resemblance to man, its embodiment of the highest humanity; and, grasping this thought, it turns to men and says, "In loving God you are only loving your own highest selves; in conforming yourselves to the Divine image you are only conforming yourselves to your own highest ideals; the unknown God whom you ignorantly worship, him declare I unto you; in serving your family, your neighbours, your country, you serve this unknown God; this God is Humanity, the race to which you belong; this is the veiled God whom all generations have worshipped in heaven, while he trod the world around them in every human form; this is the only God, the God who is manifest in the flesh:"—

> "There is no God, O son,
> If thou be none."

The first great constructive effort of the new religion is thus to transform the idea of God, and to turn all men's aspirations, all men's hopes, all men's labours, into this channel of devotion to humanity, that so the practical outcome of the new motive power may be a steady flow of loving and energetic work for man, work that begins in the family, and spreads, in ever-widening circles, over the whole race.

This transformation of the central figure necessarily transforms also the whole idea of religion, which must take its colour from that centre. Revelation from heaven being no longer possible, its place must be supplied by study on earth: revealed laws being no longer attainable, it becomes the duty of the Humanitarian to discover natural laws. This duty is the more cheering from the manifest failure of revealed laws, as exemplified in popular Christianity. "Law," in the mouth of the believer in revelation, means a command issued by God; the "laws of Nature" are the rules laid down by God, in accordance with which all things move; they are the behests of the Creator of Nature, the controlling wires of the mechanism, held by the hand of God. But "law" in the mouth of the Rationalist means nothing more than the observed and registered invariable sequence of events. Thus it is said "a stone falls to the ground in obedience to the law of gravitation." By the "law of gravitation" the Christian would mean that God had ordered that all stones *should* so fall. The Rationalist would simply mean that all stones *do* so fall, and that invariable sequence he calls the "law of gravitation." Obedience to the laws of Nature replaces, in the religion of Humanity, obedience to the laws of God. As there is no inspired revelation of these laws the student must carefully and patiently ascertain them, either by direct observation, or most often, in the books of those who have devoted their lives to the elucidation of Nature's code. Scientific books will, in fact, replace the Bible, and by the study of the laws of health, both physical, moral, and mental, the Rationalist will ascertain the conditions which surround him to which he must conform himself if he desires to retain physical, moral, and mental vigour. This difference in the authority which is obeyed leads naturally to the difference of morality between the orthodox Christian and the Rationalist. Christian morality consists of obedience to the will of God, as revealed in the Bible. The grand difficulty regarding this obedience is, that the will of Jehovah, as revealed to the Jews at different times, varies so much from age to age that the most zealous Christian must fail to obey all the conflicting behests prefaced by a "Thus saith the Lord." God would, of course, never command any one to do a thing which was directly wrong, yet God distinctly said: "Thou shalt not suffer a Witch to live;" and God sanctioned Slavery, and God commanded Persecution on account of religious convictions: true, Christians plead that all these laws are obsolete, but what is that but to acknowledge that revealed morality is obsolete, *i.e.*, that it was never revealed by God at all. For a command to persecute must be either right or wrong: if right, it is the duty of Christians to obey it, and to raise once more the stakes of Smithfield for heretics and unbelievers; if wrong, it can never have come from God at all, and must be blasphemously attributed to him. In God, Christians tell us there is no changeableness, neither shadow of turning; then what pleased him in long past ages would please him still, and what he commanded yesterday would be right to-day. Thus fatally does revealed morality fail when tested, and it becomes impossible to know which particular "will of God" he desires that we should obey. Now, once more, the Rationalist experiences the advantages of his new motive-power; he has to serve Humanity, and is unencumbered by the difficulties attendant upon "pleasing God." Not the pleasure of God, but the benefit of man, is the basis of his morality. Revealed morality is as a child's garment, into which one should try to force the limbs of a full-grown man; it is the morality of the past stereotyped for the use of to-day, and is clumsy, archaic, half-illegible from age. Rational morality, on the other hand, grows with the growth of those who follow its dictates; its errors are corrected by wider experience, its omissions are filled up by the irrefragable arguments of necessity. It is founded upon the needs of man; his happiness is its sole object; not only his physical happiness, not only the fulfilment of the desires of the body for ease and comfort, but the satisfaction also of all the cravings of his intellectual and moral powers, the love of truth, the love of beauty, the love of justice. A morality founded on this basis can never be overthrown; one sure test it affords whereby to decide on the morality or the immorality of any given action: "Is it useful to man? does it tend to the promotion of human happiness?" The will of God is doubtful, and is always disputable, and therefore it can never form the foundation of a universal system of morality, a code which shall unite all men in obedience. A code which shall unite all men must needs be founded on those human interests which are common to all men. Such a code is the utilitarian. For man's happiness is on earth, and can be known and understood; the promotion of that happiness is an intelligible aim; the test of morality may be applied by every one; it is a system which everybody can understand, and which the common sense of each must approve, for by it man lives for man, man labours for man, the efforts of each are directed to the good of all, and only in the happiness of the whole can the happiness of each part be perfected and complete.

There is much popular misconception with regard to utilitarianism: "utility" is supposed to include only those material things which are useful to the body, and which tend to increase physical comfort. But utility includes all art; for art cultures the taste and refines the nature. It thus adds a thousand charms to life, deepens, softens, purifies human happiness. Utility includes all study, for study awakens and trains the intellectual faculties, and therefore increases the sources of happiness possible to man. Utility includes all science; for science is man's true providence, foreseeing the dangers that threaten him, and shielding him against their shock. Science leads man up to those intellectual heights where to stand awhile and breathe in the keen, clear air after dwelling in the turbid atmosphere of daily toils and cares, is as the refreshment of the pure mountain wind to the weary inhabitant of the crowded city streets. Utility includes all love and search of truth; for the discovery of a truth is the keenest pleasure of which the noblest mind is susceptible. It includes all sublimest virtue; for self-sacrifice and devotion yield the purest forms of happiness to be found on earth. In a word, utility includes everything which is *useful* in building up a grander manhood and womanhood, wiser, purer, truer, tenderer than that we have to-day.

Such is the basis of the morality which is to supersede the supernatural morality of the Churches; a morality which is for this life and for this world, since we have this life, and are in this world; a morality which seeks to ensure human happiness on this side the grave, instead of dreaming of it on the other side; a morality which endeavours to carve solid heavens here, instead of seeing them in distant cloud-lands, white and soft and beautiful, but still only clouds.

One vast advantage of this humanitarian philosophy is that it endeavours to train men into unselfishness, instead of following the popular Christian plan of making self the central thought. Self is appealed to at every step in the New Testament: if we are bidden to rejoice under persecution, it is because "great is your reward in heaven;" if urged to pray, it is because "thy Father, which seeth in secret, himself shall reward thee openly;" if to be charitable, it is because at the judgment it will bring a kingdom as the recompense; if to resign home or wealth, it is because we shall receive "a hundredfold in this present life, and in the world to come life everlasting;" even the giver of a cup of cold water "shall in no wise lose his reward." It is one system of bribes, mingling the thought of personal pain with every effort of human improvement and human happiness, and thereby directly fostering and encouraging sefishness and gilding it over with the name of religion and piety. Humanitarian morality, on the other hand, while utilising the natural and rightful craving for individual happiness as a motive-power, endeavours to accustom each to look to, and to labour for, the happiness of all, making that general happiness the aim of life. Thus it gradually weakens the selfish tendencies and encourages the social, holding up ever the noble ideal by the very contemplation of its beauty transforming its votaries into its likeness. "Vivre pour autrui," is the motto of the utilitarian code; and in so living the fullest and happiest life for self is really attained; so closely drawn are the bands that bind men together that happiness and unhappiness re-act from one to another, and as the general standard of happiness rises higher and higher, the wheels of social life run more aud more easily, with less of friction, less of jar, and therefore with increased comfort to each individual member. While Christianity developes selfishness by its continual cry of "Save thyself," Utilitarianism gradually developes unselfishness by the nobler whisper, "Save others, and in so doing thou shalt thyself be saved." Delivered from every debasing fear of an unknowable and inscrutable power, Utilitarianism works with a single heart and a single eye for the happiness of the race, stamping with the brand of "wrong" every act the general repetition of which would be harmful to society, or the tendency of which is injurious, and sealing as "right" every act which brightens human life, and makes the general happiness more perfect, and more widely spread. As morality rises higher and higher, human judgment will grow keener and purer, and in the times to come probably many an act now approved on all sides will be seen to be harmful, and will therefore become marked as immoral, while, on the other hand, acts that are now considered wrong, because "offensive to God," will be seen to be beneficial to man, and will therefore be accepted by all as moral. Thus Utilitarian morality can never be a bar to progress, for it will become higher and nobler as man mounts upwards. Revealed morality is as a milestone on the road of the world's onward march: it marks how far the world had travelled when its tables of law were first set up in its place: *as a milestone*, it is useful, interesting, and instructive, and none would desire to destroy it; but if the milestone be removed from its post as a mark of distance, and be laid across the road as a barrier which none must overclimb in days to come, then it becomes necessary for the pioneers of progress to hew it to pieces that men may go on their way unchecked, and this revealed morality now lies across the upward path of the world, and must be broken in pieces with the hammer of logic and the axe of common sense, so that we may press ever higher up the mountain of progress, whose summit is hid in everlasting cloud.

And what has constructive Rationalism to say to us, when we stand face to face with the mighty destroyer of all living things? "Your creed may do well enough to live by," say objectors, "but is it good to die by?" A creed that is good in life must needs be good in death, and never yet was a hero-life closed by a coward death. What can better smooth the bed of the dying man than the knowledge that the world is the happier for his living, that he leaves it better than he found it, that he has helped to raise and to purify it? What easier pillow to rest the dying head on than the memory of a useful life? The Rationalist has no fear lurking around his death-bed; no lurid gleams from a hell on the other side lighten around him as his breath begins to fail; no angry God frowns on him from the great white throne; no devil stands beside him to drag him down into the bottomless pit; quietly, peacefully, happily, without fear and without dread, he passes out of life. As calmly as the tired child lies down to sleep in its mother's arms, and passes into dreamless unconsciousness, so calmly does the Rationalist lie down in the arms of the mighty mother, and pass into dreamless unconsciousness on her bosom.

To the Rationalist, the future of the race replaces in thought the future of the individual; for that he thinks, for that he plans, for that he labours. A heaven upon earth for those who come after him, such is his inspiration to effort and to self-devotion. He seeks the smile of man instead of the smile of God, and finds in the thought of a happier humanity the spur that Christians seek in the thought of pleasing God. His hopes for the future spread far and wide before him, but it is a future to be inherited by his children in this same world in which he himself lives; freer and fuller life, wider knowledge, deepened and more polished culture—all these are to be the heritage of the generations to come, and it is his to make that heritage the richer by every grander thought and nobler deed that he can do to-day.

Let us place side by side the dogmas of Christianity and the motive power of the Rationalist, and see which of these two is the gladder life-moulder of man. Christianity has a God in heaven, all powerful and all-wise, who in ages gone by made the universe and fore-ordained all that should happen in time to come; who created man and woman with a serpent to tempt them, and made for them the opportunity of falling; who, having made the opportunity, forced them to take it. It is said that Adam and Eve were free agents, but they were nothing of the kind, for the lamb was slain from the foundation of the world: the sacrifice was offered before the sin was committed; and the sacrifice being made, the sin was its necessary consequence. If Adam had been free, he might not have sinned, and then there would have been a slain lamb and no sin for which he could atone; but God, having provided the Saviour, was obliged to provide the sinner, and therefore he made the tree of knowledge and sent the tempter to entrap the parents of mankind. They fell, according to God's predestination, and thus became accursed, and then the waiting Redeemer was revealed, and "the divine scheme" was complete. Accursed for a sin in which they had no part, the children of Adam are born with an evil nature, and being evil they act evilly, and thereby sink lower and lower; at their feet yawns a bottomless pit, and the road to it is broad, easy, and pleasant; above their heads shines a luxurious heaven, and the path is narrow, steep, and rugged. Their nature—God-given to all—drags them downwards; the Holy Ghost—God given to some—drags them upwards: immortality is their inheritance, and "few there be that find" immortal happiness, while "many there be that go in" at the gate of hell to immortal woe; a severance, bitter beyond all earthly bitterness of parting, is in store for all, since, at the great day of judgment, "one shall be taken and the other left," and there will not be a family some of whose members will not be lost for ever. Eternal life, to the vast majority, is to mean eternal torment, and they are to be "salted with fire," burning yet never burnt up, consuming ever but never consumed. Towards the gaining of heaven, towards the avoidance of hell, all human effort must be turned. "What shall it profit a man if he gain the whole world, and lose his own soul?" All life must be one striving "to enter in at the strait gate, for many shall seek to enter in and shall not be able;" poverty, oppression, misery, what matters it? the "light affliction which is but for a moment worketh a far more exceeding and eternal weight of glory." Thus this world is forgotten for the sake of another, crushed out of sight beneath the overwhelming grandeur of eternity; the spur to human effort is blunted by the infinitessimal importance of time as compared with eternity; bad government, bad laws, injustice, tyranny, pauperism, misery, all these things need not move us, for "we seek a better country, that is a heavenly;" we are "strangers and pilgrims;" "here we have no continuing city, but we seek one to come;" "our citizenship is in heaven," and there also is our home. True, Christians do not carry out into daily life these phrases and thoughts of their creed, but in so much as they do not they are the less Christian, and the more imbued with the spirit of Rationalism. Rationalists they are, the vast majority, six days in the week, and are only Christians on the Sunday. To come out of these old world dreams into Rationalism is like coming into the open air after a hothouse. Rationalism clears away the terrible God of orthodoxy, the fall, the serpent, the Saviour, the hell, the devil. "Work, toil, struggle," it cries to man; "the ills around you are not the appointment of God, not the effects of his curse; they arise from your own ignorance, and may all be cleared away by your own study, and your own effort. Salvation? Yes, you need saviours, but the saviours must save you from earthly woes and not from the wrath of God; save yourselves, by thought, by wisdom, by earnestness. Redemption? yes, you need redeeming, but the redemption you want is from vice, from ignorance, from poverty, and must be wrought out by human effort. Prayer? yes, you need praying for, but the prayer you want is work compelling the result; not crying out for what you desire, but winning it by labour and by toil. The world stretches wide before you, capable of paying you a thousandfold for all you do for it. Life is in your hands, full of all glorious possibilities; throw away your dreams of heaven, and make heaven here; leave aside visions of the life to come, and make beautiful the life which is."

Full of hope, full of joy, strong to labour, patient to

endure, mighty to conquer, goes forth the new glad creed into the sad grey Christian world; at her touch men's faces soften and grow purer, and women's eyes smile instead of weeping; at last, at last, the heir arises to take to himself his own, and the negation of the usurped sovereignty of the popular and traditional God over the world developes into the affirmation of the rightful monarchy of man.

THE

BEAUTIES OF THE PRAYER-BOOK.

MORNING PRAYER.

"HABIT is second nature," saith a wise old saw, so it must be from custom that it has become natural to Church people to repeat placidly, week after week, the same palpable self-contradictions and absurdities. A sensible, shrewd man of business puts away his papers on the Saturday night, and apparently locks his mind up with them in his desk; certain it is that he

> "Goes on Sunday to the church,
> And sits among his boys;
> He hears the parson pray and preach,"

and yet never discovers that his boys are repeating the most contradictory responses, while the parson is enunciating as axioms the most startling propositions.

When the preliminary silence in church is broken by the "sentences," the first words that fall from the clergyman's lips are a distinct declaration of the conditions of salvation: "When the wicked man turneth away from his wickedness that he hath committed, and doeth that which is lawful and right, he shall save his soul alive;" and we are further instructed as to our sins, that "if we confess our sins, He is faithful and just to forgive us our sins, and to cleanse us from all unrighteousness." These very plain statements take high and comprehensible ground. God is supposed to desire that man should be righteous, and is, therefore, naturally satisfied when "the wicked forsakes his way and the unrighteous man his path." We proceed, then, to confess our sins, and after Mrs. A., whose eyes are straying after her neighbour's bonnet, has confessed that she is erring and straying like a lost sheep, and Mrs. B., who is devising a way to make an old dress look new, has owned plaintively that she is following the devices of her own heart; and Squire C., of the rubicund visage and broad shoulders, has sonorously remarked that there is no health in him, and his son, with the joyous face, has cheerfully acknowledged that he is a miserable sinner—after these very appropriate and reasonable confessions to a Divine Being who "seeth the heart," and may therefore be supposed to take them for what they are worth, have been duly gone through, we are somewhat puzzled to hear the clergyman announce that God "pardoneth and absolveth all them that truly repent, *and unfeignedly believe His holy Gospel.*" What is this sudden appendix to the before-declared conditions of salvation? We had been told that if we confessed our sins God's faithfulness and justice would cause him to forgive us; here we have duly done so, and surely the language is sufficiently strong; we are yet suddenly called upon to believe a "holy Gospel" as a preliminary to forgiveness. But we are not yet, to use a colloquialism, out of the wood; for while we are moodily meditating on this infraction of our contract the time slips on unobserved, and, it being a feast-day, we are startled by a stern voice conveying the cheerful intelligence, "Whosoever will be saved, *before all things*, it is necessary that he hold the Catholic Faith. Which Faith except every one do keep whole and undefiled, without doubt he shall perish everlastingly." "Before all things?" before repentance? before turning away from our wickedness? before doing that which is lawful and right? And what is this "Faith" which we must keep whole and undefiled if we would save our souls alive? A bewildering jumble of triplets and units, mingled in inextricable confusion. But as he that "will be saved must thus think of the Trinity," we will try and disentangle the thread of salvation. "The Father is God, the Son is God, and the Holy Ghost is God," says the parson. "They are not three Gods, but one God," shout out the people. We are compelled "to acknowledge every Person by Himself to be God and Lord," reiterates the parson. "We are forbidden by the Catholic Religion to say there be three Gods or three Lords," obstinately persist the people. Then, after some rather intrusive particulars about the family (and very intricate) relations of the Father to the Son, and of both to the Holy Ghost, we are told that "so"—why *so?*—"there is one Father, not three

Fathers, one Son, not three Sons, one Holy Ghost, not three Holy Ghosts." In so far as we have been able to follow the meaning, or rather the no-meaning, of the preceding sentences, no one said anything about three Fathers, three Sons, or three Holy Ghosts. The definite article *the* had been used in each case with a singular noun. We imagine the clause must have been inserted because all ideas as to the meaning of numerals must have been by this time so hopelessly lost by the congregation, that it became necessary to remark that "the Father" meant one Father, and not three. The list of necessaries for salvation is not yet complete, for "furthermore it is necessary to everlasting salvation, that he also believe rightly the Incarnation of our Lord Jesus Christ." So far, then, from its being true that the wicked man who turns from his sins shall save his soul alive, we find that our sinner must also believe the Gospel, must accept contradictory arithmetical assertions, must think of the Trinity in a way which makes thought a ludicrous impossibility, and must believe *rightly* all the details of the method by which a Divine Being became a human being. If a sinner chances to go out of church after the first sentence, and from being a drunkard becomes temperate, from being a liar becomes truthful, from being a profligate becomes chaste, and foolishly imagines that he is thereby doing God's will, and thus saving his soul alive, he will certainly, according to the Athanasian Creed, wake up from his pleasant delusion to find himself in everlasting fire. As sceptics, we need offer no opinion as to *which* is right, the creed or the text; we only suggest that *both* cannot be correct, and that it would be more satisfactory if the Church, in her wisdom, would make up her venerable mind which is the proper path, and then keep in it. After all this, we are in no way surprised to learn from a collect that being saved is dependent on quite a new support, namely, on the knowledge we have of God. How many more things may be necessary to salvation it is impossible to say at this point, but the office for Morning Prayer, at any rate, gives us no more. It would be rash to conclude, however, that we have fulfilled all, for the Church has some more scattered up and down her Prayer-Book; the end of all which double-dealing is, that we can never be sure that we have really fulfilled every condition; sad experience teaches us that when the Church says, "do so-and-so, and you shall be saved," she is, meanwhile, whispering under her breath, "provided you also do everything else."

We fail also to see the reasonableness of the constant cry, "for the sake of Jesus Christ," or "through Jesus Christ." We ask that we may lead "a godly, righteous, and sober life" *for His sake;* but this is just what we are told God wishes already, so why should He be asked to grant it for some one else's sake, as though He were unwilling that we should be righteous, and can only be coaxed into allowing us to be so by a favourite son? In the same way we are to come to God's "eternal joy," through Jesus, which is, by the way, another of these endless conditions of salvation. We ask to be defended from our enemies "through the might of Jesus Christ," as though God Himself was not strong enough for the task; and God is urged to send down His healthful Spirit for the "honour of our advocate and Mediator," although that very advocate told His disciples that God would always give that spirit to those who asked for it. To the outside critic, these continual references to Jesus, as though God grudged all good gifts, appear very dishonouring to the "Father in Heaven."

Is it considered necessary to press God vehemently to hurry himself? "O God, *make speed* to save us. O Lord, *make haste* to help us." Will not God, of his own accord, do things at the best possible time? and further, is it possible for a Divine Being to make haste?

It will, perhaps, be considered hypercritical to object to the versicles: "Give peace in our time, O Lord, *because* there is none other that fighteth for us but only thou, O God." What more do they want than an almighty reinforcement? "None other?" Well, we should have fancied that God *and* somebody else were really more than were needed. At any rate it sounds very insulting to say to God, "please give us peace, since we cannot count on any assistance except yours."

We have nothing to say about the prayers for the Royal Family, except that they do not show any very attractive results, and that it must have much edified George IV. to hear himself spoken of as a "most religious and gracious king." Never surely was a family so much prayed for, but *cui bono?* If the "Bishops, Curates, and all congregations" truly please God, he is about the only person that they succeed in pleasing, for the Bishops abuse the clergy, and the clergy abuse the Bishops, and the congregations abuse both. Of the last prayer, we must note the exceeding failure of the petition to grant the Church knowledge of truth, and we cannot help marvelling why, if they really desire to know the truth, they so invariably frown at and endeavour to crush out every earnest search after truth, every effort for clearer light. Of all things that can happen to the Church, the knowledge of the truth would be the least "expedient for" her, for she would fade away before the sunshine of truth as ghosts are said to fly at the cock-crow which announces the dawn.

A criticism on the office of Morning Prayer is scarcely complete without a few words upon the canticles appointed to be daily sung by the faithful to the glory of God. Any thing more ludicrously absurd than these from the lips of our congregations it would indeed be difficult to imagine. The *Venite* (Ps. xcv.) is the first we are called upon to take part in, and the first shock comes when we find ourselves chanting "The Lord is a great God and a *great king above all gods.*" "Above all Gods!" what terrible heresy have we been unwittingly committing ourselves to? Is there not only one God—or, at least, it may be three—but, if three, they are co-equal, and no one is above the other; who are these "all gods" that "the Lord" is "king above?" We remember for a moment that when this psalm was written the gods of the nations around Israel were believed to have a real existence, and that, therefore, it was no inconsistency in the mouth of the Hebrew to rejoice that his national god was ruler above the gods of other peoples. This explanation is reasonable, but then it does not explain why we, who believe not in this multiplicity of deities should pretend that we do. Our equanimity is not restored by the next phrase, "In his hand are all the corners of the earth;" but the earth is a globe, and has no corners. A misty remembrance floats through our mind of Iræneus stating that there were four gospels because there were four corners to the earth and four winds that blew; but since his time things have changed, and the corners have been smoothed off. Is it quite honest to say in God's praise a thing which we know to be untrue, and must we be unscientific because we are devotional? We then hear about our fathers being forty years in the wilderness, although we know that they were not there at all, unless the people—generally looked upon as amiable lunatics—are correct, who assert that the English nation is descended from the ten lost tribes of Israel. Why should we pretend to God that we are Jews, when both He and we know perfectly well that we are nothing of the kind? We come to the *Te Deum*, said to have been composed by S. Ambrose for the baptism of S. Augustine:—"To thee cherubin and seraphin continually do cry." Putting aside the manifest weariness both to God and to the cryers of the never-ceasing repetition of these words, and the degrading idea of God implied in the thought that it gives Him any pleasure to be perpetually assured of His holiness, as though it were a doubtful matter—we cannot help inquiring, "Who are these cherubin and seraphin?" According to the Bible, they are six-winged creatures, who cover their faces with two wings, and their feet with two more, and fly with the remaining pair: they may be seen in pictures of the ark, balancing themselves on their feet-covering wings, and preventing themselves from falling by steadying each other with another pair. "Lord God of Sabaoth," or of "Hosts;" is this a reasonable name for one supposed to be a "God of peace?" The elder Jewish and the Christian ideas of God here come into direct collision: according to one, "the Lord is a man of war" (Ex. xv.), while the other represents him as "the Everlasting Father, the Prince of Peace" (Isai. ix.). The *Te Deum* midway changes the object of its song, and addresses itself to the Son instead of to the Father. How far this is permissible is much disputed, for certain it is that in the early ages of Christianity prayer was addressed to the Father *only*, and that one of the Fathers* sharply rebukes those who pray to the Son, since they thereby deprive the Father of the honour due to Him alone. How this can be, when Father and Son are one, we do not pretend to explain. Then ensue those curious details regarding Christ which we shall touch upon in dealing later with the Apostles' Creed. We find ourselves, presently, asking to be kept "this day without sin;" yet, we are perfectly well aware, all the time, that God will do nothing of the kind, and that all Christians believe that they sin every day. Why does the Church teach her children to sing this in the morning, and then prepare a "confession" for the evening, unless she feels perfectly sure that God will pay no attention to her prayer? The wearisome reiteration in the *Benedicite* is so thoroughly recognised that it is very seldom heard in the church, while the *Benedictus* (Luke i.) is open to the same charge of unreality as is the *Venite*, that it is a song for

* Origen.

Jews only. Many other faults and absurdities might be pointed out which disfigure Morning Prayer, even if the whole idea of prayer be left untouched. The prayers of the Prayer-Book are dishonouring to God from their childishness, their unreality, their folly, their conflict with sound knowledge. Allowing that prayer may be reasonable, these prayers are unreasonable; allowing that prayer may be reverent, these prayers are irreverent; allowing that prayer may be sincere, these prayers are insincere. They are fragments of an earlier age transplanted into the present, and they are as ludicrous as would be men walking about in our streets to-day clad in the armour of the Middle Ages, the ages of Darkness and of Prayer.

EVENING PRAYER.

The Church, in her wisdom, fearing that the quaint conceits and impossibilities which we have referred to, the—

> "Jewels which adorn the spouse
> Of the eternal glorious King,"

should not be sufficiently appreciated and admired by her children, if presented to their adoration once only on every day, has appointed for the use of the faithful an office of Evening Prayer, which, in its main features, is identical with that which is to be "said or sung" each morning. Sentences, address, confession, absolution, Lord's Prayer, and versicles, are all exactly reproduced, and Psalms and Lessons follow in due course, varying from day to day. To take the whole Psalter, and analyse it, would be a task too long for our own patience, or for that of our readers, so we only pick out a few salient absurdities, and ask why English men and women should be found singing sentences which have no beauty to recommend them, and no meaning to dignify them. We will not lay stress on the quaintness of a congregation standing up and gravely singing: "Or ever your pots be made hot with thorns, so let indignation vex him, even as a thing that is raw" (Ps. lviii.); we will not ask what the clergyman means when he reads out to his congregation: "Though ye have lien among the pots, yet shall ye be as the wings of a dove." (Ps. lxviii.) These are isolated passages, which a pen might erase, retaining the major part of the Psalter: we go further, and challenge it as a whole, asserting that it is ludicrously inappropriate as a song-book for sensible people, even although those people may be desirous of praying to, or praising God. Our strictures are here levelled, not at prayer *as* prayer, but simply at this particular form of prayer. In the first place the Psalter is written only for a single nation; it is full of local allusions, and of references of Israelitish history, which are only reasonable in the mouth of a Jew. With what amount of sense can an English congregation every 15th evening of the month sing such a Psalm as the lxxviii., recounting all the marvels of the plagues and of the exodus, or on the following day plead with God to help them, because "the heathen are come into Thine inheritance; Thy holy temple have they defiled, and made Jerusalem an heap of stones?" (Ps. lxxix.) Is there any respect to God in telling him that "we are become an open shame to our enemies; a very scorn and derision unto them that are round about us" (*v.* 4), when, as a matter of simple fact, the speakers are become nothing of the kind? Can it be thought to be consistent with reverence to God to make these extraordinary assertions in praying to Him, and then to base upon them the most urgent pleas for His immediate aid? for we find the congregation proceeding: "Help us, O God of our salvation, for the glory of Thy Name; O deliver us and be merciful unto our sins for Thy Name's sake. . . . O let the vengeance of Thy servant's blood which is shed be openly shewed upon the heathen in our sight. O let the sorrowful sighing of the prisoners come before Thee; according to the greatness of Thy power, preserve Thou those that are appointed to die" (*vv.* 9, 10, 11). Now in all sober seriousness what does this mean? Is this addressed to God, or is it not? If it be, is it right and fit to address to him words that are absolutely untrue, and to cry urgently for aid which is not required, and which He cannot possibly give? If it be not, is it decent to solemnly sing or read phrases seemingly addressed to God, but really not intended to be noticed by him, phrases which use His name as though an appeal to Him were seriously made? It cannot be healthy to juggle thus with words, and to make emotional prayers which are utterly devoid of all meaning. Some devout persons talk very freely about the wickedness of blasphemy, but is not that kind of game with God, in wailings which are devoid of reality, appeals not intended to be answered, a far more real blasphemy in the mouth of any one who believes in Him as a hearer of prayer, than the so-called blasphemy of those who distinctly assert that to them the popular and traditional "God" is a phantom, and that they see no reason to believe in His existence? Passing from this graver aspect of the use of the Psalter as a congregational song-book, we notice how purely comic many of the psalms would appear to us had not the habit-fashion of our lives accustomed us to repeat them in a parrot-like manner, without attaching the smallest meaning to the words so glibly recited. "Every night wash I my bed and water my couch with my tears" (Ps. vi.), is sung innocently by laughing maiden and merry youth, the bright current of whose life is undimmed by the shadow of grief. "Bring unto the Lord, O ye mighty, bring young rams unto the Lord" (Ps. xxix.), is solemnly read out by the country clergyman, who would be beyond measure astonished if his direction were complied with. Then we find the congregation making the certainly untrue assertion: "Moab is my wash-pot; over Edom will I cast out my shoe; Philistia, be thou glad of me" (Ps. lx.). At another time they cry out, "O, clap your hands together, all ye people" (Ps. xlvii.); they speak of processions which have no existence, "The singers go before, the minstrels follow after, in the midst are the damsels playing on the timbrels" (Ps. lxviii.). Another phase of this Psalter, which is offensive rather than comic, is the habit of swearing and cursing which pervades it; we find Christians, who are bidden to love their enemies, and to bless them that curse them, pouring out curses of the most fearful character, and displaying the most reckless hatred: "The righteous shall rejoice when he seeth the vengeance; he shall wash his footsteps in the blood of the ungodly" (Ps. lviii.). "Let them fall from one wickedness into another, and not come into Thy righteousness" (Ps. lxix.). A nice prayer, truly, for one man to pray for his brother man, to a holy God who is supposed to desire righteousness in man. Then there is that fearful imprecation in Psalm cix., too long to quote, where the vindictive and cruel anger not only curses the offender himself, but passes on to his children: "Let there be no man to pity him, nor to have compassion upon his fatherless children." Of course, people do not really mean any of these terrible things which they repeat day after day; humanity is too noble to wish to draw down such curses from heaven; the people have outgrown the bad spirit of that cruel age when the Psalter was written, and their hearts have grown more loving; but surely it is not well that men and women should stand on a lower level in their prayers than in their lives; surely the moments, which ought to be the noblest, should not be passed in using language which the speakers would be ashamed of in their daily lives; surely the worship of the Ideal should not be degraded below the practice of the Real, or the notion of God be less lofty than the life of man. By making their worship an unreality, by being less than true in their religious feelings, by using words they do not mean, and by pretending emotions they do not experience, people become trained into insincerity, and lose that rare and beautiful virtue of instinctive and thorough honesty. When the prayer does not echo the yearning of the heart, then the habit grows of not making the word really the representative of the thought, of not making the feeling the measure of the expression. Much of the cant of the day, much of the social insincerity, much of the prevalent unreality, may be laid at the door of this crime of the Churches, of making men speak words which are meaningless to the speaker, and of teaching them to be untrue in the moments which should be the truest and the purest. At another time, we might impeach prayer as a whole; we might argue against it, either as opposed to the unchangeableness and the wisdom of God, if a prayer-hearing and prayer-answering God be believed in, or as utterly futile, and proved worthless by experience. But here we only plead for sincerity in prayer, wherever prayer is practised; we only urge that at least the prayer shall be sincere, and that the lips shall obey the heart.

Exactly the same objection applies to the "Canticles," which, in modern lips, are absolutely devoid of sense. What meaning has the "song of the blessed Virgin Mary" from an ordinary English congregation; why should English people talk about God promising His mercy "to our forefathers, Abraham, and his seed for ever," when Abraham is not their forefather at all? Why should they ask God to let them "depart in peace," when they have not the smallest desire to depart at all, and why should they assert to Him that they "have seen Thy salvation," when they have seen nothing of the kind? For the perpetually recurring *Gloria*, one cannot help wondering what it means; when was "the beginning," and is the "it" which was at that period, the "glory" which is wished to the Father, Son, and Holy

Ghost; further, what is the good of wishing glory to Him—or to Them—if He—or They—have always had, and always will have it? When we have heard a congregation reciting the Creed, we have sometimes wondered what meaning they attached to it. "The maker of heaven and earth." Do people ever try to carry the mind back to the time before this "making," and realise the period when nothing existed? Is it possible to imagine things coming into existence, "something" emerging from where before "nothing" was? And then Jesus, the only Son, conceived by the Holy Ghost, who proceeds from Himself, and son, therefore, not of "the Father," but of that spirit which only exists in and through "the Father and the Son." Again, how can a "spirit" conceive a material body? If the whole affair be miraculous, why try to compromise matters with nature, by making this kind of pseudo-father? Surely it would be simpler to leave it a complete miracle, and let the Virgin remain the solitary parent. Except for making the story match better with the elder Greek mythology, there is no need to introduce a god-parent in the affair; a child without a father is no more remarkable than a mother who remains a virgin. This attempt at reasonableness only makes the whole more outrageously unnatural, and provokes criticism which would be better avoided. A God, who suffered, was crucified, dead, buried, who rose and ascended, is a complete enigma to us. Could He, the impassive, suffer? could He, the intangible, be crucified? could He, the immortal, die? could He, the omnipresent, be buried in one spot of earth, rise from it, and ascend to some place where he was not the moment before? What kind of God is this who is to "come again" to a place where He is not now? If the answer be, that all this refers to the manhood of Jesus, then we inquire, "Is Christ divided?" if He be one God with the Father, then all He did was done by the Father as much as by Himself; if He did it only as man, then God did not come from heaven to save men; then this is not a divine sacrifice at all; then, a simple man cannot have made an atonement for the sin of the world. And where is "the right hand" of Almighty God? Is Jesus sitting at the right hand of a pure spirit, who has neither body nor parts? and, since He is one with God, is He sitting at his own right hand? Such questions as these are called blasphemous; but we fling back the charge of blasphemy on those who try to compel us to recite a creed so absurd. We decline to repeat words which convey to us no meaning, and not ours the fault, if any inquiry into the meaning produce dilemmas so inconvenient to the orthodox. We are also required to believe in "the" Holy Catholic Church, but we know of no such body. Catholic means universal, and there is no universal Church: to believe in that which does not exist would, indeed, be faith without sight. There is the Orthodox Church, but that is anathematised by the Roman; there is the Roman Church, but that is the "scarlet whore of Babylon" in the eyes of the Protestant; there are the Protestant sects, but they are many and not one, a multiformity in disunity. We are asked to acknowledge a "Communion of Saints," and we see those who severally call themselves saints excommunicating each the other; in a "forgiveness of sins," but Nature tells us of no forgiveness, and we find suffering invariably following on the disregard of law; in a "resurrection of the body," but we know that the body decays, that its gases and its juices are transmuted in the alembic of Nature into new modes of existence; in a "life everlasting," when the dark veil of ignorance envelopes the "Beyond the tomb." Only the thoughtless can repeat the creed; only the ignorant cannot see the impossibilities it professes to believe.

The two Collects, which are different in the evening prayer to those used in the morning office, call for no special remark, save that they—in common with all prayers—make no practical difference in human life. The devout Christian is no more defended from "all perils and dangers of this night," than is the most careless atheist; wisely, also, does the Christian, having prayed his prayer, walk carefully round his house, and examine the bolts and bars, mindful that these commonplace defences are more likely to be efficacious against burglars than the protecting arm of the Most High.

The remainder of the service is the same as that used in the morning, so calls for no further remark. If only people would take the trouble of *thinking* about their religion; if only they could be led, or even provoked, into trying to realise that which they say they believe, then the foundations of the popular religion would rapidly be undermined, and the banner of Freethought would soon float proudly over the crumbling ruins of that which was once a Church.

THE LITANY.

The Litany has a fault which runs throughout the Prayer-Book, that "vain repetition" which, according to the Gospel, was denounced by Jesus of Nazareth; the refrain of "Good Lord, deliver us," and "We beseech Thee to hear us, good Lord," recurs with wearisome reiteration, and is repeated monotonously by the congregation, few of whom, probably, would know from what they were requesting deliverance, if the clergyman were to stop and ask so unexpected a question. Gods the Father, Son, and Holy Ghost are severally besought to have mercy upon the miserable sinners praying to them, and then the Trinity as a whole is asked todo the same. How farthis separation is consistent with the unity of the Godhead, and whether in praying to the Son we do, or do not, implicitly pray to the Father, and *vice versâ*, those only can tell us who understand the "mystery of the Holy Trinity." This preamble over, the remainder of the Litany is addressed to "God the Son," who is the "Good Lord" invoked throughout, in spite of His reproof to the young man who knelt to Him, calling Him "Good Master;" "why callest thou Me good?" Various dogmas are alluded to in the succeeding verses in which few educated people now retain any belief. How many really care to be delivered "from the crafts and assaults of the devil," or believe in the existence of thedevilat all? He is one of those phantoms that can only be found in the darkness, and which fade away when the sun arises. How many believe in the "everlasting damnation," of the same verse, or really consider themselves in the smallest danger of it? No one who believed in hell could pray to be delivered from it in careless accents, for the smallest chance of that awful doom would force a wail of terror from the lightest-hearted of the listeners. Is it consistent to ask Christ to deliver us from His wrath? if He loved men so much as to die for them, it seems as though a great change must have come over His mind since He ascended into heaven, if He really requires to be pressed so urgently not to "take vengeance," and to spare us and deliver us from His wrath. Which is right, the wrath or the love? for they are not compatible; and does God really like to see people crouching before Him in this fashion, praising His mercy while they tremble lest He should "break out" upon them? If we were inclined to be hypercritical we might suggest that the prayer to be delivered from "all uncharitableness" gives a melancholy proof of the inadequacy of prayer; the answer to it may be read weekly in the *Church Times* and the *Rock*, more especially in the clerical contributions. The other petitions are also curiously ineffectual: "from all false doctrine, heresy, and schism," is so manifestly accepted at the Throne of Grace in these rationalising days. Jesus is then abjured to deliver His petitioners by the memory of His days upon earth, and we get the ancient idea of an incarnate God, so common to all eastern religions, and the curious picture of a God who is born, circumcised, baptised, fasts, is tempted, suffers, dies, is buried, rises, ascends. How God can do all this remains a mystery, but these suffering, and then conquering gods are familiar to all readers of mythologies; we learn further, that God the Holy Ghost can come to a place where He was not previously, although He is the infinite God, and is therefore omnipresent. Verily, it needs that our faith be great. Being delivered sufficiently, the congregation proceed to a number of additional petitions, the first of which is, unfortunately, as great a failure as the preceding ones, for it prays that the Church may be guided "in the right way;" and having regard to the multiplicity of Churches, each one of which goes doggedly in her own particular way, it is manifest that they can't all be right, as they are all different. Then follow prayers for the Royal Family and the Government, and a general request to "bless and keep all Thy people;" a request which is systematically disregarded. In these days of "bloated armaments" it is at least pleasant to dream in church of there being given "to all nations, unity, peace, and concord." The "pure affection" with which God's Word is received is also perfectly imaginary; those who do not believe it criticise and cavil; those who do believe it go to sleep over it. The last part of these verses seems designed simply to pray for everybody all round, and this being satisfactorily accomplished, we come across another trace of an ancient creed: "Lamb of God, that takest away the sins of the world;" this is a fragment of sun-worship, alluding to the sun-god, when, entering the sign of the Lamb, he bears away all the coldness and the darkness of the winter months, and gives life to the world. The remainder of the Litany is of the same painfully servile character as the earlier portions; God seems to be regarded as a fierce tyrant, longing to wreak

His fury on mankind, and only withheld by incessant entreaties. All possible evils seem to be showering down on the congregation, and, if one closed one's eyes, one could imagine a sad-faced, care-worn, haggard group of Covenanters, or Huguenots, instead of the fashionable crowd that fills the pews; and when one hears them ask that they may be "hurt by no persecutions," one is inclined to mutter grimly: "You are all safe, mother Church, and you are the persecutor, not the persecuted." The service concludes with the same unreal cant about afflictions and infirmities, till one could wish almost to hear something of the style of observation made by an angry nurse to a tiresome child: "If you don't stop crying this minute, I will give you something to cry for." If men would only be as real inside the church as they are outside; if they would think and mean what they say, this pitiful burlesque would speedily be put an end to, and they would no longer offer up that sacrifice of lying lips, which are said to be "an abomination to the Lord."

PRAYERS AND THANKSGIVINGS UPON SEVERAL OCCASIONS.

These special prayers are, perhaps, on the whole, the most childish of all the childish prayers in the Church-book before us. A prayer "for rain;" a prayer "for fair weather:" it is almost too late to argue seriously against prayers like these, except that uneducated people do still believe that God regulates the weather, day by day, and may be influenced in His arrangements by the prayer of some weather-critic below. Yet it is a literal fact that storm-signals fly before the approaching storm, and prepare people for its coming, so that when it sweeps across our seas the vessels are safely in port, which otherwise would have sunk beneath its fury; meteorology is progressing day by day, and is becoming more and more perfect, but this science—as all other science—would be impossible if God could be influenced by prayer; a storm-signal would be needless if prayer could stay the storm, and would be unreliable if a prayer could suddenly, in mid-ocean, check the course of the tempest. Science is only possible when it is admitted that "God works by laws," *i.e.*, that His working at all need not be taken into account. The laws of weather are as unchangeable as all other natural laws, for laws are nothing more than the ascertained sequence of events; not until that sequence has been found by long observation to be invariable, does the sequence receive the title of "a law." As the weather of to-day is the result of the weather of countless yesterdays, the only way in which prayers for change can be effectual is that God should change the whole weather of the past, and so let fresh causes bring about fresh results; but this seems a rather large prayer, to say the least of it, and might, by the carnal mind, be considered as somewhat presumptuous. In the prayers "in the time of dearth and famine" we find the old barbarous notion that men's moral sins are punished by physical "visitations of God," and that God's blessing will give plenty in the place of dearth: if men work hard they will get more than if they pray hard, and even long ago in Eden God could not make his plants grow, because "there was not a man to till the ground;" at least, so says the Bible. The prayer "in the time of war," is strikingly beautiful, begging the All-Father to abate the pride, assuage the malice, and confound the devices of some of His children for the advantage of the others. The "most religious and gracious" Sovereign recommended to the care of God has been known to be such a king as George IV., but yet clergy and people went on day after day speaking of him thus to a God who "searcheth the hearts." A quaint old Prayer-Book remarks upon this prayer for the High Court of Parliament, that the "right disposing of the hearts of legislators proceeds from God," and that "both disbelief and ignorance must have made fearful progress where this principle is not recognised." In these latter days we fear that disbelief and ignorance of this kind *have* made very considerable progress. The Thanksgivings run side by side with the prayers in subjects, and are therefore open to the same criticisms. None of these prayers or praises can be defended by reason or by argument; reason shows us their utter folly, and their complete uselessness. Is it wise to persist in forcing into people's lips words which have lost all their meaning, and which the people, if they trouble themselves to think about them at all, at once recognise as false? All danger in progress lies in the obstinate maintenance of things which have outlived their age; just as a stream which flows peacefully on, spreading plenty and fertility in its course, and growing naturally wider and fuller, will—if dammed up too much—burst at length through the dam, and rush forward as a torrent, bearing destruction and ruin in its course; so will gradual and gentle reform in ancient habits change all that needs changing, without abrupt alterations, letting the stream of thought grow wider and fuller; but if all Reform be delayed, if all change be forbidden, if the dam of prejudice, of custom, of habit, bar the stream too long, then thought hurls it down with the crash of revolution, and many a thing is lost in the swirling torrent which might have remained long, and might have beautified human life. Few things call more loudly for Reform than our hitherto loudly-boasted Reformation.

THE

BEAUTIES OF THE PRAYER-BOOK.

THE COMMUNION SERVICE.

NO doctrine, perhaps, has done so much to cause disunion in the Church as the doctrine of Communion enshrined in the Lord's Supper. A feast of love in idea, it has been pre-eminently a feast of hate in reality, and the fiercest contests have been waged over this "last legacy of the Redeemer." Down to the time of the Reformation it was the central service of the Church universal, Eastern and Western alike: it was the Liturgy, distinguished from every other office by this distinctive name. Round this rite revolved the whole of the other services, as week-days around the Lord's Day; on its due performance was lavished everything of beauty and of splendour that wealth could bring; sweetest incense, most harmonious music, richest vestments, rarely jewelled vessels, pomp of procession, stateliness of ceremony, all brought their glory and their beauty to render magnificent the reception of the present God. Among the Reformed Churches the festival was shorn of its grandeur; it became once more the simple "supper of the Lord," no memorial sacrifice, but only a commemorative rite; no coming of the Lord to men, but only a sign of the union through faith of the believer with the Saviour. At the present time the old contest rages, even within the bosom of the Reformed Church of England; one party still clings to the elder belief of a real presence of Christ in the elements themselves, or in indissoluble connection with them, and, therefore, celebrates the service with much of the ancient pomp; while the other furiously rejects this so-called idolatry, and makes the service as bare and as simple as possible. Both parties can claim parts of the Communion Office as upholding their special views, for the English service has passed through much of tinkering from High and Low, and retains the marks of the alterations that have been made by each.

To those outside the Church this office has particular attraction, as being, in a special manner, a link between the past and the present, and being full of traces of the ancient religion of the world, that catholic sun-worship of which Christianity is a modernised revival. From the Nicene Creed, in which Jesus is described as "God of God, *Light of Light*, very God of very God, Begotten not made, Being of one substance with the Father, By whom all things were made"—from this point we breathe the full atmosphere of the elder world, and find ourselves engaged in the worship of that Light of Light, who, being the image of the invisible God, the first-born of every creature, has for ages and ages been adored as incarnate in Mithra, in Christna, in Osiris, in Christ. We give thanks for "the redemption of the world by the death and passion of 'the Sun-Saviour, who suffered on the Cross for us,' who lay in darkness and in the shadow of death;" we praise Him who fills heaven and earth with His glory, and who rose as "the Paschal Lamb," and has "taken away the sin of the world," bearing away in the sign of the Lamb the darkness and dreariness of the winter; we remember the Holy Ghost, the fresh spring wind, who, "as it had been a mighty wind," came to bring us "out of darkness" into "the clear light" of the sun; then we see the priest, with his face turned to the sun-rising, take the bread and wine, the symbols of the God, and bless them for the food of men, these symbols being changed into the very substance of the deity, for are they not, in very truth, of him alone? "How naturally does the eternal work of the sun, daily renewed, express itself in such lines as

> 'Into bread his heat is turned,
> Into generous wine his light.'

And imagining the sun as a person, the change to 'flesh' and 'blood' becomes inevitable; while the fact that the solar forces are actually changed into food, without forfeiting their solar character, finds expression in the doctrines of transubstantiation and the real presence." ("Keys of the Creeds," page 91.) After this union with the Deity, by partaking of his very self, we praise once more the "Lamb of God that takest away the sins of the world," and is "most high in the glory of God the Father." The resemblance is made the nearer in the churches where much of ceremony is found (although noticeable in all, since that resemblance is stereotyped in the formulas themselves; but in the more elaborate performances the old rites are more clearly apparent) in the tonsured head of the priest, in the suns often embroidered on vestment and on altar-cloth, in the rays that surround the sacred monogram on the vessels, in the cross imprinted on the bread, and marking each utensil, in the lighted candles, in the grape-vine chiselled on the chalice—in all these, and in many another symbol, we read the whole story of the Sun-god, written in hieroglyphics as easily decipherable by the initiated as is the testimony of the rocks by the geologian.

But passing by this antiquarian side of the Office, we will examine it as a service suitable for the use of educated and thoughtful people at the present time. The Rubric which precedes the Office is one of those unfortunate rules which are obsolete as regards their practice, and yet which—from their preservation—appear to simple-minded parsons to be intended to be enforced, whereby the said parsons fall into the clutches of the law, and suffer grievously. "An open and notorious evil-liver" must not be permitted to come to the Lord's Table, and this expression seems to be explained in the Exhortation in the Office, wherein we read: "if any of you be a blasphemer of God, an hinderer or slanderer of His word, an adulterer, or be in malice, or envy, or in any other grievous crime, repent you of your sins, or else come not to that holy Table; lest, after the taking of that holy Sacrament, the devil enter into you, as he entered into Judas, and fill you full of all iniquities, and bring you to destruction both of body and soul." In a late case, the Sacrament was refused to one who disbelieved in the devil and who slandered God's word, on those very grounds, and it would seem to be an act of Christian charity so to deny it; for surely to say that part of God's word is "contrary to religion and decency" must be to slander it, if words have any meaning, and people who do not believe in the devil ought hardly to be sharers in a rite after which the devil will enter into them with such melancholy consequences. It would seem more consistent either to alter the formulas or else to carry them out; true, one clergyman wrote that the responsibility lay with the unworthy recipient who "did nothing else but increase" his "damnation," but it is scarcely a pleasing notion that the clergyman should stand inviting people to the Lord's table and, coolly handing to one of those who accept, the body of Christ, say, "The Body of our Lord Jesus Christ preserve thy body and soul unto everlasting life," when he means—in the delicate language used by the above-mentioned clergyman—"The Body of our Lord Jesus Christ damn thy body and soul unto everlasting death." No one but a clergyman could dream of so offensive a proceeding, and, to those who believe, one so terribly awful.

The Ten Commandments which stand in the fore-front of the service are very much out of place as regards some of them, to say nothing of the want of truthfulness in the assertion, that "God spake these words," &c. In the second we are forbidden to make any graven image, or any likeness of any thing, a command which would destroy all art, and which no member of the congregation can have the smallest notion of obeying. The Jews, who made the cherubim over the ark, upon which God sat, are popularly supposed not to have disobeyed this command, because the cherubim were not the likeness of anything in heaven, earth, or water: they were, like unicorns, creatures undiscovered and undiscoverable. Yet in direct opposition to this command, Solomon made brazen oxen to support his sea of brass (1 Kings vii. 25, 29), and lions on the steps of his ivory throne (1 Kings x. 19, 20), and God himself is said to have ordered Moses to make a Brazen Serpent. God is described, in this same Commandment, as "a jealous God"—which is decidedly immoral and unpleasant—who visits "the sins of the fathers upon the children, unto the third and fourth generation of them that hate me;" the injustice of this is so obvious that no comment on it is necessary. The fourth Commandment is another which no one dreams of attending to; in the first place, we do not keep the seventh day at all, and in the second, our man-servant, our maid-servant, and our cattle do all manner of work on the day we keep the Sabbath. Further, who in the present day believes that "in six days the Lord made heaven and earth, the sea, and all that in them is, and rested the seventh day;" geology, astronomy, ethnology have taught us otherwise, and, among those who repeat the response to this commandment in a London church, not one could probably be found who believes it to be true. The fifth Commandment is equally out of place, for dutiful children do not live any longer than undutiful. The remainder touch simple moral duties, enforced by all creeds alike, and are noticeable for their omissions and not for their commissions: the insertion of the Buddhist Commandment against intoxication, for instance, would be an improvement, although such a commandment is naturally not to be found in the case of so gross and sensual a people as the ancient Jews. The alternative prayers for the Queen, which follow next, are only worth noting, because the first enshrines the doctrine of divine right, which is long since dead and buried, except in church; and the other says "that the hearts of Kings are in thy rule and governance," and suggests the thought that, if this be so, it is better to be out of that "rule and governance," the effects on the hearts of Kings not having been specially attractive. The Nicene Creed comes next, and is open to the objections before made against the Apostles' Creed; the last clauses relating to the Holy Ghost are historically interesting, since the "and the Son" forms the *Filioque* which severed Eastern from Western Christendom;* "Who with the Father and the Son together" ought to be "worshipped and glorified," would be more true to fact than "is," since the Holy Ghost is sadly ignored by modern Christendom, and has a very small share of either prayers or hymns: yet he is the husband of the Virgin Mary, and the Father of Jesus Christ; he is, therefore, a very important, though puzzling, person in the Godhead, being the Father of him from whom he himself proceeds: this is a mystery, and can only be understood by faith. The texts that follow are remarkable for their ingenious selection: "Who goeth a warfare," &c. (1 Cor. ix. 7); "If we have sown," &c. (1 Cor. ix. 9); "Do ye not know," &c. (1 Cor. ix. 13); "He that soweth little" (2 Cor. ix. 6); "Let him that is taught" (Gal. vi. 6). The pervading selfishness of motive

* A short but very graphic account of the shameful transaction by which the Filioque clause was, so to speak, smuggled into the Nicene Creed, is to be found in the first ten or twelve pages of the shilling pamphlet written by Edmund S. Ffoulkes, B.D., entitled "The Church's Creed, or the Crown's Creed," published by J. T. Hayes, Lyall-place, Eaton-square, London. The following short prayer, "Mentes nostras, quæsumus, Domine, Paráclitus, qui à te procedit, illuminet: et inducat in omnem, sicut tuus promisit Filius, veritatem" (*vide* Præparatio ad Missam, in the "Missale Romanum"), clearly proves, too, that the Church of Rome once held that the Holy Ghost only proceeded from the Father, as the Dominus in it can only refer to the Father.

is also worth nothing: Give now in order that ye may get hereafter; "Never turn thy face from any poor man, *and then the face of the Lord shall not be turned away from thee;*" "He that hath pity upon the poor lendeth unto the Lord: *and look, what he layeth out, it shall be paid him again;*" "If thou hast much, give plenteously; if thou hast little, do thy diligence gladly to give of that little; *for so gathered thou thyself a good reward in the day of necessity.*"* No free, glad giving here; no willing, joyful aid to a poorer brother, because he needs what I can give; no ready offer of the cup of cold water, simply because the thirsty is there and wants the refreshment; ever the hateful whisper comes: "thou shalt in no wise lose thy reward." These time-serving offerings are then presented to God by being placed "upon the Holy Table," and we then get another prayer for Queen, Christian Kings, authorities, Bishops, and people in general, concluding with thanks for the dead, not a cheerful subject to bless God for, if there chance to be present any mourner whose heart is sore with the loss of a beloved one. At this point the service is supposed to end, when no celebration of the Holy Communion is intended, and here we find two Exhortations, or notices of celebration, from the first of which we have already quoted:† in the second, we cannot help remarking the undignified position in which God is placed; it is a "grievous and unkind thing" not to come to a rich feast when invited thereto, wherefore we are to fear lest by withdrawing ourselves from this holy Supper, we "provoke God's indignation against" us. "Consider with yourselves how great injury ye do unto God:" what a very curious expression. Is God thus at the mercy of man? Surely, then, of all living Beings the lot of God must be the saddest, if his happiness and his glory are in the hands of each man and woman; the greater his knowledge the greater the misery, and as his knowledge is perfect, and the vast majority of human kind know and care nothing about him, his wretchedness must be complete. All things being ready,

* As if the clergy, with very few exceptions, are not sufficiently provided for by the tithes, &c., without having to go a-begging like either Buddhist or Roman Catholic monks, to both of whom P.P. and P.M. are not inappropriately applied (Professors of Poverty and Practisers of Mendicancy).

† It is, however, only just to say that that portion of it contained between "*The Way and Means thereto,*" and "Offences at God's Hands," is one of the best bits in the whole Prayer-Book, and which far surpasses the generality of sermons one hears afterwards.

the clergyman begins by another Exhortation, of somewhat threatening character: "So is the danger great if we receive the same unworthily." For then we are guilty of the Body and Blood of Christ our Saviour; we eat and drink our own damnation, not considering the Lord's Body; we kindle God's wrath against us; we provoke him to plague us with divers diseases, and sundry kinds of death." (Surely we cannot be plagued with more than one kind of death at once, and we can't die sundry times, even after the Communion.) One almost wonders why any-one accepts this very threatening invitation, even though there are advantages promised to "meet partakers." The High Church party have indeed the right to talk much of the real presence, since ordinary bread and wine have none of these fearful penalties attached to the eating and drinking, and some curious change must have taken place in them before all these terrible consequences can ensue. What would happen if some consecrated bread and wine chanced to be left by mistake, and a stray comer into the vestry eat it unknowingly? One thinks of Anne Askew, who, told that a mouse eating a crumb fallen from the Host would infallibly be damned, replied, "Alack, poor mouse!" Then follows a Confession of the most cringing kind, fit only for the lips of some coward suppliant crouching at the feet of an Eastern monarch; it is marvellous that free English men and women can frame their lips into phrases of such utter abasement, even to a God; manliness in religion is sorely needed, unless, indeed, God be something smaller than man, and be pleased with the degradation painful to human eyes. The prayer of consecration is the central point of the ordinance; of old they prayed for the descent of the Holy Ghost on the elements, "for whatsoever the Holy Ghost toucheth is sanctified and clean"—it is not explained how the Holy Ghost, being omnipresent, manages to avoid touching everything—and now the priest asks that in receiving the bread and wine we "may be partakers of" Christ's Body and Blood, and repeats the words, "This is my Body," "This is my Blood," laying his hand alternately over the bread and the wine: now if this means anything, if it is not mere mockery, it means that after the consecration the bread and wine are other than they were before; if it does not mean this, the whole prayer is simply a farce, a piece of acting scarcely decent under the circumstances. But flesh and blood! Putting aside the extreme repulsiveness of the idea, the coarseness of the act, the utter unpleasantness of eating flesh and drinking blood, all of which has become non-disgusting by habit and fashion, and the distastefulness of which can scarcely be realised by any believer—putting aside all this, is there any change in the bread and wine? Examine it; analyse it; test it in any and every fashion; still it answers back to the questioner, "bread and wine." Are our senses deceived? Then try a hundred different persons; all cannot be deceived alike. Unless every result of experience is untrustworthy, we have here to do with bread and wine, and with nothing more. "But faith is needed." Ah yes! There is the secret: no flesh and blood without faith; no miracle without credulity. Miracle-working priests are only successful among credulously-disposed people; miracles can only be received by those who think it less likely that Nature should speak falsely than that man should deceive; those who believe in this change through consecration cannot be touched by argument; they have closed their eyes that they may not see, their ears that they may not hear; no knowledge can reach them, for they have shut the gateways whereby it could enter, they are literally dead in their superstition, buried beneath the stone of their faith. The reception of the Body and Blood of Christ being over, the people having knelt to eat and drink, as is only right when eating and drinking Christ (John vi. 57), the Lord's Prayer is said for the second time, a prayer and thanksgiving follows, confined to "we and all thy whole Church," for the spirit is the same as that of the prayer of Christ, "I pray not for the world, but for them whom thou hast given me" (John xvii. 9), and then the service winds up with the *Gloria in Excelsis* and the Benediction. Such is the "bounden duty and service" offered by the Church to God, the service of which the central act must be either a farce or a falsehood, and therefore insulting to the God to whom it is offered. Regarded as a service to God, the whole Communion Office is objectionable in the highest degree; regarded as an antiquarian survival, it is very interesting and instructive; it is surely time that it should be put in its right place, and that its true origin should be recognised. The day is gone by for these barbarous, though poetic, ceremonials; the "flesh and blood," which was a bold figure for the heat and light of the sun, becomes coarse when joined in thought to a human being; ceremonies that fitted the childhood of the world are out of place in its manhood, as the play that is graceful in the child would be despicable in the man; these rites are the baby-clothes of the world, and cannot be stretched to fit the stalwart limbs of its maturer age, cannot add grace to its form, or dignity to its graver walk.

THE BAPTISMAL OFFICES.

For all purposes of criticism the Offices for "Public Baptism of Infants, to be used in the Church," for "Private Baptism of Children in houses," and "Baptism to such as are of riper years, and able to answer for themselves," may be treated as one and the same, the leading idea of each service being identical; this idea is put forward clearly and distinctly in the preface to the Office: "Dearly beloved, forasmuch as all men are conceived and born in sin; and that our Saviour Christ saith, None can enter into the kingdom of God, except he be regenerate and born anew of water and of the Holy Ghost; I beseech you to call upon God the Father, through our Lord Jesus Christ, that of his bounteous mercy he will grant to this Child that thing which by nature he cannot have." According to the doctrine of the Church, then, baptism is absolutely necessary to salvation: "*None can enter* . . . except he be . . . born anew of water;" thus peals out the doom of condemnation on the whole human race, save that fragment of it which is sprinkled from the Christian font; there is no evasion possible here; no exception made in favour of heathen peoples; no mercy allowed to those who have no opportunity of baptism; none can enter save through "the laver of regeneration." Can any words be too strong whereby to denounce a doctrine so shameful, an injustice so glaring? A child is born into the world; it is no fault of his that he is conceived in sin; it is no fault of his that he is born in sin; his consent was not asked before he was ushered into the world; no offer was made to him which he could reject of this terrible gift of a condemned life; flung is he, without his knowledge, without his will, into a world lying under the curse of God, a child of wrath, and heir of damnation. "By nature he *cannot* have." Then why should God be wrath with him because he hath not? The whole arrangement is of God's own making. He fore-ordained the birth; he gave the life; the helpless, unconscious infant lies there, the work of his own hands; good or bad, he is responsible for it; heir of love or of wrath, he has made it what it is; as wholly is it his doing as the unconscious vessel is the doing of the potter; as reasonably may God be angry with the child as the potter swear at the clay he has clumsily moulded: if the vessel be bad, blame the potter; if the creature be bad, blame the Creator. The congregation pray that God "of his bounteous mercy," "for thine infinite mercies," will save the child, "that he, being delivered from thy wrath," may be blessed. It is no question of mercy we have to do with here; it is a question of simple justice, and nothing more; if God, for his own "good pleasure," or in the pursuance of the designs of his infinite wisdom, has placed this unfortunate child in so terrible a position, he is bound by every tie of justice, by every sacred claim of right, to deliver the blameless victim, and to place him where he shall have a fair chance of well-being. "It is certain by God's Word," says the Rubric, "that children *which are baptized*, dying before they commit actual sin, are undoubtedly saved." And those which are not baptized? The Holy Roman Church sends these into a cheerful place called Limbo, and the baby-souls wander about in chill twilight, cursed with immortality, shut out for ever from the joys of Paradise. Many readers will remember Lowell's pathetic poem on this subject, and the ghastly baptism; they will also know into what devious paths of argumentative indecency that Church has wandered in deciding upon the fate of unbaptized infants;—how, when mothers have died in childbirth, the yet unborn children have been baptized to save them from the terrible doom pronounced upon them by their Father in heaven, even before they saw the light;—how it has been said that in cases where mother and child cannot both be saved the mother should be sacrificed that the child may not die unbaptized. Into the details of these arguments we cannot enter; they are only fit for orthodox Christians, in whose pages they may read them who list. Truly, the Lord is a jealous God, visiting the sins of the fathers upon the children, since unborn children are condemned for the untimely death of their mother, and unbaptized infants for the carelessness of their parents or nurses. Of course, the majority of English clergymen believe nothing of this kind; but then why do they read a service which implies it? Why do they use words in a non-natural sense? Why do they put off their honesty when they put on their surplices?

And why will the laity not give utterance to their thoughts on these and all such objectionable parts of the Service? In the Office for adults, as regards the necessity of the Sacrament, the words come in: "where it may be had;" but the phrase reads as though it had been written in the margin by some kindly soul, and had from thence crept into the text, for it is in direct opposition to the whole argument of the address wherein it occurs, and to the rest of the office, as also to the other two offices for infants. The stress laid upon right baptism, *i.e.*, baptism with water, accompanied by the "name of the Father, and of the Son, and of the Holy Ghost," appears specially in the office to follow the private baptism of a child, should the child live; for the Rubric directs that if there be any doubt of the use of the water and the formula, "which are essential parts of Baptism," the priest shall perform the baptismal ceremony, saying, "If thou art not already baptized, I baptize thee," &c. Surely such care and pains to ensure correct baptism speak with sufficient plainness as to the importance attached by the Church to this initiatory rite; this importance she gives to it in other places: none, unbaptized, must approach her altar to take the "bread of life:" none, unbaptized, must be buried by her ministers, "in sure and certain hope of the Resurrection to eternal life." The baptized are within the ark of the Church; the unbaptized are struggling in the waves of God's wrath outside; no hand can be outstretched to save them; they are strangers, aliens, to the covenant of promise; they are without hope. The whole office for infants reads like a play: the clergyman asks that the infant "may receive remission of his sins;" what sins? The people are admonished "that they defer not the Baptism of their children longer than the first or second Sunday next after their birth." What sins can a baby a week old have committed? from what sins can he need release? for what sins can he ask forgiveness? And yet, here is a whole congregation prostrate before Almighty God, praying that a tiny long-robed baby may be forgiven, may be pardoned his sins of—coming into the world when God sent him! The ceremony would be ludicrous were it not so pitiful. And supposing that the infant does need forgiveness, and has sins to be washed away, why should a few drops of water, sprinkled on the face—or bonnet—of the baby, or even the immersion of his body in the font, wash away the sins of his soul? The water is "sanctified;" we pray: "Sanctify this water to the mystical washing away of sin." As the hymn sweetly puts it:

> "The water in this font
> Is water, by gross mortals eyed;
> But, seen by faith, 'tis blood
> Out of a dear friend's side."

Blood once more! how Christians cling to the revolting imagery of a bygone and barbarous age of gross conceptions. And, applied by faith, it cleanses the soul of the child from sin. Well, the whole thing is consistent: the invisible soul is washed from invisible sin by invisible blood, and to all outward appearance the child remains after baptism exactly what it was before—except it chance to get inflammation of the lungs, as we have known happen, from High Church free use of water, which is, perhaps, the promised baptism of fire. The promises of the sponsors are in full accordance with the rest of the services; promises made by other people, in the child's name, as to his future conduct, over which they have no control. The baby renounces the devil and all his belongings, believes the Apostles' Creed, and answers "that is my desire," when asked if he will be baptized; all which "is very pretty acting," but jars somewhat on the feeling of reality which ought surely to characterize a believer's intercourse with his God. The child being baptized and signed with the Cross, "is regenerate," according to the declaration of the priest. Some contend that the Church of England does not teach baptismal regeneration, but it is hard to see how any one can read this service, and then deny the teaching; it is clearer and fuller than is the teaching of her voice upon most subjects. The ceremony of baptism and the idea of regeneration are both derived from the sun-worship of which so many traces have already been pointed out: the worshippers of Mithra practised baptism, and it is common to the various phases of the solar faith. Regeneration, in some parts, especially in India, was obtained in a different fashion: a hole through a rock, or a narrow passage between two, was the sacred spot, and a worshipper, squeezing himself through such an opening, was regenerated, and was, by this literal representation of birth, born a second time, born into a new life, and the sins of the former life were no longer accounted to him. Many such holes are still preserved and revered in India, and there can be little doubt that the ancient Druidic remains bear traces of being adapted for this same ceremony, although a natural fissure appears ever to have been accounted the most sacred.*

One ought scarcely to leave unnoted the preamble to the first prayer in the baptismal service: "Who of thy great mercy didst save Noah and his family in the ark from perishing by water; and also didst safely lead the children of Israel thy people through the Red Sea, figuring thereby thy holy baptism; and by the baptism of thy well-beloved Son Jesus Christ, in the river Jordan, didst sanctify water to the mystical washing of sin." In the two first examples given the choice of the Church appears to be peculiarly unfortunate, as in each case water was the element to be escaped *from*, and it was a source of death, not of life; perhaps, though, there is a subtle meaning in the *Red* Sea, it points to the blood of Christ: but then, again, the Red Sea drowned people, and surely the anti-type is not so dangerous as that? It must be a mystery. It would be interesting to know how many of the educated clergymen who read this prayer believe in the story of the Noachian deluge, and of the miraculous passage of the Red Sea; and further, how many of them believe that God, by these fables, figured his holy baptism. Will the nineteenth century ever summon up energy enough to shake off these remnants of a dead superstition, and be honest enough to stop using a form of words which is no longer a vehicle of belief? When the Prayer Book was compiled these words had a meaning; to-day they have none. Shall not a second Reformation sweep away these dead beliefs, even as the first away for its own age the phrases which represented an earlier and coarser creed?

THE ORDER OF CONFIRMATION.

"These signs shall follow them that believe: In my name shall they cast out devils; they shall speak with new tongues; they shall take up serpents; and if they drink any deadly thing, it shall not hurt them; they shall lay hands on the sick, and they shall recover." In those remarkable days the "order of Confirmation" might have

* Even in this country, at Brimham Rocks, near Ripon, in Yorkshire, the dead form of the custom is, or was, until very lately, kept u by the guide sending all visitors, who chose to avail themselves of th privilege, through such a fissure.

been in consonance with its surroundings, a state of things which is very far from being its present position. Mr. Spurgeon, writing for the benefit of street preachers, lately pointed out very sensibly that as the Holy Ghost no longer gave the gift of tongues, they had "better stick to their grammars," and in these degenerate days honest effort is more likely to show results more satisfactory than those which ensue from the laying on of Bishops' hands. When the Apostles performed this ceremony, which the Bishop now performs after their example, definite proofs of its efficacy were said to have been seen; so much so, indeed, that Simon, the sorcerer, wished to invest some money in heavenly securities, so that "on whomsoever I lay hands he may receive the Holy Ghost." A Simon would manifestly never be found nowadays ready to pay a Bishop for the power of causing the effects of Confirmation. So far as the carnal eye can see, the white-robed, veiled young ladies, and the shame-faced black-coated boys, who throng the church on a Confirmation day, return from the altar very much the same as they went up to it: no one begins to speak with tongues; if they did, the beadle would probably interfere and quench the Spirit with the greatest promptitude. They are supposed to have received some special gifts: "the spirit of wisdom and understanding; the spirit of counsel and ghostly strength; the spirit of knowledge and true godliness;" and in addition to these six spirits, there is one more: "the spirit of thy holy fear." No less than seven spirits, then, enter these lads and lasses. Wisdom and understanding are easily perceptible: are they wiser after Confirmation than they were before? do they understand more rapidly? do they know more? if there be no perceptible difference is the presence of the Holy Spirit of none effect? if of none effect can his presence be of any use, of the very smallest advantage? if of no use, why make all this parade about giving a thing whose gift makes the recipient no richer than he was before? Besides, what certainty can there be that the Holy Ghost is given at all? Allowing—what seems to an outsider a gross piece of irreverence—that the Holy Ghost is in the fingers of the Bishop to be given away when it suits the Bishop's convenience, or is in a sort of reservoir, of which the Bishop turns the tap and lets the stream of grace descend—allowing all this as possible, ought not some "sign to follow them that believe"? How can we be sure that the Bishop is not an impostor, going through a conjuror's gestures and mutterings, and no magic results accruing? If, in the ordinary course of daily life, any one came and offered us some valuable things he said that he possessed, and then went through the form of giving them to us, saying: "Here they are; guard and preserve them for the rest of your life;" and the outstretched hand contained nothing at all, and we found ourselves with nothing in our grasp, should we be content with his assurance that we had really got them, although we might not be able to see them, and we ought to have sufficient faith to take his word for it? Should we not utterly refuse to believe that we had received anything unless we had some proof of having done so, and were in some way the better or the worse for it? The truth is that people's religion is, to them, a matter of such small importance that they do not trouble themselves about proof—Faith is enough to comfort them; the six week-days require their brains, their efforts, their thought: the Sunday is the Lord's day, and he must see to it: earth needs all their earnest attention, but heaven must take care of itself; the validity of an earthly title is important, and the confirmation of a right to inherit property in this world is eagerly welcomed, but the Confirmation to a heavenly inheritance is a mere farce, which it is the fashion to go through about the age of fifteen, but which is only a fashion, the confirmation of a faith in nothing in particular to an invisible heritage of nothing at all.

THE FORM OF THE SOLEMNIZATION OF MATRIMONY.

One of the most curious blunders regarding orthodox Christianity is, that it has tended to the elevation of woman. As a matter of fact, the Eastern ideas about women are embodied in Christianity, and these ideas are essentially degraded and degrading. From the time when Paul bade women obey their husbands, Augustine's mother was beaten, unresisting, by Augustine's father, and Jerome fled from woman's charms, and monks declaimed against the daughters of Eve, down to the present day, when Peter's authority is used against woman suffrage, Christianity has consistently regarded woman as a creature to be subject to man, because, being deceived, she was first in transgression. The Church service for matrimony is redolent of this barbarous idea, relic of a time when men seized wives by force, or else purchased them, so that the wives became, in literal fact, the property of their husbands. We learn that matrimony was "instituted of God in the time of man's innocency, signifying unto us the mystical union that is between Christ and his Church." It would be interesting to know how many of those joined by the Church believe in the Paradise story of man's innocency and fall. It seems that Christ has adorned the holy estate by his first miracle in Cana; but the adornment is rather of a dubious character, when we reflect that the probable effect of the miracle would be a scene somewhat too gay, from the enormous quantity of wine made by Christ for men who already had "well drunk." Christ's approval of marriage may well be considered doubtful when we remember that a virgin was chosen as his mother, that he himself remained unmarried, and that he distinctly places celibacy higher than marriage in Matt. xix. 11, 12, where he urges: "he that is able to receive it let him receive it." St. Paul also, though he allows it to his converts, advises virginity in preference: "I say to the unmarried and widows, It is good for them if they abide even as I;" "he that giveth her not in marriage doeth better" (see throughout 1 Cor. vii.) The reasons given for marriage are surely misplaced; last of all, it is said that marriage is "ordained for the mutual society, help, and comfort that the one ought to have of the other;" this, instead of "thirdly," ought to be "first." "As a remedy against sin and to avoid fornication, that such persons as have not the gift of continency might marry," is not a reason very honourable to the marriage estate, nor very delicate to read out before a mixed congregation to a young bride and bridegroom; so strongly objectionable is the heedless coarseness of this preface felt to be that in many churches it is entirely omitted, although it is retained—as are all remains of a coarser age—in the Prayer-Book as published by authority. The promise exchanged between the contracting parties is of far too sweeping a character, and is immoral, because promising what may be beyond the powers of the promisers to perform; "to love" "so long as ye both shall live," and "till death us do part," is a pledge far too wide; love does not stay by promising, nor is love a feeling which can be made to order. A promise to live always together might be made, although that would be unwise in this changing world, and the endless processes in the Divorce Court are a satire on this so-called joined by God; "what God hath joined together" man does continually "put asunder," and it would be wiser to adapt the service to the altered circumstances of the times in which we live. The promise of obedience and service on the woman's part should also be eliminated, and the contract should be a simple promise of fidelity between two equal friends. The declaration of the man as he places the ring on the woman's finger is as archaic as the rest of this fossil service, and about as true: "With all my worldly goods I thee endow," says the man, when, as a matter of fact, he becomes possessed of all his wife's property and she does not become possessed of his. One of the concluding prayers is a delightful specimen of Prayer-Book science: "O God, who of thy mighty power hast made all things of nothing." What was the general aspect of affairs when there was "nothing?" how did something emerge where "nothing" was before? if God filled all space, was he "nothing?" is the existence of nothing a conceivable idea? can people think of nothing except when they don't think at all? "who also (after other things set in order) didst appoint that out of man (created after thine own image and similitude) woman should take her beginning:" "out of man," that is out of one of man's ribs; has any one tried to picture the scene: Almighty God, who has no body nor parts, taking one of Adam's ribs, and closing up the flesh, and "out of the rib made he a woman." God, a pure spirit, holding a man's rib, not in his hands, for he has none, and "making" a woman out of it, fashioning the rib into skull, and arms, and ribs, and legs. Can a more ludicrous position be imagined; and Adam? What became of his internal economy? was he made originally with a rib too much, to provide against the emergency, or did he go, for the rest of his life, with a rib too little? And the Church of England endorses this ridiculous old-world fable. Man was created "after thine own image and similitude." What is the image of God? He is a spirit and has no similitude. If man is made in his image, God must be a celestial man, and cannot possibly be omnipresent. Besides, in Genesis i. 27, where it is stated that "God created man in his own image," it distinctly goes on to declare: "in the image of God created he him; *male and female* created he them. Thus the woman is made in God's image as much as the man, and God's image is "male and female." All students know that the ancient ideas of God give him this double nature, and that no trinity is complete without the addition of the female element; but the pious compilers of the Prayer-Book did not probably intend thus to transplant the simple old nature-worship into their marriage office. Once more we hear of Adam and Eve in the next prayer, and we cannot help thinking that, considering all the trouble Eve brought upon her husband by her flirtation with the serpent, she is made rather too prominent a figure in the marriage service. The ceremony winds up with a long exhortation, made of quotations from the Epistles, on the duties of husbands and wives. Husbands are to love their wives because Christ loved a church—a reason that does not seem specially *à propos*, as husbands are not required to die for their wives or to present to themselves glorious wives, not having spot or wrinkle or any such thing (!); nor would most husbands desire that their wives' conversation should be "coupled with fear." Why should women be taught thus to abase themselves? They are promised as a reward that they shall be the daughters of Sarah; but that is no great privilege, nor are English wives likely to call their husbands "lord;" if they did not adorn themselves with plaited hair and pretty apparel, their husbands would be sure to grumble, and the only defence that can be made for this absurd exhortation is that nobody ever listens to it.

Among the various reforms needed in the Marriage Laws one imperatively necessary is that all marriages should be made civil contracts—that is, that the contract which is made by citizens of the State, and which affects the interests of the State, should be entered into before a secular State official; if after that the parties desired a religious ceremony, they could go through any arrangements they pleased in their own churches and chapels, but the civil contract should be compulsory and should be the only one recognised by the law. Of course the Church might maintain its peculiar marriage as long as it chose, but it would probably soon pass out of fashion if it were not acknowledged as binding by the State.

THE ORDER FOR THE VISITATION OF THE SICK.

Of all the services in the Prayer-Book this is, perhaps, the most striking relic of barbarism, the most completely at variance with sound and reasonable thought. The clergyman entering into a house of sickness, and as he enters the sick man's room and catches sight of him, kneeling down and exclaiming, as though horror-stricken: "Remember not, Lord, our iniquities, nor the iniquities of our forefathers; spare us, good Lord, spare Thy people whom Thou hast redeemed with Thy most precious blood, and be not angry with us for ever." This clergyman reminds one of nothing so much as of one of Job's friends, who appear to have been an even more painful infliction than Job's boils. The sickness, the patient is told, "is God's visitation," and "for what cause soever this sickness is sent unto you: whether it be to try your faith for the example of others, . . . or else it be sent unto you to correct and amend in you whatsoever doth offend the eyes of your heavenly Father; know you certainly, that if you truly repent you of your sins, and bear your sickness patiently, . . . it shall turn to your profit, and help you forward in the right way that leadeth unto everlasting life." One might question the justice of Almighty God if the theory be correct that the sickness may be sent "to try your patience for the example of others;" why should one unfortunate victim be tormented simply that others may have the advantage of seeing how well he bears it? If we are to endeavour to conform ourselves to the image of God, then it would seem that we should be doing right if we racked our neighbours occasionally to "try their patience for the example of others." And is the idea of God a reverent one? What should we think of an earthly father who tortured one of his children in order to teach the others how to bear pain? if we should condemn the earthly father as wickedly cruel, why should the same action be righteous when done by the Father in heaven? If we accept the second reason given for the sickness, it is difficult to see the rationale of it. Why should illness of the body correct illness of the mind; does pain cure fretfulness, or fever increase truthfulness? Is not sickness likely rather to bring out and strengthen mental faults than to weaken them? And how far is it true that sickness is, in any sense, the visitation of God for moral delinquencies? Is it not true, on the contrary, that a man may lie, rob, cheat, slander, tyrannise, and yet, if he observe the laws of health, may remain in robust vigour, while an upright, sincere, honest and truthful man, disregarding those same laws, may be miserably feeble and suffer an early death? Is it, or is it not, a fact, that in the Middle Ages, when people prayed much and studied little, when the peasant went to the shrine for a cure instead of to the doctor, when sanitary science was unknown, and cleanliness was a virtue undreamed of,—is it, or is it not, true, that pestilence and black death then swept off their thousands, while these terrible scourges have been practically driven away in modern times by proper attention to sanitary measures, by improved drainage and greater cleanliness of living? How can that be a visitation of God for moral transgressions, which can be prevented by man if he attends to physical laws? Is man's power greater than God's, and can he thus play with the thunderbolts of the divine displeasure? The clergyman prays that "the sense of his weakness may add strength to his faith;" what fine irony is here, as body and mind grow weak faith grows strong; as a man is less able to think, he becomes more ready to believe. It is impossible to pass, without a word of censure, over the passage in the exhortation, taken from the Epistle to the Hebrews, which says, "for they (fathers of our flesh) verily for a few days chastened us after their own pleasure." Good earthly fathers do not chasten their children for their own amusement, while God does it "for our profit;" on the contrary, they do it for the improvement of their children, while God alone, if there be a hell, tortures his children for his own pleasure and for no gain to them. The succeeding portion of the Exhortation, that, "our way to eternal joy is to suffer here with Christ," is full of that sad asceticism which has done so much to darken the world since the birth of Christ; men have been so engaged in looking for the "eternal joy" that they have let pass unnoted the misery here; they have been so busy planting flowers in heaven that they have let weeds grow here; yes, and they have rejoiced in the misery and in the weeds, because they were only strangers and pilgrims, and the tribulation, which was but temporal, increased the weight of the glory that was eternal. Thus has Christianity blighted the flowers of this world, and entwined the brows of its followers with wreaths of thorns. The concluding portion of the exhortation deals with the duty of self-examination and self-accusation, that you may "not be accused and condemned in that fearful judgment." Very wholesome teaching for a sick man; sickness always makes a person morbid, and the Church steps in to encourage the unwholesome feeling; sickness always makes a person timid and unnerved, and the Church steps in to talk about a "fearful judgment," and bewilders and stuns the confused brain by the terrible pictures called up to the mind by the thought of the last day.

But worse follows; for after the sick person has said that he steadfastly believes the creed, the clergyman is bidden by the rubric to "examine whether he repent him truly of his sins, and be in charity with all the world." Imagine a sick person being worried by an examination of this kind, putting aside the gross impertinence of the whole affair. Further, "the minister should not omit earnestly to move such persons as are of ability to be liberal to the poor." When every one remembers the terrible scandals of by-gone days, when priests drew into the net of the Church the goods of the dying, using threat of hell and promise of heaven to win that which should have been left for the widow and the orphan, one marvels that such a rubric should be left to recall the rapaciousness and the greed of the Church, and to invite priests to grasp at the wealth slipping out of dying hands. And here the sick person is to "be moved to make a special confession of his sins, if he feel his conscience troubled with any weighty matter," and the priest is bidden to absolve him, for Christ having "left power to his Church to absolve by his authority committed to me," says the priest, "I absolve thee." Confession, delegated authority, priestly absolution, such is the doctrine of the Church of England: all the untold abominations of the confessional are involved in this rubric and sentence; for if the man can absolve a man at one time, he can do it at another. The precious power should surely not be left unused and wasted; whenever sin pressos, behold the remedy, and thus we are launched and in full sail. But never in England shall the confessional again flourish; never again shall English women be corrupted by the foul questions of the priests; never again shall Englishmen have their mental vigour and virility destroyed by such degradation. Let the Church fall that countenances such an accursed thing, and leave English purity and English courage to grow and flourish unchecked.

The devil is in great force in this service, as is only right in a so generally barbarous an office: "Let the enemy have no advantage of him;" "defend him from the danger of the enemy;" "renew in him whatsoever hath been decayed by the fraud and malice of the devil;" "the wiles of Satan;" "deliver him from fear of the enemy;" all this must convey to the sick person a cheerful idea of the devil lingering about his bed, and trying to get hold of him before it is too late to drag him down to hell.

Is there any meaning at all in the expression, "the Almighty Lord . . . . to whom all things in heaven, in earth, and *under the earth* do bow and obey. Where is "under the earth"? The sun is under some part of the earth to some people at any given time; the stars are under, or above, according to the point of view from which they are looked at. Of course, the expression is only a survival from a time when the earth was flat and the bottomless pit was under it, only it seems a pity to continue to use expressions which have lost all their meaning and are now thoroughly ridiculous. People seem to think that any old things are good enough for God's service.

The last two prayers are remarkable chiefly for their melancholy and craven tone towards God: "we humbly commend," "most humbly beseeching thee." Surely God is not supposed to be an Eastern despot, desiring this kind of cringing at his feet. Yet the "Prayer for persons troubled in mind or in conscience" is one pitiful wail, as though only by passionate entreaty could God be moved to mercy, and he were longing to strike, and with difficulty withheld from avenging himself. When will men learn to stand upright on their feet, instead of thus crouching on their knees? When will they learn to strive to live nobly, and then to fear no celestial anger, either in life or in death?

THE ORDER FOR THE BURIAL OF THE DEAD.

It is a little difficult to write a critical notice of a funeral office, simply because people's feelings are so much bound up in it that any criticism seems a cruelty, and any interference seems an impertinence. Round the open grave all controversy should be hushed, that no jarring sounds may mingle with the sobs of the mourners, and no quarrels wring the torn hearts of the survivors. Our criticism of this office, then, will be brief and grave.

The opening verses strike us first as manifestly inappropriate: "Whosoever liveth and believeth in me shall never die;" yet the dead is then being carried to his last home, and the words seem a mockery spoken in face of a corpse. In the Fourth Gospel they preface the raising of Lazarus, and of course are then very significant, but to-day no power raises our dead, no voice of Jesus says to the mourners,

"Weep not." The second verse from Job is—as is well known—an utter mistranslation: "without my flesh" would be nearer the truth than "in my flesh," and "worms" and "body" are not mentioned in the original at all. It seems a pity that in such solemn moments known falsehoods should be used.

The whole argument in the 15th chap. of 1 Corinthians is the reverse of convincing. Christ is not the first fruits of them that slept. A dead man had been raised by touching the bones of Elisha (2 Kings xiii. 21). Elisha, in his life-time, had raised the dead son of the Shunamite (2 Kings iv.); Elijah, before him, had raised the son of the widow of Zarephath (2 Kings xvii.); Christ had raised Lazarus, the daughter of Jairus, and the son of the widow of Nain. In no sense, then, if the Scriptures of the Christians be true can it be said that Christ has become the first fruits, the first begotten from the dead. "For since by man came death;" but death did not come by man; myriads of ages before man was in the world animals were born, lived and died, and they have left their fossilised remains to prove the falsity of the popular belief. We notice also that "flesh and blood cannot inherit the kingdom of God." If this be so, what becomes of the resurrection of the flesh," spoken of in the Baptismal and Visitation Offices? What has become of the "flesh and bones" which Christ had after his resurrection and with which, according to the 4th Article, he has gone into heaven? Cannot Christ "inherit the kingdom of God"? It is hard to see how, in any sense, the resurrection of Christ can be taken as a proof of the resurrection of man. Christ was only dead thirty-six or thirty-seven hours before he is said to have risen again; there was no time for bodily decay, no time for corruption to destroy his frame: how could the restoration to life of a man whose body was in perfect preservation prove the possibility of the resurrection of the bodies which have long since been resolved into their constituent elements, and have gone to form other bodies, and to give shape to other modes of existence? People talk in such superior fashion of the resurrection that they never stoop to remember its necessary details, or to think where is to be found sufficient matter where-with to clothe all the human souls on the resurrection morn. The bodies of the dead make the earth more productive; they nourish vegetable existence; transformed into grass they feed the sheep and the cattle; transformed into these they sustain human beings; transformed into these they form new bodies once more, and pass from birth to death, and from death to birth again, a perfect circle of life, transmuted by Nature's alchemy from form to form. No man has a freehold of his body; he possesses only a life-tenancy, and then it passes into other hands. The melancholy dirge which succeeds this chapter sounds like a wail of despair: man "hath but a short time to live and is full of misery. He cometh up and is cut down like a flower; he fleeth as it were a shadow, and never continueth in one stay." Can any teaching be more utterly unwholesome? It is the confession of the most complete helplessness, the recognition of the futility of toil. And then the agonised pleading: "O Lord God most holy, O Lord most mighty, O holy and most merciful Saviour deliver us not into the bitter pains of eternal death." But if he be most merciful, whence all this need of weeping and wailing? If he be most merciful, what danger can there be of the bitter pains of eternal death? And again the cry rises: "Shut not thy merciful ears to our prayer; but spare us, Lord most holy, O God most mighty, O holy and merciful Saviour, thou most worthy Judge Eternal, suffer us not, at our last hour, for any pains of death, to fall from thee." It is nothing but the wail of humanity, face to face with the agony of death, feeling its utter helplessness before the great enemy, and clinging to any straw which may float within reach of the drowning grasp; it is the horror of Life facing Death, a horror that seems felt only by the fully living and not by the dying; it is the recoil of vigorous vitality from the silence and chilliness of the tomb.

After this comes a sudden change of tone, and the mourners are told of God's "great mercy" in taking the departed, and of the "burden of the flesh," and they are bidden to give "hearty thanks" for the dead being delivered "out of the miseries of this sinful world." Can anything be more unreal? There is not one mourner there who desires to share in the great mercy, who wants to be freed from the burden of the flesh, or desires deliverance from the miseries of this world. Why should people thus play a farce beside the grave? Do they expect God to believe them, or to be deceived by such hypocrisy?

It is urged by some that the Church cannot have a "sure and certain hope of the Resurrection to eternal life" as regards some of those whom she buries with this service;

and it is manifest that, if the Bible be true, drunkards and others who are to be cast into the lake of fire, can scarcely rise to eternal life at the same time, and therefore the Church has no right to express a hope where God has pronounced condemnation. The Rubric only shuts out of the hope the unbaptized, the excommunicated, and the suicide; all others have a right to burial at her hands, and to the hope of a joyful resurrection, in spite of the Bible.

We may hope that the day will soon come when people may die in England and may be buried in peace without this cry of pain and superstition over their graves. Wherever cemeteries are within reasonable distance the Rationalist may now be buried, lovingly and reverently, without the echo of that in which he disbelieved during life sounding over his grave; but throughout many small towns and country villages the Burial Service of the Church is practically obligatory, and is enforced by clerical bigotry. But the passing knell of the Establishment sounds clearer and clearer, and soon those who have rejected her services in life shall be free from her ministrations at the tomb.

THE

BEAUTIES OF THE PRAYER-BOOK.

A COMMINATION;

OR, DENOUNCING OF GOD'S ANGER AND JUDGMENTS AGAINST SINNERS.

THIS service is too beautiful to be passed over without a word of homage; the spectacle of the Church raving and cursing is too edifying to be ungratefully ignored. "Brethen, in the primitive Church there was a godly discipline that, at the beginning of Lent, such persons as stood convicted of notorious sin were put to open penance and punished in this world, that their souls might be saved. . . . Instead whereof (until the said discipline may be restored again, which is much to be wished), it is thought good," &c. That is, in other words: "In days gone by, we were able to bite, as well as to bark; now that our mouths are muzzled we can only snarl; but, until the old power comes back, which is much to be wished, let us, since we cannot bite, show our teeth and growl as viciously as we can, so that people may understand that it is only the power that is wanting, and not the will, and that, if we could, we would torture and burn as vigorously as we curse and damn." And promptly the priest begins with his curses, and all the people say Amen: what a pretty sight—a whole church full of Christians with one consent cursing their neighbours! Then comes an exhortation; as so many curses are flying about we must take care of our heads: "Let us, remembering the dreadful judgment hanging over our heads, and *always ready to fall upon us*, return to our Lord God." Always ready to fall; but is God, then, always lying in wait to catch us tripping, and crush us with his judgments? Does he punish gladly, and keep his blow suspended, to fall at the first chance our weakness gives him? If so, by no means let us return to our Lord God, but let us rather try to put a considerable distance between himself and us, and endeavour, like the prophet Jonah, to flee from the presence of the Lord. "It is a fearful thing to fall into the hands of the living God: he shall pour down rain upon the sinners, fire and brimstone, storm and tempest." And who made the sinners? Who called them into the world without their own consent? Who made them with an evil nature? Who moulded them as the potter the clay? Who made it impossible for them to go to Jesus unless he drew them, and then did not draw them? If God wants to pour fire and brimstone on anybody, he should pour it on himself, for he made the sinners, and is responsible for their existence and their sin. "It shall be too late to knock when the door shall be shut; too late to cry for mercy when it is the time of justice." How utterly repulsive is this picture of the popular and traditional God: how black the colours wherein is painted this Moloch; surely the artist must have been sketching a picture of the devil, and by mistake wrote under it the name of God when he should have put the name of Satan. If, however, we submit ourselves, and walk in his ways, and seek his glory, and serve him duly—that is, if we acknowledge injustice to be justness, and cruelty to be mercy, and evil to be good—then we shall escape "the extreme malediction which shall light upon them that shall be set on the left hand." On the whole, brave men and women will prefer to do rightly and justly here, caring much about serving man, and nothing about glorifying such a God, and leaving the malediction alone, very sure that no punishment can befal a man for living nobly, and that no fear need cloud the death-bed of him who has made his life a blessing to mankind.

Of course, after all this preface, come cringing confessions of sin. The 51st Psalm leads the way, the congregation having by this time become so thoroughly confused that they see no incongruity in saying that when God has built the walls of Jerusalem, he will be pleased with burnt offerings and oblations, and that "then shall they offer young bullocks upon thy altar." As a matter of fact, they have no intention of offering young bullocks at all—bullocks having become too useful to be wasted in that fashion, but they have so thoroughly left the realm of common sense that they have become unconscious of the absurdities which they repeat. The gross exaggeration of the concluding prayers must be patent to everyone; they are full of the hysteria which passes for piety. "We are grieved and wearied with the burden of our sins," although most of the congregation will forget all about the burden before they leave the church: we are "vile earth and miserable sinners;" we "meekly acknowledge our vileness." One longs to shake them all, and tell them to stand up like men and women, instead of cringing there like cowards, whining about their vileness. If they are vile, why don't they mend, instead of saying the same thing every year? They should be ashamed to tell God of their miserable condition year after year, when his grace is sufficient for them, and they might be perfect as their Father in heaven.

The Church in all this service reminds one of nothing so much as a wicked old crone, who whines to the parson and scolds all the children. In days gone by the old woman has been the terror of the village, and her sturdy arm has been shown on many a black eye and bruised face; now she can no longer strike, she can only curse; she can no longer tyrannise, she can only scowl; her palsied tongue still mutters the curses which her shrivelled arm can no longer translate into act, and in her bleared eye, in her wrinkled cheeks, in her shaking frame, we read the record of an evil youth, wherein she abused her strength, and we see descending upon her the gloom of a dishonoured age, and the night of a fathomless despair.

FORMS OF PRAYER

TO BE

USED AT SEA.

There is now a special service used at the launching of her Imperial Majesty's war-vessels which has not yet found its way into the Prayer-Book; curious thoughts arise in the mind in contemplating that fashion, conjoined to the office to be "used in her Majesty's navy every day." How does God protect "the persons of us, thy servants, and the fleet in which we serve?" Does prayer make bad ships more seaworthy, or supply the place of stout iron and sound wood? If the ship is not safe without prayer, will prayer make it so?

If not, what is the use of praying over it? Either the ship is seaworthy or it is not; if it is, it will sail safely without prayer; if it is not, will prayer carry the rotten ship through the storm? If prayer be so efficacious, would it not be cheaper to use less wood and more prayer? Bad materials roughly put together would serve, for a curate would be cheaper than a shipwright, and much prayer would enable us to dispense with much labour. In "storms at sea," a special prayer is to be used; "O most powerful and glorious Lord God, at whose command the winds blow, and lift up the waves of the sea, and who stillest the rage thereof:" "O send thy word of command to rebuke the raging winds and the roaring sea." Is not this the prayer of utter ignorance, the prayer of an unscientific age? For what does the prayer imply? Only the modest request that the state of the atmosphere round the whole globe may be modified to suit the convenience of a small ship! And not only that, but also that the whole course of weather may be changed during countless yesterdays, the weather of to-day being only an effect caused by them. Such prayers were offered up in former days by a people who knew nothing of the inviolability of natural order, and who imagined that the weather might be changed at their bidding as the clerk may push on the hands of the church clock. The sailors are very frank in their confession: "When we have been safe and seen all things quiet about us, we have forgot thee, our God. . . . But now we see how terrible thou art in all thy works of wonder; the great God to be feared above all." At any rate they cannot be accused of hypocrisy in their dealings with God! Nor is this all. Short prayers are provided for those who have no time for the long ones; and if the danger grows very pressing, everybody who can be spared is to join in a special confession of sins, taken from the Communion Office. It would surely be well to avoid a very pious crew, as they might be wasting the time in prayer which might save the ship by work. One serious thought presents itself for consideration in connection with this supposed power of God to smooth the turbulent billows. Many ships go down year after year; many thousands of lives sink in the pitiless ocean; many a bitter wail goes up from drowning crews; how wickedly cruel to have such power and to see the ship sink in the storm! how icily stony to have such power and to watch unmoved the agony of the perishing!

The prayers against the enemy are beautiful effusions; some of the children praying the All-father to enable them to slay his other children: "Stir up thy strength, O Lord, and come and help us." What a curious request! Does the All-strong require to stir up his strength before he can crush a few men? "Judge between us and our enemies." But suppose the enemy is in the right, what then? Suppose English sailors are on the wrong side, as in the dispute between George III. and the American Colonies, such a prayer then becomes a prayer for defeat, not an encouraging thought with which to go into battle. The prayers are also offensive for their cowardice of tone: "Let not our sins now cry against us for vengeance; but hear us thy poor servants begging mercy, and imploring thy help." The praises after victory are as objectionable as the prayers before: "The Lord hath covered our heads and made us to stand in the day of battle." And what of the poor wounded, groaning below in the cockpit, whose heads the Lord hath not covered? "The Lord hath overthrown our enemies, and dashed in pieces those that rose up against us." How thoroughly savage and bloodthirsty the thanksgiving! Is God supposed to rejoice over the sufferings of the defeated? Is he to be thanked for slaying his creatures? And then the victory is to be improved to the "advancement of thy gospel;" the gospel of so-called peace and goodwill is to be advanced by cannon-ball and torpedo, by sabre and cutlass. Truly they must believe that Jesus came to send a sword through the earth. And yet this is the true spirit of Christianity; of the creed which has shed more human blood than any other faith; of the creed which won its way through Europe with the crucifix in one hand, and the battle-axe in the other; of the creed that tortured innumerable victims on the rack, and which lit the funeral pyres of the martyrs; of the creed whose cross has ever been crimson-red, not with the blood of one who died to save humanity, but with the blood of a humanity sacrificed to the glory of God.

THE FORM AND MANNER OF MAKING, ORDAINING, AND CONSECRATING OF BISHOPS, PRIESTS, AND DEACONS, ACCORDING TO THE ORDER OF THE UNITED CHURCH OF ENGLAND AND IRELAND.

If the Church of England confined herself in her ministrations to offices which had some demonstrable effect, her occupation would be gone. These Ordination offices stand on a par with that of Confirmation. In both, the Holy Ghost is given by imposition of episcopal hands; in both, no appreciable results follow the gift. The preface to these offices says: "It is evident unto all men diligently reading the Holy Scripture and ancient authors, that from the Apostles' time there have been these orders of ministers in Christ's Church: Bishops, Priests, and Deacons." The "evidence" of this appears doubtful, seeing that all Presbyterians acknowledge no such triple order, and regard bishops as an invention of the devil, and "the pride of prelacy" as "a rag of the scarlet" lady. The three offices before us may, to all intents and purposes, be treated as one, for they are the progressive steps of the ladder which reaches from earth to heaven, from the poor deacon-curate on 70*l.* a year at the bottom, to the archbishop luxuriating on 15,000*l.* a year at the top. There is much of solemn farce in the opening: the archdeacon presents the candidates for ordination to the bishop, and the reverend father in God, who has had them examined, who knows all about them, and has probably dined with them the night before, gravely responds: "Take heed that the persons whom ye present unto us be apt and meet, for their learning and godly conversation, to exercise their ministry duly, to the honour of God and the edifying of his Church." For the learning of some young clergymen, the less said about it the better, but those presented have at least scraped through the bishop's examination, and will not now be turned back. The question is simply a sham, and both candidates and bishop would be thoroughly astonished if the archdeacon replied that any one of them was deficient.

The Litany follows after this, and then the Communion Office, with special Collect, Epistle, and Gospel. After the Oath of Supremacy, the bishop examines the candidates for the diaconate: "Do you trust that you are inwardly moved by the Holy Ghost to take upon you this office?" is asked of each, and each answers: "I trust so." This ought to be a solemn question: to be inwardly moved by the Holy Ghost is surely an important thing; and when one remembers how very little many of these young men, fresh from college, seem to think of the matter, and how one chooses the Church because it is "gentlemanly," and another because there is a fat living in the family, and another because he is too stupid for any other profession, we can scarcely help wondering at the workings of the Holy Spirit in the heart of man. They are also asked if they "unfeignedly believe all the Canonical Scriptures." If they really do believe them at their ordination much change must take place in after life, judging by the amount of scepticism among the clergy. Much of the fault lies in pledging young men of three-and-twenty to absolute belief in what they have probably studied but little; at college all their instruction is in Christian *Evidences*, not in attacks on Christianity; they really know but little of the anti-Christian arguments, and therefore are naturally shaken when they learn them further on. Then the deacon is to read Homilies in Church, and promises to do so, although he never fulfils the promise, and he vows to obey his "Ordinary and other chief ministers of the Church . . . following with a glad mind and will their godly admonitions." How well the deacons and priests keep this pledge may be seen in the daily struggles between them and their bishops, and in the necessity of passing a Public Worship Regulation Act for the easier suppression of rebellious priests. A year must intervene between the diaconate and the priesthood, and when this year has run, the youthful aspirant to the power of the keys presents himself once more before the Father in God, and the same farce of question and answer is repeated. The service runs as in that for deacons, save the special Epistle and Gospel, until after the Oath of Supremacy; and then comes a long exhortation, wherein what strikes us most is the complete contrast between the priest in theory and the priest in practice: "If it shall happen the same Church, or any member thereof, to take any hurt or hindrance by reason of your negligence, ye know the greatness of the fault, and also the horrible punishment that will ensue . . . see that you never cease your labour, your care and diligence, until you have done all that lieth in you, according to your bounden duty, to bring all such as are or shall be committed to your charge, unto that agreement in the faith and knowledge of God, and to that ripeness and perfectness of age in Christ, that there be no place left among you, either for error in religion, or for viciousness in life." Now change the scene to six weeks later, and our young priest is playing croquet and flirting meekly with his rector's daughters, oblivious of the "horrible punishment" he is incurring from Hodge at the public-house getting drunk unrebuked. "Consider how studious ye ought to be in reading and learning the Scriptures . . . and for this self-same cause how ye ought to forsake and set aside (as much as you may) all worldly cares and studies." Alas for the special vanities of country clergymen; this one botanizes, and that one zoologizes, and another one geologizes, and a fourth is devoted to his garden, and a fifth to his poultry, and a sixth to his farming, not to speak of those who adorn the bench of magistrates and sternly sentence wicked poachers, and sinful old women who pick up sticks, and children who steal flowers. It may be urged that no set of men could possibly live the life sketched in this exhortation: granted; but, then, why pretend that they are bound to live it, and threaten horrible punishments if they do not perform the impossible? Besides, the bishop expresses his hope that they have well considered the whole matter, and have "clearly determined, by God's grace . . . you will apply yourself wholly to this one thing, and draw all your cares and studies this way." When the time comes to put the questions to the candidates, this very point forms one of them: "Will you be diligent in prayers, and in reading of the Holy Scriptures, and in such studies as help to the knowledge of the same, laying aside the study of the world and the flesh?" And the candidates solemnly promise to do that which they must know they have no intention of doing. One might further urge, that the perpetual meddlesomeness enjoined in this Office on the priest would make that individual a perfect nuisance to his parishioners if he tried to carry it into practice, and that he would probably very often find his ministrations cut short with unpleasant emphasis. The consecration follows in due course: "Receive the Holy Ghost for the Office and work of a priest in the Church of God . . . Whose sins thou dost forgive they are forgiven; and whose sins thou dost retain, they are retained." And yet some people pretend that the Church of England does not sanction an absolving priesthood! If these words have any meaning, they mean that the young men now ordained have the most awful power given into their hands, that they can, in very truth, lock and unlock heaven, for by their absolution the forgiven sinner may enter, while through their retainment of his sins he may be shut out. How tremendous then is the authority thus given into hands so young and so untried! And surely such power is not to be wasted? Surely it is the duty of these priests to be continually urging people to seek, and continually to be giving, absolution. Why should one sinner die unshriven, when such death may be prevented by the diligence of the priest? Life would be impossible were all this really believed; what priest could live in reasonable comfort if this were true and were realised? All earthly things would sink into insignificance, and life would become a desperate struggle to save and absolve the perishing; real belief would end its days in a lunatic asylum.

The Consecration of Archbishop or Bishop is somewhat more ceremonious, but is one in character with the preceding offices. The promise to banish and drive away all erroneous and strange doctrine contrary to God's word is one the fulfilment of which brings unfortunate bishops nowadays into much trouble in the flesh. For when a Colenso "comes down like a wolf on the fold," and a faithful Bishop of Oxford forbids him to tear the lambs of his flock, immediately people mutter "bigoted," "narrow-minded," "tyranny," with sundry other unpleasant adjectives and nouns. Yet can there be no doubt that he of Oxon was only obeying his ordination vow. In truth the present spirit of liberty is thoroughly at issue with the spirit of these offices, and the only effect of maintaining them is to create hypocrites and vow breakers. Nor is it fair to judge too harshly those who break these foolish vows, for a man may honestly think that he can best serve his generation as clergyman, and may have a general belief in Christianity, and he may then argue that he cannot permit himself to be kept out of a wide sphere of usefulness by a few obsolete vows. The pity is that men, whose common sense is too strong to be bound by foolish promises taken in ignorance in their youth, do not join earnestly together to remove this stumbling-block from before the feet of the next generation, so that, if they deem their church valuable, they may preserve her by adapting her to the realities of the nineteenth instead of the sixteenth century, and may make her services something more than a farce, her ceremonies something better than a show.

THE ARTICLES.

It is a little difficult to make out how far the Thirty-nine Articles of the Church of England—"the forty stripes save one"—are binding or non-binding on her members. There is, of course, no question that they accurately sketch her doctrines, and that all her faithful children should accept and believe them with devout piety, but scarcely any dogma can be enforced by law against the laity, the whole spirit of the time being directly antagonistic to such enforcement. But there is no doubt that these Articles are both legally and morally binding on the clergy, as they voluntarily submit themselves to them, and declare their full and free belief in them when entering upon the enjoyment of any benefice of the Establishment. The Royal Declaration, prefixed to the Articles, is sweeping and decisive enough. "The Articles of the Church of England do contain the true doctrine of the Church of England agreeable to God's word; which we do therefore ratify and confirm, requiring all our loving subjects to continue in the uniform profession thereof, and prohibiting the least difference from the said Articles." After this distinct declaration we are commanded "That no man hereafter shall either print, or preach, to draw the Article aside either way, but shall submit to it in the plain and full meaning thereof; and shall not put his own sense or comment to be the meaning of the Article, but shall take it in the literal and grammatical sense." When any outsider has read this declaration it becomes to him one of the mysteries of the faith how it is that English gentlemen, honest, honourable men in everything else, manage to accept livings on condition of declaring their full concord with these Articles, and then deliberately twist them into non-natural meanings, in order that they may be Roman Catholic or Latitudinarian, according to the opinions of the readers. It may, certainly, be conceded that the "literal and grammatical sense" is very often nonsense, and therefore cannot be believed; perfectly true: but these honest men have no right to give the weight of their culture and their goodness to bolster up this falling Church, whose dogmas they can never accept, except by transfiguring their unreason into reason, and their folly into wisdom. Many who are ignorant, and careless, and uncultured are kept as nominal members of the Anglican Church because a glamour is thrown over it by the Broad Church clergy; but their position cannot be too strongly reprobated, *so long as they make no effort to alter that in which they do not believe, so long as they silently support superstitions which without their aid would, long ago, have crumbled into ruin.*

Article I. deals with "Faith in the Holy Trinity." Most creeds, certainly all Oriental creeds, cluster around a Trinity; the root of the worship of the Trinity is struck deep into the nature of man, for it is the worship of the life universal, localised in the giver of the life individual, under the symbol of the phallic emblem, the creator of each new existence. The Christian Trinity has, naturally, outgrown the primal barbarism of Nature-worship, although preserving the Trinity in unity: "There is but one living and true God, everlasting, without body, parts, or passions . . . and in unity of this Godhead there be three persons, of one substance, power, and eternity; the Father, the Son, and the Holy Ghost." So far have we travelled under the guidance of the Church, and we have before our mind's eye, one God, uncorporeate, passionless, indivisible, and yet divided into three "persons," thus implying three individualities, separate the one from the other. Let us remember that the Father is God, the Son is God, and the Holy Ghost is God, but that since there is but one God, the Father is the Son, and the Son is the Holy Ghost, and since the Father is the same as the Son, and the Son is the same as the Holy Ghost, the Father and the Holy Ghost must necessarily be identical. Article II. teaches us that "the Son, which is the word of the Father, begotten from everlasting of the Father, the very and eternal God, and of one substance with the Father, took man's nature in the womb of the blessed Virgin, of her substance;" the Son: that is, the Second Person in the undivided and indivisible Trinity: "begotten from everlasting of the Father;" but the Father is one with the Son, for both are God, and yet there is but one God, and therefore Son and Father are interchangeable terms; the Son then is begotten from everlasting of himself, for in the one true God no division is possible, and "such as the Father is such is the Son;" and further, the Son, being the Son, and at the same time identical with his own Father, takes man's nature: then the Father and the Holy Ghost must also take man's nature, for "such as the Son such is the Father, and such is the Holy Ghost:" and God, "without body," takes man's body, and "without parts" is crucified, and "without passions" suffers. But the Son dies "to reconcile his Father to us;" but he is his Father, and his Father is himself. Can the one living and true God die to reconcile himself to himself, and to offer himself up a sacrifice to himself to appease his own wrath? The bodiless is nailed on the cross: the impassible suffers: the undying dies: the one God on earth is offered to appease the one God in heaven, and there is but one living and true God. If this be so, either the God in heaven or the God on earth must have been a false God, for there is but one true God: and the Father, Son, and Holy Ghost, who must be kept indivisible in thought, hang upon the cross, as a sacrifice to the Father, Son, and Holy Ghost, and cry, being the one true God, to "my God, my God" who has forsaken himself. And all this "to reconcile the Father to us:" the Father who is "without passions," and who therefore cannot be angry or need reconcilement. "As Christ died for us, and was buried, so also it is to be believed that he went down into hell." *Down* into hell; which way is down from a round globe? In the ancient conception of the universe the earth was flat, with heaven above and hell underneath, and Korah, Dathan, and Abiram, when the earth opened her mouth, "went down quick (alive) into hell:" did Jesus do the same? But, hanging on the cross, he said to the penitent thief: "*To-day* shalt thou be with me in Paradise:" is Paradise the same hell? and is heaven identical with both? Jesus ascended, went up, not down, to heaven: if this be so, might not some confusion arise on the way, for a soul starting downwards from Australia on its way to hell, might be found soaring upwards from England after a few hours' journey. Are heaven and hell both all round the world, and if so, why is one "up" and the other "down"? Rome was right and wise when she set her face sternly against the heliocentric theory; a revolving globe destroys all the old notions of the "heaven above," and of "the water under the earth," and of hell below; and it was a strong argument against the sphericity of the earth that "in the day of judgment, men on the other side of the globe could not see the Lord descending through the air." The Fourth Article teaches us that Christ "took again his body, with flesh, bones, and all things appertaining to the perfection of man's nature; *wherewith* he ascended into heaven, and there sitteth." Body, flesh, bones, and all things appertaining to man's nature; wishes, and appetites, and needs, heart and lungs, for instance; and he took these beyond the atmosphere? lungs to breathe where no air is? heart to pulse where no oxygen can purify the blood? flesh and bones among pure spirits? the form of man sitting on the throne of God? and this flesh, bones, &c., all one with the indivisible, from the God without body and parts, and Jesus the Son of Mary, the crucified man, sitting in his flesh and bones in heaven, not to be separated in thought from the one living and true God, without body, parts, or passions.* Such is the "literal and grammatical sense" of the first four Articles, and to analyse the Fifth, "of the Holy Ghost," would be simply to repeat all that has been said above, since "such is the Son, such is the Holy Ghost." May it not justly be said that belief in the Trinity in Unity is the negation of thought, and that faith is only possible where reason ends?

Article VI. deals with "the sufficiency of the Holy Scriptures for Salvation," and lays down the Canon that anything not capable of proof from the Bible must not be "required of any man that it should be believed as an article of the faith, or be thought requisite or necessary to salvation." The converse of this proposition, that dogmas that can be proved therefrom *are* necessary to salvation, is said not to be binding on the Church, and some notable "depravers" of the Scriptures have successfully slipped through this Article. The list of books given as those "of whose authority was never any doubt in the Church" seems open to grave objections, as the authority of many of the books now accounted canonical has been distinctly challenged. "The history of Jonah is so monstrous that it is absolutely incredible." "Job spake not therefore as it stands written in his book." "Isaiah hath borrowed his whole art and knowledge from David." Thus, among many other staid criticisms, wrote Luther. To go further back, is to find much sharp challenging. The Epistle to the Hebrews is of most doubtful authenticity. The 2nd Epistle of Peter and that of Jude are debateable. The Revelation of St. John the Divine was very slowly received, and the two shorter Epistles which bear his name are dubiously recognised. If only the books are to be received of which there "was never any doubt in the Church," the canonical list must be shorn of most of its ornaments. When Article VII. tells us that the ceremonial and civil precepts of the Old Testament are not binding upon us, it seems a pity that some test is not given whereby unlearned people may be

* 1 Cor. xv. 50.

able to distinguish between the "Commandments which are called moral" and the others. Is the command to persecute non-believers in Jehovah (Deut. xiii., xvii. 2—7) binding to-day? Is the command to put Witches to death (Lev. xx. 27) binding to-day? John Wesley said that belief in witchcraft was incumbent on all those who believed the Bible, and if witchcraft was possible then, why not now? or has God changed his mind as to the proper method of dealing with such persons? Are the commands enjoining and regulating Slavery (Ex. xxi. 2—6, and 20, 21; Lev. xxv. 44—46; Deut. xv. 12—18) intended for the guidance of slave-holders to-day? What is there to make the "Commandments which are called moral"—by which we may presume are meant the Ten Commandments—more binding on "Christian men" than the other parts of the law? The Fourth Commandment is essentially a Jewish one, and is not obeyed among Christians. The Second Commandment is invariably ignored, and the Fifth promises a reward which is not given. The Commandments touching murder, adultery, stealing, lying are not peculiar to the Mosaic code. They are found in all moral legislation, and are binding—not because taught by Moses or by Buddha, but—because their observance is necessary to the existence of society. Of the three Creeds of the Church we have already spoken, so pass to Article IX., "of Original or Birth-sin." It seems that a fault and corruption of Nature are naturally "engendered of the offspring of Adam," and that this fault "in every person born into the world deserveth God's wrath and damnation." That seems scarcely fair, since the infant's consent is not asked before he is born into the world, and the fault of being born is, therefore, none of his. How, then, can the babe *deserve* God's wrath and damnation? And seeing that the very next Article (X.) informs us that our condition is such that a man "cannot turn and prepare himself, by his own natural strength and good works, to faith and calling upon God," it appears terribly unjust that either child or man should be held accursed because they do not do what God has made them incapable of doing. It would be as reasonable to torture a man for not flying without wings, as for God to punish man for being born of the race of Adam, and for not turning to God when the power so to do is withheld; for "we have *no power to do good works* . . . . without the grace of God by Christ," and when that grace is not given we lie helpless and strengthless, unable to do right. Nor can any deed of ours make us fit recipients of the grace of God, for (Article XIII.) "works done before the grace of Christ and the Inspiration of his Spirit *are not pleasant* to God . . . . neither do they make men meet to receive grace . . . . yea, rather, for that they are not done as God hath willed and commanded them to be done, *we doubt not but that they have the nature of sin.*" So that if a good and noble heathen, who has never heard of Christ, and whose good deeds cannot therefore "spring of faith in Jesus Christ," does some high-minded action, or shows some kindly charity, his good deeds are of "the nature of sin," and in fact make him rather worse off than he was before: as Melancthon said, his virtues are only "splendid vices" because done without faith in a person of whom he has never heard. For (Art. XVIII.) they "are to be accursed that presume to say that every man shall be saved by the law or sect which he professeth, so that he be diligent to frame his life according to that law, and the light of nature:" "we are accounted righteous before God (Art. XI.) *only* for the merit of our Lord and Saviour Jesus Christ by Faith, and *not for our own works and deservings.*" Thus we learn that God cares not for righteousness of life, but only for blind faith, and that he sends us out into a world lying under his curse, without any chance of salvation except by attaining a faith which he gives or withholds at his pleasure, and which we can of ourselves do nothing to deserve, much less to obtain. To crown this beautiful theory we learn,—Article XVII. "of Predestination and Election:"—predestination to life, it seems, "is the everlasting purpose of God whereby (before the foundations of the world were laid) he hath constantly decreed by his counsel, secret to us, to deliver from curse and damnation those whom he hath chosen in Christ out of mankind, and to bring them by Christ to everlasting salvation, as vessels made to honour." But if this be true, man has no choice of any kind in the matter; for not only is grace to do right the gift of God, but man's acceptance of the gift is also compulsory. God has arranged, before he made the world how many and whom he will save. What, then, becomes of man's boasted free will? Before the creation God drew the plan of every human life, and as the potter moulds the ductile clay into the shape he desires, so God moulds his human pottery after his own will into "vessels made to salvation" or made to dishonour. To talk of man's freedom is a mockery. What freedom had Adam and Eve in Paradise? "They might have stood:" nay; for was not "the Lamb slain from the foundation of the world?" Before the sin was committed God had made the atonement for it. If Adam were free not to sin, then it would be possible that he might not have sinned, and then God would have offered a needless sacrifice, and would have a Saviour with no one to save, so that it would have been necesssary to provide a sinner in order to utilise the sacrifice. All idea of justice is here hideously impossible; God has predestinated some human beings *out of mankind.* These "in due season" he calls; "through grace they obey the calling;" "they be justified freely . . . and at length, by God's mercy, they attain to everlasting felicity." And the rest—those who are *not* predestined; those who are *not* called; those to whom *no* grace is given; those who are *not* justified freely; those who have no God's mercy to aid them;—what of them? Made by God, the creatures of his hand, the vessels of his moulding, the clay of his shaping, are they cast into the lake of brimstone, into the fire that never shall be quenched, simply because God in "his sovereingty" put them—unconscious—under his curse and left them there, adding to the cruelty of creation the more savage cruelty of preservation? No! whether such deeds should be wrought by God or man, they would be wickedly wrong. Almighty power is no excuse for crime, and the God of the Articles of the Church of England is a gigantic criminal, who uses his Almightiness to make life that he may torment it, and to create sentient beings foredoomed to bitterest agony, to keenest woe. Such frightful misuse of power can only meet with strongest reprobation from all moral beings; unlimited power turned to evil purposes may trample upon and crush us into helplessness, but it can never force us to worship, nor compel us to adore.

These first eighteen Articles of the Church may be said to contain the more salient points of the Church's teaching, and it is needless to point out the utter impossibility of reasonable and gentle-hearted men and women believing in the "plan of salvation" sketched out in them. They are instinct with the cruel theology of Calvin and of Zwingli, and imply (though they do not so plainly word) the view of the Lambeth Articles of 1595, that "God from eternity hath predestinated certain men unto life; *certain he hath reprobated.*" These Anglican Articles must be taken as teaching predestination to damnation as well as to salvation, since those not called to life must inevitably fall to death. The next section—so to speak—of the Articles deals with Church affairs, defining the authority of Churches and of Councils, and explaining the doctrine of the Sacraments. It is with these that the High Church party chiefly fall out, for the Twenty-first Article, acknowledging that General Councils may err and have erred, strikes at the root of the infallibility of the Church Universal, so dear to the priestly soul. The Articles on the Sacraments also tend somewhat to the Low Church view of them, and dwell more on the faith of the recipient than on the consecration of the priest. The Article (XXXIII.) levelled against "excommunicate persons," commanding that such an one shall "be taken of the whole multitude of the faithful, as an Heathen and Publican, until he be openly reconciled by penance," is duly believed and subscribed by clergymen, but has no real meaning to-day. If the Thirty-fifth Article were acted upon, some curiosities of English literature would enliven the Churches; for this Article bids the clergy read the Homilies: "we judge them to be read in Churches by the Ministers, diligently and distinctly, that they may be understanded of the people." It is really a pity that this direction is not carried out, for some of the barbarous doctrines of popular Christianity would then be seen as they are described by men who thoroughly believed in them, instead of being known only as they are presented to us to-day, with some of their deformity hidden under the robes woven for them by modern civilisation, wherein humanity has outgrown the old Christianity, and men's reason chastens their faith. The last three Articles touch on civil matters, acknowledging the Royal Supremacy and dealing with other matters pertaining to Cæsar, but on the borderland between him and God.

Such are the Articles of the Church; believed by few, unknown to many, winked at by all, because religion is practically a matter of indifference to most, and while custom and fashion enforce conformity with the Church, the brain troubles not itself to analyse the claim, or to weigh the conditions of allegiance. Men have become so sceptical as to regard all creeds with indifference, and the half-conceived unbelief of the clergy, signing with mental reservations, and formally asserting belief where the thought and the lips are at variance, appears to have eaten the heart out of all religious honesty in England, and men lie to God who would revolt at lying to man. If belief in the Articles is now a thing of the past, then the Articles should also pass away; if Churchmen have outgrown these dogmas, why do they suffer them to deface their Prayer-Book, to barb "the shafts of the sceptic, and to give power to the sneer of the scoffer?"

THE

CHURCH OF ENGLAND CATECHISM.

WISE men, in modern times, are striving earnestly and zealously to, as far as possible, free religion from the cramping and deadening effect of creeds and formularies, in order that it may be able to expand with the expanding thought of the day. Creeds are like iron moulds, into which thought is poured; they may be suitable enough to the day in which they are framed; they may be fit enough to enshrine the phase of thought which designed them; but they are fatally unsuitable and unfit for the days long afterwards, and for the thought of the centuries which succeed. "No man putteth new wine into old bottles, else the new wine doth burst the bottles, and the wine is spilled, and the bottles will be marred; but new wine must be put into new bottles." The new wine of nineteenth century thought is being poured into the old bottles of fourth century creeds and sixteenth century formulas, and the strong new wine bursts the bottles, while the weak new wine that cannot burst them ferments into vinegar in them, and often becomes harmful and poisonous. Let the new wine be poured into new bottles; let the new thought mould its own expression; and then the old bottles will be preserved unbroken as curious specimens of antiquity, instead of being smashed to pieces because they get in the way of the world. Nothing is more to be deprecated in a new and living movement than the formulating into creeds of the thoughts that inspire it, and the imposition of those creeds on those who join it. The very utmost that can be done to give coherency to a large movement is to put forward a declaration of a few cardinal doctrines that do not interfere with full liberty of divergent thought. Thus, Rationalists might take as the declaration of their central thought, that "reason is supreme," but they would be destroying the future of Rationalism if they formulated into a creed any of the conclusions to which their own reason has led them at the present time, for by so doing they would be stereotyping nineteenth century thought for the restraint of twentieth century thought, which will be larger, fuller, more instructed than their own. Freethinkers may declare as their symbol the Right to Think, and the Right to express thought, but should never claim the declaration by others of any special form of Freethought, before acknowledging them as Freethinkers. Bodies of men who join together in a society for a definite purpose may fairly formulate a creed to be assented to by those who join them, but they must ever remember that such creed will lose its force in the time to come, and that while it adds strength and point to their movement now, it also limits its useful duration, if it is to be maintained as unalterable, for as circumstances change different needs will arise, and a fresh expression of the means to meet those needs will become necessary. A wise society, in forming a creed, will leave in the hands of its members full power to revise it, to amend it, to alter it, so that the living thought within the society may ever have free scope. A creed must be the expression of *living thought*, and be moulded by it, and not the skeleton of dead thought, moulding the intellect of its heirs. The strength of a society lies in the diversity, and not in the uniformity, of the thought of its members, for progress can only be made through heretical thought, *i.e.*, thought that is at variance with prevailing thought. All Truth is new at some time or other, and the fullest encouragement should therefore be given to free and fearless expression, since by such expression only is the promulgation of new truths possible. An age of advancement is always an age of heresy; for advancement comes from questioning, and questioning springs from doubt, and hence progress and heresy walk ever hand-in-hand, while an age of faith is also an age of stagnation.

Every argument that can be brought against a stereotyped creed for adults, tells with tenfold force against a stereotyped catechism for children. If it is evil to try and mould the thought of those whose maturity ought to be able to protect them against pressure from without, it is certainly far more evil to mould the thought of those whose still unset reason is ductile in the trainer's hand. A catechism is a sort of strait-waistcoat put upon children, preventing all liberty of action; and while the child's brain ought to be cultured and developed, it ought never to be trained to run in one special groove of thought. Education should teach children *how* to think, but should never tell them *what* to think. It should sharpen and polish the instruments of thought, but should not fix them into a machine made to cut out one special shape of thought. It should send the young out into the world keen-judging, clear-eyed, thoughtful, eager, inquiring, but should not send them out with answers cut-and-dried to every question, with opinions ready made for them, and dogmas nailed into their brains. Most churches have provided catechism-sawdust for the nourishment of the lambs of their flock; Roman Catholics, Church of Englanders, Presbyterians, they have all their juvenile moulds. The Church of England catechism is, perhaps, the least injurious of all, because the Church of England is the result of a compromise, and has the most offensive parts of its dogmas cut out of the public formularies. It wears some slight apron of fig-leaves in deference to the effect produced by the eating of the tree of knowledge. But still, the Church of England catechism is bad enough, training the child to believe the most impossible things before he is old enough to test their impossibility. To the age which believes in Jack-and-the-bean-stalk, and the adventures of Cinderella, all things are possible; whether it be Jonah in the whale's belly, or Tom Thumb in the stomach of the red cow, all is gladly swallowed with implicit faith; the children grow out of Tom Thumb, in the course of nature, but they are not allowed to grow out of Jonah.

When the baby is brought to the font to make divers promises, of the making of which he is profoundly unconscious—however noisily he may at times convey his utter disgust at the whole proceeding—the godfathers and godmothers are directed to see that the child is "brought to the bishop to be confirmed by him, so soon as he can say the creed, the Lord's Prayer, and the Ten Commandments, in the vulgar tongue, and be further instructed in the Church Catechism set forth for that purpose." It is scarcely necessary to say that these words—being in the Prayer-Book—are not meant to be taken literally, and that the bishop would be much astonished if all the small children in the Sunday School who can glibly repeat the required lesson, were to be brought up to him for confirmation. As a matter of fact, the large majority of godfathers and godmothers do not trouble themselves about seeing their godchildren brought to confirmation at all, and the children are sent up when they are about fifteen, at which period most of them who are above the Sunday School going grade, are rapidly "crammed" with the Catechism, which they as rapidly forget when the day of confirmation is over.

The Christian name of the child being given in answer to the first question of the Catechism, the second inquiry proceeds: "Who gave you this name?" The child is taught to answer—"My godfathers and godmothers in my baptism; wherein I was made a member of Christ, the child of God, and an inheritor of the kingdom of heaven." Thus, the first lesson imprinted on the child's memory is one of the most objectionable of the dogmas of the Church, that of baptismal regeneration. In baptism he is "made" something; then he becomes something which he was not before; according to the baptismal office, he is given in baptism "that thing which by nature he cannot have," and being under the wrath of God, he is delivered from that curse, and is received for God's "own child by adoption;" he is also "incorporated" into the "holy Church," and thus becomes "a member of Christ," being made a part of the body of which Christ is the head; this being done, he is, of course, an "inheritor of the kingdom of heaven" through the "adoption."

Thus the child is taught that, by nature, he is bad and accursed by God; that so bad was he as an infant, that his parents were obliged to wash away his sins before God would love him. If he asks what harm he had done that he should need cleansing, he will be told that he inherits Adam's sin; if he asks why he should be accursed for being born, and why, born into God's world at God's will, he should not by nature be God's child, he will be told that God is angry with the world, and that everyone has a bad nature when they are born; thus he learns his first lesson of the unreality of religion; he is cursed for Adam's sin, which he had no share in, and forgiven for his parent's good deed, which he did not help in. The whole thing is to him a play acted in his infancy in which he was a puppet, in which God was angry with him for what he had not done, and pleased with him for what he did not say, and he consequently feels that he has neither part nor lot in the whole affair, and that the business is none of his; if he be timid and superstitious, he will hand over his religion to others, and trust to the priest to finish for him what Adam and his parents began, shifting on to them all a responsibility that he feels does not in reality belong to him.

The unreality deepens in the next answer which is put into his mouth—"What did your godfathers and godmothers then for you?" "They did promise and vow three things in my name: First, that I should renounce the devil and all his works, the pomps and vanities of this wicked world, and all the sinful lusts of the flesh. Secondly, that I should believe all the articles of the Christian Faith. And thirdly, that I should keep God's holy will and commandments, and walk in the same all the days of my life." Turning to the Baptismal Service again, we find that the godparents are asked, "Dost thou, *in the name of this child*, renounce," &c., and they answer severally, "I renounce them all," "All this I steadfastly believe;" and, asked if they will keep God's holy will, they still answer for the child, "I will." What binding force can such promises as these have upon the conscience of anyone when he grows up? The promises were made without his consent; why should he keep them? The belief was vowed before he had examined it; why should he profess it? No promise made in another's name can be binding on him who has given no authority for such use of his name, and the unconscious baby, innocent of all knowledge of what is being done, can never, in justice, be held liable for breaking a contract in the making of which he had no share. Bentham rightly and justly protests against "the implied—the necessarily implied—assumption, that it is in the power of any person—not only with the consent of the father or other guardian, but without any such consent—to fasten upon a child at its birth, and long before it is itself even capable of giving consent to anything, with the concurrence of two other persons, alike self-appointed, load it with a set of obligations—obligations of a most terrific and appalling character—obligations of the nature of *oaths*, of which just so much and no more is rendered visible as is sufficient to render them terrific—obligations to which neither in quantity nor in quality are any limits attempted to be, or capable of being, assigned."

This obligation, laid upon the child in its unconsciousness, places it in a far worse position, should it hereafter reject the Christian religion, than if such an undertaking had not been entered into on its behalf. It becomes an "apostate," and is considered to have disgracefully broken its faith; it lies under legal disabilities which it would not otherwise incur, for heavy statutes are levelled against those who, after having "professed the Christian religion," write or speak against it. Thus in early infancy a chain is forged round the child's neck which fetters him throughout life, and the unconsciousness of the baby is taken advantage of to lay him under terrible penalties. In English law a minor is protected because of his youth; surely we need an ecclesiastical minority, before the expiration of which no spiritual contracts entered into should be enforceable. From the religiuos point of view, apostacy is far more fatal than simple non-Christianity. Keble writes:

> "Vain thought, that shall not be at all!
> Refuse me, or obey,
> Our ears have heard the Almighty's call,
> We cannot be as they."

Is it fair not to ask the child's assent before making his case worse than that of the heathen should he hereafter reject the faith which his sponsors promise he shall believe?

Besides, how absurd is this promising for another; a child is taught not to break *his* baptismal vow, when he has made no such vow at all; how can the god-parents ensure that the child shall renounce the devil and believe in Christianity, and obey God? It is foolish enough to make a promise of that kind for oneself, when changing circumstances may force us into breaking it, but it is sheer madness to make such a promise on behalf of somebody else. The promise to "believe all the Articles of the Christian Faith," cannot take effect until the judgment has grown ripe enough to test, to accept, or to reject, and who then can say for his brother, "he shall believe." Belief is not a matter of will, it is a matter of evidence; if evidence enough supports an assertion, we *must* believe it, while if the evidence be insufficient we *must* doubt it. Belief is neither a virtue nor a vice; it is simply the consequence of sufficient evidence. Theological belief is demanded on insufficient evidence; such belief is called, theologically, "faith," but in ordinary matters it would be called "credulity." First amongst the renouncings comes "the devil and all his works." Says Bentham—"The *Devil*, who or what is *he*, and how is it that he is *renounced?* The *works* of the Devil, what are *they*, and how is it that they are renounced? Applied to the Devil, who or whatever he is—applied to the Devil's works, whatever they are—what sort of an operation is *renouncement* or *renunciation?*"

Pertinent questions, surely, and none of them answerable. A Court of Law lately sat upon the Devil, and could not find him; how is the Christian to explain to the child whom it is he has renounced in his infancy? "And in the first place, the Devil himself—of whom so decided and familiar a mention, as of one whom everybody knows, is made—

Where lives he? Who is he? What is he? The child itself, did it ever see him? By any one, to whom for the purpose of the inquiry the child has access, was he ever seen? The child, has it ever happened to it to have any dealings with him? Is it in any such danger as that of having, at any time, to his knowledge, any sort of dealings with him? If not, then to what purpose is this *renouncement?* and, once more, what is it that is meant by it?"

But supposing there were a devil, and supposing he had works, how could the child renounce him? The devil is not in the child's possession that he might give him up as if he were an injurious toy. In days gone by the phrase had a definite meaning; people were supposed to be able to hold commerce with the devil, to commune with familiar spirits, and summon imps to do their bidding; to "renounce the devil and all his works" was then a promise to have nothing to do with witchcraft, sorcéry, or magic; to regard the devil as an enemy, and to take no advantage by his help. All these beliefs have long since passed away into "The Old Curiosity Shop" of Ecclesiastical Rubbish, but children are still taught to repeat the old phrases, to rattle the dry bones which life has left so long. The "pomps of this wicked world" might be renounced by Christians if they wanted to do so, but they show a strange obliviousness of their baptismal vow. A reception at court is as good an instance of the renunciation of the vain pomp and glory of this wicked world as we could wish to see, and when we remember that the children who are taught the Catechism in their childhood are taught to aim at winning these pomps in their youth and maturity, we learn to appreciate the fact that spiritual things can only be spiritually discerned. Would it not be well if the Church would publish an "Explanation of the Catechism," so that the children may know what they have renounced?

"Dost thou not think that thou art bound to believe, and to do as they have promised for thee?" "Yes, verily; and by God's help so I will. And I heartily thank our heavenly Father, that he hath called me to this state of salvation, through Jesus Christ our Saviour. And I pray unto God to give me his grace, that I may continue in the same unto my life's end." "Bound to believe . . . as they have promised for thee!" In the name of common sense, why? What a marvellous claim for any set of people to put forward, that they have the right to promise what other people shall believe. And the child is taught to answer to this preposterous question, "Yes, verily." The Church does wisely in training children to answer thus before they begin to think, as they would certainly never admit so palpably unjust a claim as that they were bound to believe or to do anything simply because some other persons said that they should. The hearty thanks due to God "that he hath called me to this state of salvation," seem somewhat premature, as well as unnecessary. God, having made the child, is bound to put him in some "state" where existence will not involve a curse to him; the "salvation" is very doubtful, being dependent on a variety of things in addition to baptism. Besides, it is doubtful whether it is an advantage to be in a "state of salvation," unless you get finally saved, some Christian authors appearing to think that damnation is the heavier if it is incurred after being put in the state of salvation, so that, on the whole, it would probably be less dangerous to be a heathen. The child is then required to "rehearse the articles of his belief," and is taught to recite "the Apostles' Creed," *i.e.*, a creed with which the apostles had nothing in the world to do. The act of belief ought surely to be an intelligent one, and anyone who professes to believe a thing ought to have some idea of what the thing is. What idea can a child have of conception by the Holy Ghost and being born of the Virgin Mary, in both which recondite mysteries he avows his belief? Having recited this, to him (as to everyone else) unintelligible creed, he is asked, "What dost thou chiefly learn in these articles of thy belief?" a most necessary question, since they can have conveyed no idea at all to his little mind. He answers: "First, I learn to believe in God the Father, who hath made me and all the world. Secondly, in God the Son, who hath redeemed me and all mankind. Thirdly, in God the Holy Ghost, who sanctifieth me and all the elect people of God." Curiously, the last two paragraphs have no parallels in the creed itself; there is no word there that the Son is God, nor that he redeemed the child, nor that he redeemed all mankind; neither is it said that the Holy Ghost is God, nor that he sanctifies anyone at all. How is the child to believe that God the Son redeemed *all mankind*, when he is taught that only by baptism has he himself been brought into "this state of salvation?" if all are redeemed, why should he specially thank God that he himself is called and saved? if all are redeemed, what is the meaning of the phrase that "all the elect people of God" are sanctified by the Holy Ghost? Surely all who are redeemed must also be sanctified, and should not the two passages touch only the same people? Either the Holy Ghost should sanctify all mankind, or Christ should redeem only the elect people of God. A redeemed, but unsanctified, person would cause confusion as to his proper place when he arrived in the realms above; St. Peter would not know where to send him to. Bentham caustically remarks: "Here, then, in this word, we have the name of a sort of *process*, which the child is made to say is going on within him; going on within him at all times—going on within him at the very instant he is giving this account of it. This process, then, what is it? Of what feelings is it productive? By what marks and symptoms is he to know whether it really is or is not going on within him, as he is forced to say it is? How does he feel, now that the Holy Ghost is *sanctifying* him? How is it that he would feel, if no such operation were going on within him? Too often does it happen to him in some shape or other, to commit *sin;* or something which he is told and required to believe is *sin:* an event which cannot fail to be frequently, not to say continually, taking place, if that be true, which in the Liturgy we are all made so decidedly to confess and assert,—viz., that we are all—all of us without exception—so many '*miserable sinners.*' In the *schoolroom*, doing what by this Catechism he is forced to do, saying what he is forced to say, the child thus declares himself, notwithstanding, a *sanctified* person. From thence going to church, he confesses himself to be no better than '*a miserable sinner.*' If he is not always this miserable sinner, then why is he always forced to say he is? If he is always this same miserable sinner, then this sanctification, be it what it may, which the Holy Ghost was at the pains of bestowing upon him, what is he the better for it?" Besides, how can the child be taught to believe in one God if he finds three different gods all doing different things for him? As clear a distinction as possible is here made between the redeeming work of God the Son and the sanctifying work of God the Holy Ghost, and if the child tries to realise in any fashion that which he is taught to say he believes, he must inevitably become a Tri-theist and believe in the creator, the redeemer, the sanctifier, as three different gods. The creed being settled, the child is reminded: "You said that your godfathers and godmothers did promise for you that you should keep God's commandments. Tell me how many there be? *Ans.* Ten. *Ques.* Which be they? *Ans.* The same which God spake in the twentieth chapter of Exodus, saying, I am the Lord thy God, who brought thee out of the land of Egypt, out of the house of bondage. Thou shalt have none other gods but me." But God has not brought the child, nor the child's ancestors, out of the land of Egypt, nor out of the house of bondage: therefore the first commandment, which is made dependent on such out-bringing, is not spoken to the child. The argument runs: "Seeing that I have done so much for thee, thou shalt have no other God instead of me." The second commandment is rejected by general consent, and it is almost certain that the child will be taught that God has commanded that no likeness of anything shall be made in a room with pictures on the walls. Christians conveniently gloss over the fact that this commandment forbids all sculpture, all painting, all moulding, all engraving; they plead that it only means nothing that shall be made for purposes of worship, although the distinct words are: "*Thou shalt not make any* likeness of *anything*." In order to thoroughly understand the state of the child's mind who has learned that "I the Lord thy God am a jealous God, and visit the sins of the fathers upon the children," when he comes to read other parts of the Bible it will be well to put side by side with this declaration, Ezekiel xviii. 19, 20: "Yet say ye, why? doth not the son bear the iniquity of the father? When the son hath done that which is lawful and right, and hath kept all my statutes, and hath done them, he shall surely live. The soul that sinneth it shall die. The son shall not bear the iniquity of the father." The fourth commandment is disregarded on all sides; from the prince who has his fish on the Sunday from the fishmonger down to the costermonger who sells cockles in the street, all nominal Christians forget and disobey this command; they keep their servants at work, although they ought to "do no manner of work," and drive in carriage, cab, and omnibus as though God had not said that the cattle also should be idle on the Sabbath day. Although the New Testament is, on this point, in direct conflict with the Old,—Paul commanding the Colossians not to trouble themselves about Sabbaths, yet Christians read and teach this commandment, while in their lives they carry out the injunction of Paul. To complete the demoralising effect of this fourth commandment on the child, he is taught that "in six days the Lord made heaven and earth, the sea, and all that in them is," while, in his day-school he is instructed in exactly the opposite sense, and is told of the long and countless ages of evolution through which the world passed, and the marvellous creatures that inhabited it before the coming of man. The fifth commandment is also evil in its effect on the child's mind from that same fault of unreality which runs throughout the teaching of the Established Church. "Honour thy father and thy mother *that thy days may be long in the land.*" He will know perfectly well that good children die as well as bad, and that, therefore, there is no truth in the promise he recites. The rest of the commandments enjoin simple moral duties, and would be useful if taught without the preceding ones; as it is, the unreality of the first five injures the force of the later ones, and the good and bad, being mixed up together, are not likely to be carefully distinguished and thus they lose all compelling moral power.

The commandments recited, the child is asked—"What dost thou chiefly learn by these commandments?" and he answers that—"I learn two things: my duty towards God and my duty towards my neighbour." We would urge here that man's duty to man should be the point most pressed upon the young. Supposing that any "duty to God" were possible—a question outside the present subject—it is clear that the duty to man is the nearest, the most obvious, the easiest to understand, and therefore the first to be inculcated. Surely, it is only by discharge of the immediate and the plain duty that any discharge becomes possible of one less near and less plain. Besides, the duty to God taught in the Catechism is of so wide and engrossing a nature that to discharge it fully would take up the whole time and thoughts. For in answer to the question, "What is thy duty towards God?" the child says:—"My duty towards God is to believe in him, to fear him, and to love him with all my heart, with all my mind, with all my soul, and with all my strength; to worship him, to give him thanks, to put my whole trust in him, to call upon him, to honour his holy name and his word, and to serve him truly all the days of my life." First, "to believe in him;" but how can the child believe in him until evidence be offered of his existence? But to examine such evidence is beyond the still weak intellectual powers of the child, and therefore belief in God is beyond him, for belief based on authority is utterly valueless. Besides, it can never be a "duty" to believe; if the evidence of a fact be convincing, belief in that fact naturally follows, and non-belief would be very stupid; but the word "duty" is out of place in connection with belief. "To fear him:" that the child will naturally do, after learning that God was angry with him for being born, and that another God, Jesus Christ, was obliged to die to save him from the angry God. "To love him;" not so easy, under the circumstances, nor is love compatible with fear; "perfect love casteth out fear . . . he that feareth is not made perfect in love." "With all my heart, with all my mind, with all my soul, and with all my strength." Four different things the child is to love God with: What does each mean? How is heart to be distinguished from mind, soul, and strength? In human love, love of the heart might, perhaps, be distinguished from love of the mind, if by love of the heart alone a purely physical passion were intended; but this cannot explain any sort of love to God, to whom such love would be clearly impossible. Once more, we say that the Church of England should publish an explanation of the Catechism, so that we may know what we ought to do and believe for our soul's health. Bentham urges that to put the "whole trust" in God would prevent the child from putting "any part of his trust" in second causes, and that disregard of these would not be compatible with personal safety and with the preservation of health and life; and that further, as all these services are "unprofitable" to God, they might "with more profit be directed to the service of those weak creatures, whose need of all the service that can be rendered to them is at all times so urgent and so abundant." The duty to God being thus acknowledged, there follows the duty to the neighbour, for which there seems no room when the love, trust, and service due to God have been fully rendered. "*Ques.* What is thy duty toward thy neighbour? *Ans.* My duty towards my neighbour is to love him as myself, and to do to all men as I would they should do unto me. To love, honour, and succour my father and mother. To honour and obey the king, and all that are put in authority under him. To submit myself to all my governors, teachers, spiritual pastors, and masters. To order myself lowly and reverently to all my betters. To hurt nobody by word or deed. To be true and just in all my dealings. To bear no malice nor hatred in my heart. To keep my hands from picking and stealing, and my tongue from evil-speaking, lying, and slandering. To keep my body in temperance, soberness, and chastity. Not to covet nor desire other men's goods; but to learn and labour truly to get mine own living, and to do my duty in that state of life unto which it shall please God to call me." The first phase reproduces the morality which is as old as successful social life. "What word will serve as a rule for the whole life?" asked one of Confucius. "Is not reciprocity such a word?" answered the sage. "What thou dost not desire done to thyself, do not to others. When you are labouring for others, let it be with the same zeal as if for yourself." The second phrase is true and right; the next is often foolish and impossible. Who could honour such a king as George IV.? while to "obey" James II. would have been the destruction of England. Honour and obedience to constituted authorities is a duty only when those authorities discharge the duties that they are placed in power to execute; the moment they fail in doing this, to honour and to obey them is to become partners in their treason to the nation. The doctrine of divine right was believed in when the Catechism was written, and then the voice of the king was a divine one, and to resist him was to resist God. The two following phrases breathe the same cringing spirit, as though the main duty towards one's neighbour were to submit to him. Reverence to any one better than one's-self is an instinct, but "my betters" is simply a cant expression for those higher in the social scale, and those have no right to any lowlier ordering than the simple respect and courtesy that every man should show towards every other. This kind of teaching saps a child's mental strength and self-respect, and is fatal to his manliness of character if it makes any impression upon him. The remainder of the answer is thoroughly good and wholesome, save the last few words about "that state of life unto which it shall please God to call me." A child should be taught that his "state of life" depends upon his own exertions, and not upon any "calling" of God, and that if the state be unsatisfactory, it is his duty to set diligently to work to mend it; not to be content with it when bad, not to throw on God the responsibility of having placed him there, but so to labour with all hearty diligence as to make it worthy of himself, honourable, respectable, and comfortable. At this point the child is informed: "Thou art not able to do these things of thyself, nor to walk in the commandments of God, and to serve him, without his special grace; which thou must learn at all times to call for by diligent prayer." But if the child cannot do these things without God's "special grace," then the responsibility of his not doing them must of necessity fall upon God; for the child cannot pray unless God gives him grace; and without prayer he can't get special grace, and without special grace he can't "do these things;" so that clearly the child is helpless until God sends him his grace, and therefore the whole responsibility lies upon God alone, and he can never blame the child for not doing that which he himself has prevented him from beginning. Diligent prayer for special grace being thus wanted, the child is taught to recite the Lord's Prayer, in which grace is not mentioned at all, and he is then asked—"What desirest thou of God in this prayer?" "I desire my Lord God, our Heavenly Father, who is the giver of all goodness, to send his grace to me and to all people; that we may worship him, serve him, and obey him, as we ought to do." We rub our eyes; not one word of all this is discoverable in the Lord's Prayer! "Send his grace to me and to all people"? not a syllable conveying any such meaning: "that we may worship him, serve him, and obey him"? not the shadow of such a request. Is it supposed to train a child in the habit of truthfulness to make him recite as a religious lesson what is utterly and thoroughly untrue? "And I pray unto God that he will send us all things that be needful both for our souls and bodies, and that he will be merciful unto us, and forgive us our sins." "All things that be needful both for our souls and bodies" is, we presume, summed up in "our daily bread." Simple people would scarcely imagine that "daily bread" was all they wanted both for their souls and bodies; perhaps the souls want nothing, not being discoverable by any real needs which they express. "And that it will please him to save and defend us in all dangers, ghostly and bodily; and that he will keep us from all sin and wickedness, and from our ghostly enemy, and from everlasting death." Here, again, nothing in the prayer can be translated into these phrases; there is nothing about saving and defending from all dangers, ghostly and bodily, nor a syllable as to defence from our ghostly enemy, by whom a child will probably understand a ghost in a white sheet, and will go to bed in terror after saying the Catechism which thus recognises ghosts—nor from everlasting death. The prayer is of the simplest, but the translation of it of the hardest. "And this I trust he will do of his mercy and goodness, through our Lord Jesus Christ; And therefore I say Amen, so be it." Why should the child trust God's mercy and goodness to protect him? There would be no dangers, ghostly and bodily, no ghostly enemy, and no everlasting death, unless God had invented them all, and the person who places us in the midst of dangers is scarcely the one to whom to turn for deliverance from them. Mercy and goodness would not have surrounded us with such dangers; mercy and goodness would not have encompassed us with such foes; mercy and goodness would have created beings whose glad lives would have been one long hymn of praise to the Creator, and would have ever blessed him that he had called them into existence.

The child is now to be led further into the Christian mysteries, and is to be instructed in the doctrine of the sacraments, curious double-natured things of which we have to believe in what we don't see, and see that which we are not to believe in. "How many sacraments hath Christ ordained in his Church?" "Two only, as generally necessary to salvation, that is to say, Baptism and the Supper of the Lord." "Generally necessary"; the word "generally" is explained by commentators as "universally," so that the phrase should run, "universally necessary to salvation." The theory of the Church being that all are by nature the children of wrath, and that "*none* are regenerate," except they be born of water and of the Holy Ghost, it follows that baptism is universally necessary to salvation; and since Jesus has said, "Except ye eat the flesh of the Son of man and drink his blood, ye have no life in you" (John vi. 53), it equally follows that the Lord's Supper is universally necessary to salvation. Seeing that the vast majority of mankind are not baptized Christians at all, and that of baptized Christians the majority never eat the Lord's supper, the heirs of salvation will be extremely limited in number, and will not be inconveniently crowded in the many mansions above. "What meanest thou by this word *sacrament?* I mean an outward and visible sign of an inward and spiritual grace given unto us, ordained by Christ himself, as a means whereby we receive the same, and as a pledge to assure us thereof." If this be a true definition of a sacrament, no such thing as a sacrament can fairly be said to be in existence. What is the inward and spiritual grace given unto the baby in baptism? If it be given, it must be seen in its effects, or else it is a gift of nothing at all. A baby after baptism is exactly the same as it was before; cries as much, kicks as much, fidgets as much; clearly it has received no inward and spiritual sanctifying grace; it behaves as well or as badly as any unbaptized baby, and is neither worse nor better than its contemporaries. Manifestly the inward grace is wanting, and therefore no true sacrament is here, for a sacrament must have the grace as well as the sign. The same thing may be said of the Lords Supper; people do not seem any the better for it after its reception; a hungry man is satisfied after his supper, and so shows that he has really received something, but the spirit suffers as much from the hunger of envy and the thirst of bad temper after the Lord's Supper as it did before. But why should the grace be "inward," and why is the soul thought of as *inside* the body, instead of all through and over it? There are few convenient hollows inside where it can dwell, but people speak as though man were an empty box, and the soul might live in it. The sacrament is "a means whereby we receive the same, and a pledge to assure us thereof." God's grace, then, can be conveyed in the vehicles of water, bread, and wine; it must surely, then, be something material, else how can material things transmit it? And God becomes dependent on man to decide for him on whom the grace shall be bestowed. Two infants are born into the world; one of them is brought to church and is baptized; God may give that child his grace: the other is left without baptism; it is a child of wrath, and God may not bless it. Thus is God governed by the neglect of a poor, and very likely drunken, nurse, and the recipients of his grace are chosen for him at the caprice or carelessness of men. Strange, too, that Christians who received God's grace need "a pledge to assure" them that they have really got it; how curious that the recipient should not know that so precious a gift has been bestowed upon him until he has also been given a little bit of bread and a tiny sip of wine. It is as though a queen's messenger put into one's hand a hundred £1000 notes, and then said solemnly: "Here is a farthing as a pledge to assure you that you have really received the notes." Would not the notes themselves be the best assurance that we had received them, and would not the grace of God consciously possessed be its own best proof that God had given it to us? "How many parts are there in a sacrament? Two; the outward visible sign, and the inward spiritual grace." This is simply a repetition of the previous question and answer, and is entirely unnecessary. "What is the outward visible sign, or form, in baptism? Water; wherein the person is baptized *in the name of the Father, and of the Son, and of the Holy Ghost.*" This answer raises the interesting question as to whether English Christians—save the Baptists—are really baptized. They are not baptized "in," but only "with" water. The rubric directs that the minister "shall *dip it in* the water discreetly and warily," and that only where "the child is weak it shall suffice to pour water upon it." It appears possible that the salvation of nearly all the English people is in peril, since their baptism is imperfect. The formula of baptism reminds us of a curious difference in the baptism of the apostles from the baptism in the triune name of God; although Jesus had, according to Matthew, solemnly commanded them to baptize with this formula, we find, from the Acts, that they utterly disregarded his injunction, and baptized "in the name of Jesus Christ," instead of in the name of "Father, Son, and Holy Ghost." (See Acts ii. 38, viii. 16, x. 48, xix. 5, etc.) The obvious conclusion to be drawn from this is, that if the Acts be historical, Jesus never gave the command put into his mouth in Matthew, but that it was inserted later when such a formula became usual in the Church. "What is the inward and spiritual grace? A death unto sin, and a new birth unto righteousness; for being by nature born in sin, and the children of wrath, we are hereby made the children of grace." What? a baby die unto sin? how can it, when it is unconscious of sin, and therefore cannot sin? "A new birth unto righteousness?" but it is only just born, surely there can be no need that it should be born over again so soon? And if it be true that this is the inward grace given, would it not be well—as did many in the early Church—to put off the ceremony of baptism until the last moment, so that the dying man, being baptized, may die to all the sins he has committed during life, and be born again into spiritual babyhood, fit to go straight into heaven? It seems a needless cruelty to baptize infants, and so deprive them of the chance of getting rid of all their life sins in a lump later on. This is not the only objection to baptism. Bentham powerfully urges what has often been pressed:—

"Note well the sort of story that is here told. The Almighty God,—maker of all things, visible and 'invisible,'—'of heaven and earth, and all that therein is,'—makes, amongst other things, a child: and no sooner has he made it, than he is '*wrath*' with it for being made. He determines accordingly to consign it to a state of endless torture. Meantime comes somebody,—and pronouncing certain words, applies the child to a quantity of water, or a quantity of water to the child. Moved by these words, the all-wise Being changes his design; and, though he is not so far appeased as to give the child its pardon, vouchsafes to it a *chance*,—no one can say *what* chance,—of ultimate escape. And this is what the child gets by being 'made'—and we see in what way made—'*a child of grace*.'"

"What is required of persons to be baptised? Repentance, whereby they forsake sin; and Faith, whereby they steadfastly believe the promises of God made to them in that Sacrament. Why then are infants baptised when by reason of their tender age they cannot perform them? [Why, indeed!] Because they promise them both by their sureties, which promise, when they come of age, themselves are bound to perform." Surely it would be better if these things are "required" before baptism, to put off baptism until repentance and faith become possible, instead of going through it like a play, where people act their parts and represent somebody else. For suppose the child for whom repentance and faith are promised does not, when he comes to full age, either repent of his sins or believe God's promises, what becomes of the inward and spiritual grace? It must either have been given, or not have been given; if the former, the unrepentant and unbelieving person has got it on the faith of his sureties' promises for him; if the latter, God has not given the grace promised in Holy Baptism, and his promises are therefore unreliable in all cases.

"Why was the Sacrament of the Lord's Supper ordained? For the continual remembrance of the sacrifice of the death of Christ, and of the benefits which we receive thereby." What very bad memories Christians must have! God has come down from heaven on purpose to die for them, and they cannot remember it without eating and drinking in memory of it. The child is then taught that the outward part in the Lord's Supper is bread and wine, and that the inward part is "The Body and Blood of Christ, which are verily and indeed taken and received by the faithful in the Lord's Supper," the body and blood nourishing the soul, as the bread and wine do the body. If the body and blood convey as infinitesimal an amount of nourishment to the soul as the small portions of bread and wine do to the body, the soul must suffer much from spiritual hunger. But how do they nourish the soul? The body and blood must be somehow in the bread and wine, and how is it managed that one part shall nourish the soul while the rest goes to the body? "verily and indeed taken and received." From the eager protestation one would imagine that there must be some doubt about it, and that there might be some question as to whether the invisible and intangible thing were really and truly taken. It needs but little insight to see how woefully confusing it must be to an intelligent child to teach him that bread and wine are only bread and wine one minute and the next are Christ's body and blood as well, although none of his senses can distinguish the smallest change in them. Such instruction will, if it has any effect on his mind, incline him to take every assertion on trust, without, and even contrary to, reason and experiment; it lays the basis of all superstition, by teaching belief in what is not susceptible of proof.

"What is required of them who come to the Lord's supper? To examine themselves, whether they repent them truly of their former sins, steadfastly purposing to lead a new life; have a lively faith in God's mercy through Christ, with a thankful remembrance of his death; and be in charity with all men." It is the custom in many churches now to have weekly, and in some to have daily, communion; can the communicants who attend these steadfastly purpose to lead a new life every time? and how many "former sins" are they as continually repenting of? Here we find the overstrained piety which throughout disfigures the Prayer-Book; people are moaning about their sins, and crying over their falls, and resolving to mend their ways, and vowing they will lead new lives, and the next time one sees them they are once more proclaiming themselves to be as miserable sinners as ever. How weary the Holy Ghost must get of sanctifying them!

Such is the Catechism that "The curate of every parish shall diligently upon Sundays and Holy Days, after the second lesson at evening prayer, openly in the Church" teach to the children sent to him, and which "all fathers, mothers, masters, and dames shall cause their children, servants, and apprentices (which have not learned their Catechism) to come to the Church at the time appointed," in order to learn; such is the nourishment provided by the Church for her lambs: such is the teaching she offers to the rising generation. Thus, before they are able to think, she moulds the thinking-machine; thus, before they are able to judge, she biases the judgment; thus, from children puzzled and bewildered, she hopes to make men and women supple to her teaching, and out of the Catechism she winds round the children's brains, she forges the chain of creeds which fetters the intellect of the full-grown members of her communion.

London: Printed by Annie Besant and Charles Bradlaugh, 28, Stonecutter Street, E.C.